Lin MacDonald
Set Decorator

urban furniture for a new city life

ICI CONSULTANTS
Sophie BARBAUX

Assisted by: Sara LUBTCHANSKY
Direction: Chia-Ling CHIEN
Editorial Coordination: Nicolas BRIZAULT
English Translation: Alison CULLIFORD
Graphic Design & Layout &: Linh VU

urban furniture for a new city life

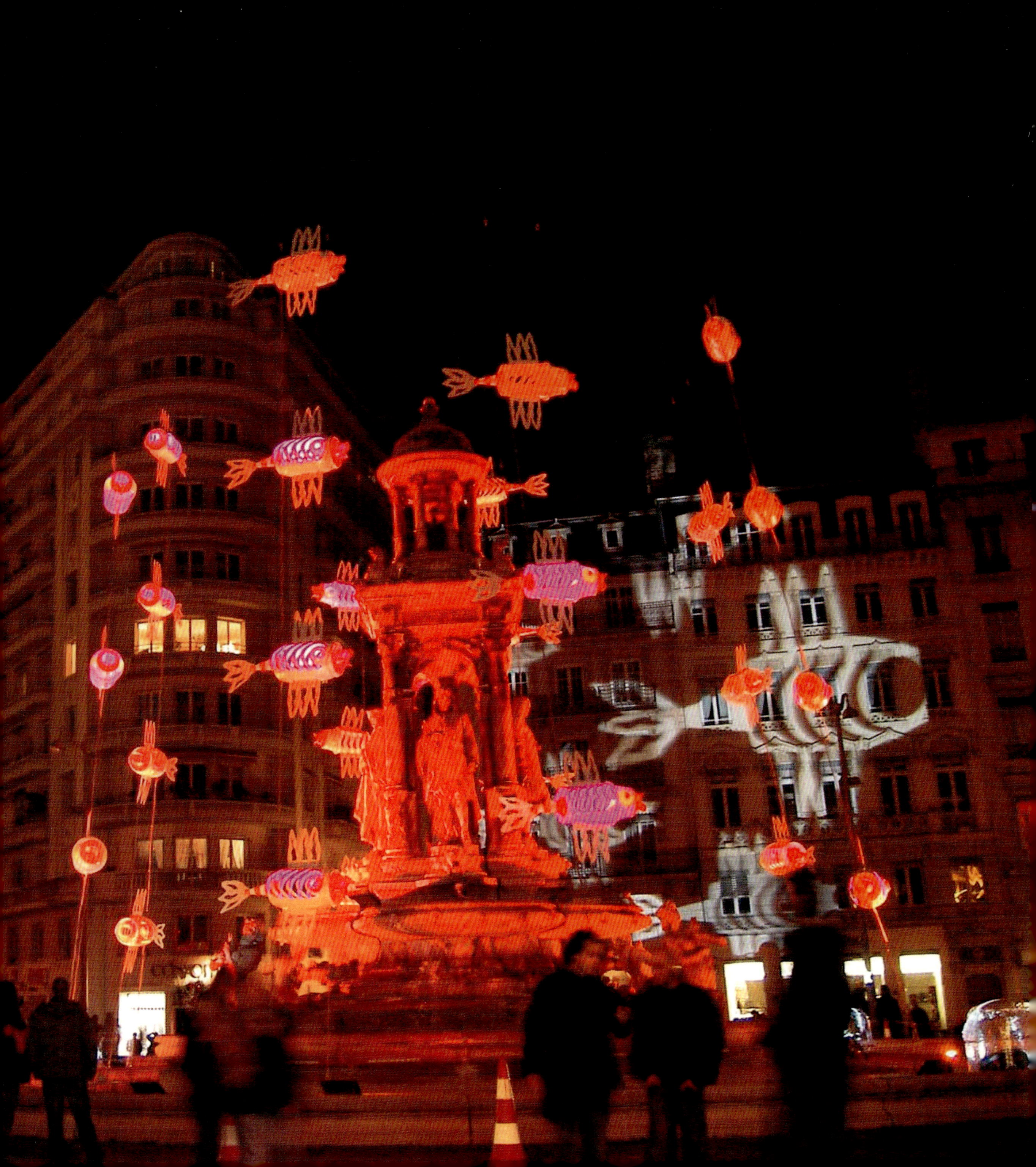

CONTENTS

PREFACE — 007

01 SEATS OF CONVIVIALITY — 018

02 CLEAN CITY! — 094

03 ENCHANTING THE CITY — 118

04 URBAN EXPRESSIONS — 170

05 SHELTER — 200

06 CITY GAMES — 222

07 ON YOUR BIKE! — 254

08 GREEN CITY — 268

ANNEX — 308

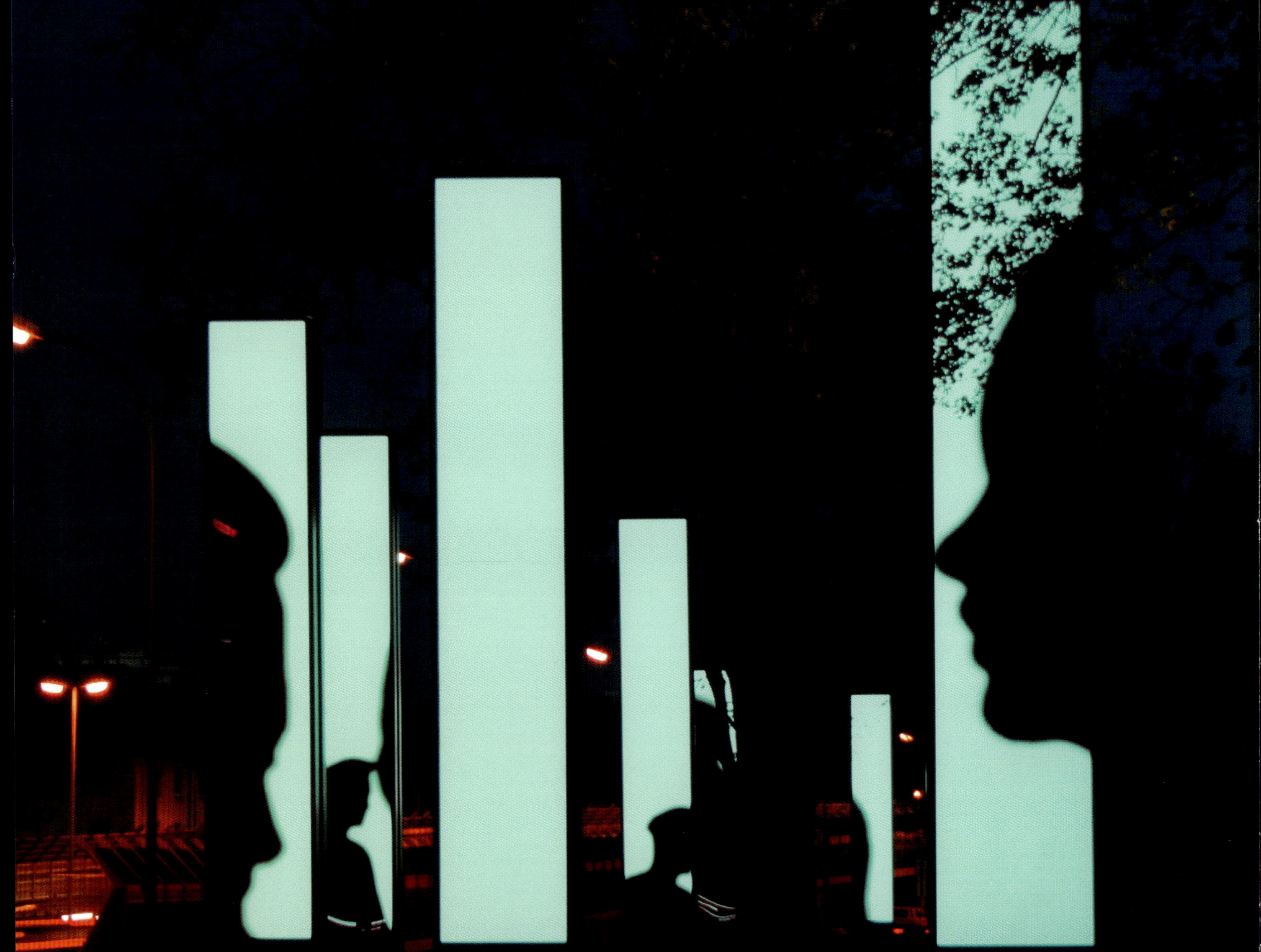

preface

dresses for Wallace fountains - 2009
Collectif France Tricot / Solène Couturier
page 2

the fish fountain - 2008
BIBI
Agence Tagada / Magnum
Fêtes des Lumières, Lyon
Page 4

reprojected – 2006
Mader Stublic Wiermann
Osram light consulting

Installed in front of the Osram head office in Munich, 7 screens 6 m high use a sophistical system based on LEDs. They project different sized silhouettes of characters like shadow puppets, giving the impression that they are also walking in the street, like the real passers-by who watch them and who participate through their presence in the interface between reality and artifice.

Pages 6 & 7

Urban furniture groups together the elements and systems installed in the public space, offering different services and functions to users. Today, within its richly varied typology one finds seating and waste bins, lighting and means of information and communication, as well as fountains, playground apparatus, signage systems, bike racks, road signs and plant containers, shelters and other types of protection.

In bringing together 400 objects and projects and illustrating them, this book doesn't see itself as exhaustive but as prospective – a panorama of contemporary creation in this field, showing the most recent and innovative aspects. The relevance of the design of this type of furniture, whether it is formal, aesthetic, functional, or even playful, cannot be ignored at a time when urban planning concerns us more and more, with demographers announcing that in 2026 84% of the population of industrialised countries will be living in the large cities!

007

Cities have forged their identity over the centuries. And in the modern era they have defined a style for this planning of their exterior spaces, a component in their development that can be qualified as historic. But, over time, this unity is frequently degraded by parameters such as wear and tear, and the deterioration or evolution of sites, uses and security standards. As a result the urban space often resembles a motley collection of heterogeneous objects that doesn't make any sense.

The focus of various debates on its ethical, aesthetic, political, economical and social environment, the city represents a primordial challenge that assembles all the current problematics, and which often finds solutions in the public space, the space for everyone. A world that is too often standardised, it must again become a place of sharing and hospitality, two dimensions that it has lost, thus raising the stakes in our willingness to live together. For this mutation to be successful, urban furniture is one of the key elements in the city's transformation, the carrier of new functions and new directions for our societies.

flight- 2008
Sophie Barbaux & Roberto Cabot
França.br 2009

Flight is a tribute to two Brazilian personalities, Alberto Santos Dumont, aviation pioneer and Roberto Burle Marx, botanist, landscape architect and artist.
page 8

phonemes - 2006
Vincent Bécheau & Marie-Laure Bourgeois
Atelier des Bois Perennes

Taking forms borrowed from the postures of the body and the syntax of the bench, Phonemes deploy their architecture in acacia wood for several different uses, both as a place for meetings and for transversality in the city.
page 9

009

The powers that be therefore have the exciting task of restoring charm to the world by responding to the change in mentality, using the skills of designers, artists, architects, landscape architects... These people are both the bearers of the spirit of place and the creators of stylistic forms that are very diverse, an essential factor in the rediscovery of identity in the true sense of the term.

They are also progressively integrating the new technologies that are impossible to ignore, and the pressing need for ecology and nature. So that the city can accommodate new practices that have yet to be born, they free up the space to a maximum by bringing together several functions or services in a single object or by making it mobile. It is these new approaches that we find in this book, in the form of projects that may or may not have been made real, but that are all reflections of a permanent questioning on what the city of tomorrow may be.

moodwall – 2009
Remco Wilcke / CUBE & Jasper Klinkhamer / Studio Klink
Hans van Helden and Matthijs ten Berge / Illuminate & Matthias Oostrik
Ville d'Amsterdam

In Amsterdam, this pilot project gives an underground passageway an interactive wall with LEDs and presence detectors, thus creating a feeling of security. Moodwall accompanies the slightest movement of passers-by with a calming, mimetic wave of colours.

Page 10

boxing - 2008
Sarah Bittel
Workshop Mobilier Urbain / HEAD Genève

In Geneva, to create one of the rare direct access points to the water of the Rhône, Boxing unfolds a checkerboard structure, alternating wooden decking of different heights and shallow pools, allowing one to enjoy the river and to walk from one island to another.

Page 11

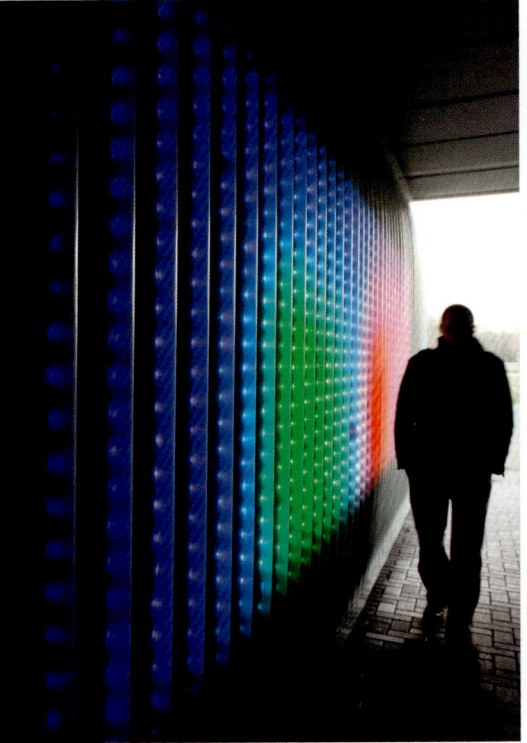

011

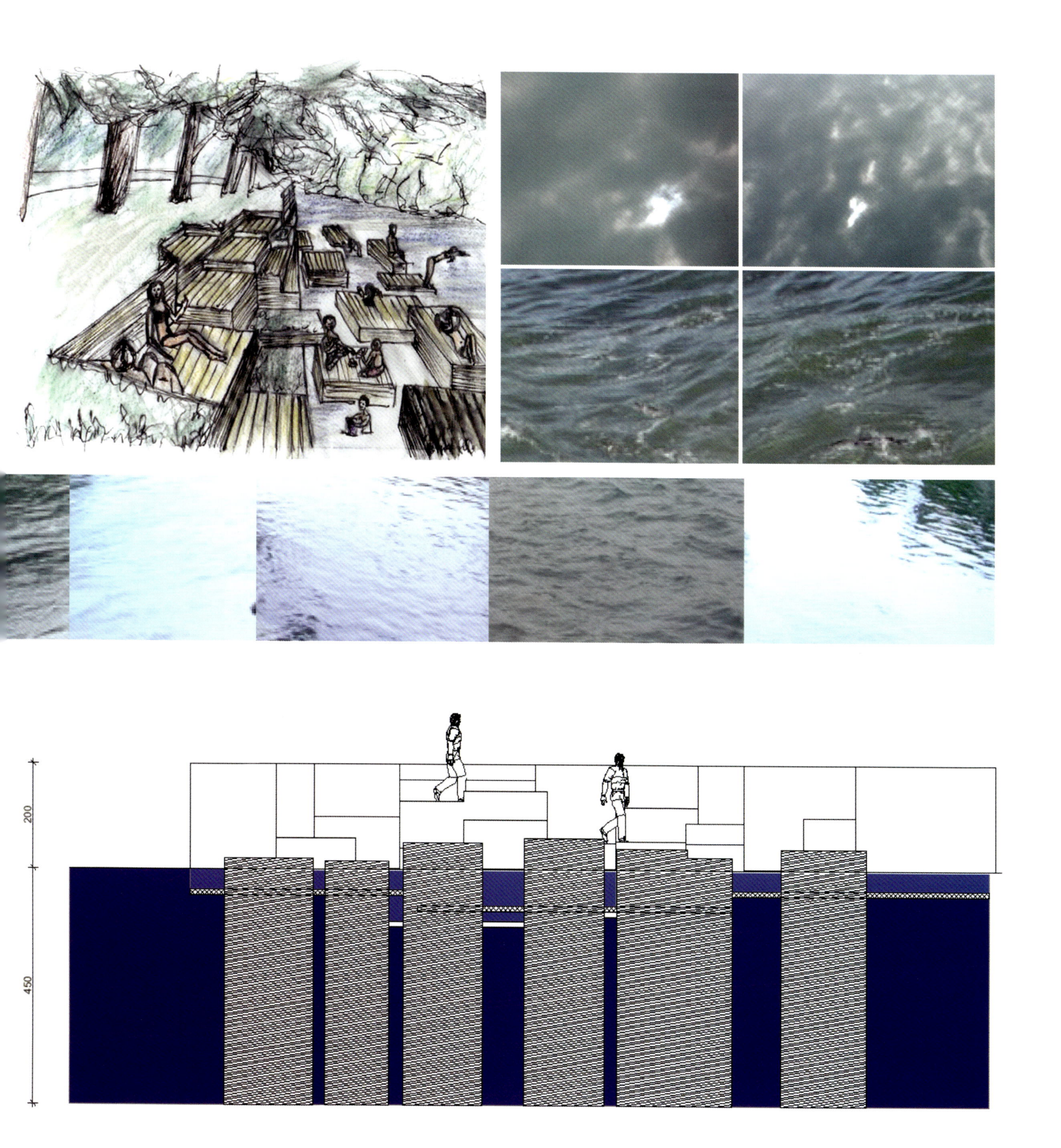

Legoville
Fonds d'art contemporain (Fmac)
Service d'aménagement urbain et de la mobilité, Geneva
Editions Dasein

urban botanics

2008 2009

Taking the Castle Park in Geneva as its study and exhibition site, this project establishes a methodical inventory of urban furniture and creates an artistic-scientific classification. A score of objects is identified and a Latin name is given to each, as if it was a plant belonging to a new family, *Mobilia urbana*. The history of each species is thus described in an erudite manner on an information panel offered to curious walkers. A botanical manual accompanies this juicy nomenclature, testifying to the evolution of human space and strategies to control it, the confrontation of pedestrians, animals and vehicles and the putting in place of different networks of public services.

012 preface

LES ESPÈCES DU MOBILIER URBAIN AU PARC DES BASTIONS

LA BORNE

La borne constitue la première espèce connue du mobilier urbain. Dans le Proche-Orient ancien, l'existence de bornes et de stèles frontières est attestée, notamment pour délimiter des domaines sacrés. Chez les Romains, représentant la divinité Terminus, garantissaient l'intégrité spatiale de l'Empire tout en soutenant son expansion ; dans les villes, elles délimitaient les quartiers, et les routes, elles servaient de signalisation.

Cette espèce était fréquemment ornée d'inscriptions en l'honneur d'un dieu ou d'un roi. Elle servait enfin de support d'informations quant au souverain y faisait inscrire ses hauts-faits ou témoignait de sa générosité à l'égard de son peuple.

Les bornes assuraient aussi la sécurité des piétons dans des rues sans trottoirs ; ceux-ci étaient déjà fréquents à Londres à la fin du XVIIIe siècle, leur développement rendra les bornes obsolètes. Néanmoins, au cours du XIXe siècle, le trottoir s'avéra être une protection insuffisante pour les piétons face à l'invasion de l'automobile.

Ainsi, piquets métalliques (*Terminus palus*), barrières continues en métal (*Transenna terminalis*), potelets avec chaînes (*Catena terminalis*), bornes escamotables (*Terminus fortivus*) ou plots de béton (*Terminus mutus*, *fig. 1*) sont quelques-unes des nouvelles espèces qui ont repris la place perdue par les anciennes bornes. Parfois, ces objets sont également destinés à protéger un autre mobilier urbain. En définitive, ayant perdu ses nobles fonctions d'antan, la borne n'a aujourd'hui plus qu'un humble statut de serviteur.

fig. 1

LA BORNE-FONTAINE

Les fontaines sont des espèces déjà présentes dans la ville antique. Les Grecs avaient leurs fontaines publiques, petites, simples et dépourvues d'ornementation architecturale. Les ruines de Pompéi montrent quant à elles une abondance de points d'eau, sobrement ornés.

Jusqu'à l'époque moderne, il fallait chercher l'eau à la source, ou la faire acheminer à domicile par porteurs d'eau. La fontaine était un lieu de rencontre et d'échange social pour tous ceux qui ne disposaient pas d'un puits privé. Les fontaines de puisage, courantes à Paris jusqu'au XIXe siècle, remplissaient également une fonction d'hygiène publique ; coulant sur le pavé en permanence, leurs eaux entraînaient les déjections de toutes sortes. A Londres, l'eau était disponible à l'intérieur des maisons dès le début du XVIIe siècle. Cependant, les réseaux privés et payants ne desservaient pas toute la population.

À partir de 1830, une nouvelle espèce du mobilier urbain colonisa Paris auquel elle fit la part des bouches d'eau, jusqu'alors souterraines, muèrent en borne-fontaines (*Fons terminalis*, *fig. 2*). En 1871, l'Anglais Richard Wallace introduisit une espèce en fonte (*Fons Wallacei*) qui se multiplia dans plusieurs villes occidentales.

De nos jours, en raison de la généralisation de l'adduction d'eau dans les logements, les fontaines des rues ne font plus guère partie du paysage de la ville contemporaine, et seules les fontaines monumentales restent en tant qu'éléments du décor urbain. Genève, en revanche, a su conserver ses bornes-fontaines, pour le bonheur des enfants et des passants assoiffés.

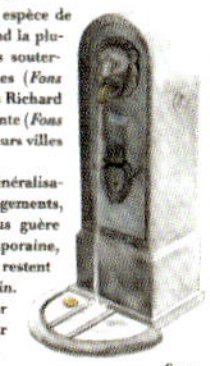

fig. 2

LA BORNE D'INCENDIE

L'histoire de l'hydrant remonte au XVIIe siècle. Arrivés sur le lieu de l'incendie, les pompiers avaient à cette époque l'habitude de creuser dans le sol jusqu'à ce qu'ils rencontrent la conduite principale ; puis, après avoir percé ce tuyau en bois, ils acheminaient l'eau vers l'incendie, d'abord au moyen de seaux, ultérieurement par des pompes manuelles.

Après un grand incendie de 1666, la ville de Londres implanta un nouveau type de conduites auxquelles étaient raccordés, à intervalles réguliers, des tuyaux remontant à la surface, précurseurs des bouches d'incendie.

Le premier exemplaire d'une borne d'incendie (*Hydra terminalis*, *fig. 3*) fut décrit à Philadelphie en 1803, par Frederick Graff Sr, ingénieur des Philadelphia Water Works. L'hydrant en fer forgé était implanté de façon permanente et constamment sous pression. L'office des brevets des Etats-Unis ayant brûlé en 1836, on ne peut catégoriquement attribuer à Graff Sr la découverte de cette espèce.

Depuis le début du XIXe siècle, les villes du monde entier ont cultivé la borne d'incendie dans toutes ses variantes, cherchant à conjurer ainsi un de leurs plus grands ennemis, l'incendie géant. En définitive, les bornes d'incendie ont évolué vers deux formes perfectionnées, la variété « Wet Barrel » (*Hydra terminalis umida*) sous pression en permanence, répandue dans les zones tropicales et subtropicales, et la « Dry Barrel » (*Hydra terminalis sicca*) répandue dans les zones tempérées et boréales, une variété munie d'une valve souterraine pour protéger l'armature des dégâts occasionnés par le gel.

fig. 3

L'ARMOIRE TECHNIQUE

L'histoire des réseaux énergétiques commence au début du XIXe siècle. On y retrouve des espèces comme l'éclairage public, puis à la cuisine et au chauffage. La ville s'enrichit ensuite de réseaux de tous types : au gaz et à l'eau s'ajoutèrent la vapeur, l'hydraulique et l'air comprimé. Les tuyaux de ces réseaux tissaient un maillage de plus en plus dense, tantôt souterrain, tantôt ornant les façades et les espaces intérieurs, transformant profondément la ville.

À cette époque, l'électricité n'était que d'un usage discret, on vantait ses qualités de prédateur. Pourtant, elle éliminera tour à tour tous ses concurrents directs, enserrant les réseaux complémentaires et donnant naissance aux réseaux de télécommunication.

Avec la révolution industrielle, l'équipement d'un bâtiment n'est pas pleinement destinée aux usagers, elle confère également à l'espèce des caractères insolites comme la lampe téléphonique, l'horodateur, le sanitaire public à entretien automatique ou encore le feu de signalisation.

fig. 4

LE TERRAIN DE JEUX

Le terrain de jeu constitue un micro-écosystème très favorable à la culture du mobilier urbain. On y retrouve des espèces comme le bac à sable (*Arena puerorum*), le toboggan (*Clivulus lapsans*), la balançoire (*Oscillum publicum*) ou le carrousel (*Sellulae circumvertentes*, *fig. 5*).

Avec la révolution industrielle, la condition des enfants dans les villes était devenue un problème social. À Leipzig, en 1868, le médecin allemand Daniel Gottlob Moritz Schreber préconisa des exercices visant à soulager leurs pulsions sexuelles « malsaines » chez les enfants et les adolescents. Ses appareils gymnastiques, prédécesseurs des équipements de fitness, transformaient le mouvement répétitif en énergie thermique. Schreber réclama ensuite des terrains à l'extérieur des villes, sur lesquels les enfants pouvaient jouer et s'exercer à des travaux agricoles « sains », contribuant ainsi à la naissance du mouvement des jardins ouvriers.

Parallèlement, le premier terrain de jeux apparut en 1854 à Birmingham et, quatre ans plus tard à Paris, des balançoires furent installées à l'accès régulier le long des Champs-Elysées. Mais ce fut aux Etats-Unis, à la fin du XIXe siècle, que le terrain de jeux devint une véritable institution. Le « Playground Movement » associait à la création des centres de chemin de fer danois furent équipées de rangées de crochets destinés à la suspension des bicyclettes.

L'usage du cadenas se généralisa dans la seconde moitié du XXe siècle. Le remplacement du modèle intégré au cadre par des cadenas en chaîne entraîna la mutation du parking pour bicyclettes en demi-lune recueillant au profit des rangées qui permettaient d'attacher solidement le cadre de la bicyclette. Ainsi, les dispositifs anti-vol, encombrants et disgracieux, prennent une place de plus en plus prépondérante tant sur la bicyclette que dans l'espace public.

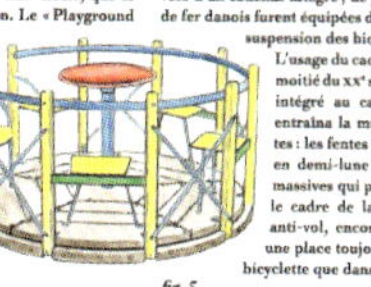

fig. 5

LE RÂTELIER À BICYCLETTES

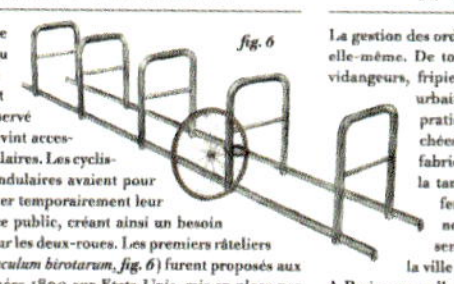

Le cyclisme utilitaire commença à la fin du XIXe siècle quand la bicyclette, auparavant réservée aux classes aisées, devint accessible aux classes populaires. Les cyclistes travailleurs et pendulaires avaient pour coutume d'abandonner temporairement leur véhicule dans l'espace public, créant ainsi un besoin de parking urbain pour les deux-roues. Les premiers râteliers à bicyclettes (*Receptaculum birotarum*, *fig. 6*) furent proposés aux cyclistes dans les années 1890 aux Etats-Unis, mis en place par les fabricants de vélos aux fins publicitaires.

En Europe, le premier parking surveillé pour bicyclettes apparut en 1936 à Bonn. Lors de la seconde guerre mondiale, face à la recrudescence du vol de bicyclettes, le Danemark systématisa la numérotation des cadres et obligea les fabricants à munir chaque vélo d'un cadenas intégré ; de plus, toutes les stations de chemin de fer danoises furent équipées de rangées de crochets destinés à la suspension des bicyclettes.

fig. 6

LA CORBEILLE À DÉCHETS

La gestion des ordures est une activité aussi ancienne que la ville elle-même. De tout temps, les balayeurs, éboueurs, râteliers, vidangeurs, fripiers ou chiffonniers vivaient des immondices urbaines. Ainsi à Londres, jusqu'au XIXe siècle, on pratiquait l'élevage des cochons dans les cours jonchées d'ordures, on utilisait les cendres pour la fabrication des briques, les excréments canins de la tannerie et on vendait du fumier de rue comme fertilisant. Cependant, ces activités de recyclage dans une ville pré-industrielle offraient de bien piètres conditions hygiéniques dans la ville pré-industrielle.

À Paris, une collecte régulière des ordures fut mise en place en 1667. En 1883, le préfet Eugène René Poubelle réorganisa le ramassage des ordures ménagères ; dans son système, trois boîtes étaient prévues pour le tri des déchets : matières putrescibles ; papier et chiffons ; verre, faïence et coquilles d'huîtres.

Mais, alors que la ville industrielle semblait venir à bout de ses immondices grâce à la canalisation et à l'évacuation, la société de consommation fit surgir de nouveaux déchets urbains : le papier et l'emballage. Les premières corbeilles de la voie publique (*Cista purgamentorum*, *fig. 7*) furent implantées à Paris en 1908.

Vers la fin du XXe siècle, avec la recrudescence du tri des déchets entrainée le développement de nouvelles variétés de cette espèce. Au Parc des Bastions, le promeneur peut observer, outre la population résidentielle de corbeilles à déchets, l'apparition éphémère de certaines de ces variétés, florissant les jours de fête.

fig. 7

LA COLONNE MORRIS

Au cours du XIXe siècle, la multiplication des lieux de divertissement, comme les théâtres, les salles de bal et les cirques, entraîna une accumulation chaotique d'affiches publicitaires.

À partir de 1855, l'imprimeur et éditeur Ernst Litfass cultiva à Berlin des colonnes pour annonces, les « Litfaßsäulen », déshérenant l'affichage sauvage de manière radicale. Leur nouvelle espèce (*Columna nuntiorum*, *fig. 8*) fut très appréciée, car elle empêcha que les annonces furent recouvertes. En outre, les autorités lui étaient favorables, car elle leur permit de placarder des informations officielles et de surveiller les affichages.

En 1868 à Paris, l'imprimeur Gabriel Morris implanta cent cinquante colonnes similaires.

Sa société couvrait les frais de culture et s'occupait de la pose des affiches. Les employés municipaux assuraient l'entretien du meuble ; on considérait par exemple la colonne Morris, quoique centenaire, ne puisse échapper à cette analyse et à ses conséquences.

fig. 8

LA TABLE D'INFORMATION

La table d'information partage des racines communes avec l'enseigne antique (*Nota negotii*), une des toutes premières espèces du mobilier urbain. L'enseigne régna jusqu'au XIXe siècle, période durant laquelle elle recula au profit de l'affiche. Celle-ci en réaction à cette conception du mobilier urbain dans la seconde moitié du XXe siècle.

En France, l'affiche était l'un des principaux moyens utilisés par les autorités pour faire connaître les lois. L'affiche avait besoin de tables ou de panneaux porteurs ; ainsi, le genre Monitor proliféra dans la ville moderne, et évolua vers des espèces destinées tant à la publicité qu'aux informations touristiques. Les espèces actuelles en sont distinguées par leurs finalités et par leurs formes.

Au parc des Bastions, le promeneur peut apprécier des panneaux montrant un plan de situation, ainsi que des informations sur l'histoire, les monuments et la végétation (*Monitor situs*, *fig. 9*). À l'extérieur du parc, les espèces cultivées correspondent à la variété publicitaire (*Monitor propagans merces*), durant la saison électorale, on observe l'abondante floraison d'une variété éphémère destinée à l'affichage politique (*Monitor propagans publicus res*).

fig. 9

LE POTEAU INDICATEUR D'ARRÊT

L'ère des transports collectifs urbains commença au début du XIXe siècle avec l'omnibus tiré par des chevaux. À cette époque-là, la ligne et ses points d'arrêt n'étaient pas définis de façon très nette ; on pouvait pour repère une enseigne ou un édifice caractéristiques. Plus tard, le tramway détermina un trajet exclusif et, étant donné son succès, demanda une exploitation plus rationnelle. Des arrêts furent donc définis, ce qui, toutefois, n'empêcha pas les usagers de monter et de descendre du véhicule en marche, surtout dans les centres-villes.

D'habitude, la description de la ligne était affichée en toutes lettres à l'avant des véhicules, et les arrêts intermédiaires sur les côtés. La densification des réseaux créant la confusion, les règles commencèrent à identifier leurs lignes au moyen de numéros.

Après avoir introduit la systématisation des arrêts fixes en 1899, la ville de Paris implanta le premier poteau d'arrêt (*Monitor stationis*, *fig. 10*) en bordure de la voie en 1911. Proches d'un porte-bannière, ces indicateurs affichaient sur le poteau le nom de l'arrêt, ainsi que le numéro et le nom des lignes qui le desservaient.

Coriace, cette espèce s'est avérée prolifique dans le monde entier en s'adaptant aux conditions locales et à l'évolution technologique. Les variétés récentes abritent des écrans informant les passagers en attente de la progression du véhicule espéré.

fig. 10

LA PLAQUE DE RUE

La plaque de rue (*Nota nominis-viae*, *fig. 11*) apparut au XVIIe siècle, portant parfois le nom de la ville qu'elle indiquait, parfois seulement la désignation des quartiers ou du nom ; en peu, on pouvait repérer une enseigne qu'elle délimitait. En France, l'usage des plaques de rue remonte à son règne de Louis XIV. À Paris, l'obligation de signaler les rues par l'apposition de leurs noms date de 1728.

Les numéros, en revanche, étaient quasi inconnus à cette époque. Dès 1770, Vienne cultiva la numérotation continue de toutes les édifices, afin de faciliter le travail des facteurs et le recrutement militaire. Quand cette ville adopta les plaques de rue au XIXe siècle plus tard, le système viennois, un modèle d'ordre et de rationalité, se révélait complexe ; des plaques ovales identifiaient les voies radiales, des plaques rectangulaires les voies transversales ; la couleur de leur contour changeait en fonction des neuf arrondissements de la ville.

Dans les villes modernes, l'expansion géographique, même que la mobilité croissante des biens et des personnes, appelèrent à une identification générale des rues et des immeubles. Aujourd'hui, les plaques sont implantées à presque chaque fin du XXe siècle, la loi relative à la surpopulation. Le promeneur peut observer aux alentours du parc des Bastions un éventail remarquable de formes, de couleurs et de matières qui se prêtent mieux aux éventuels changements de nom des rues.

fig. 11

LE PANNEAU DE SIGNALISATION

La culture de la borne kilométrique (*Terminus terminus*) pendant l'Empire Romain marque le début de la signalisation routière. Inconnus au Moyen Age, les signes routiers réapparaissent en 1698 en Angleterre, quand une loi astreignit les municipalités à implanter des indicateurs de direction (*Nota itinerum*) aux intersections des routes.

À la fin du XIXe siècle, les associations de cyclistes introduisirent les panneaux d'avertissement (*Nota cautionis*), relatifs à l'état des routes. C'est de la systématisation de ces panneaux sauvages que naquirent en 1909 les premiers quatre signes internationaux : cassis (dos d'âne), virage, croisement, passage à niveau.

Cependant, leur implantation était encore difficile en ville. En effet, confrontées à une circulation dense, les villes avaient développé une attitude différente : elles ne devaient ni renseigner ni avertir, mais réglementer. Les agents de circulation intervenaient par des gestes et des coups de sifflet, mais s'avéraient bientôt dépassés par la circulation motorisée.

En zone urbaine, le panneau de réglementation (*Nota regularum deambulationis*, *fig. 12*) apparut d'abord à Detroit, en 1914 : las de crier, un agent de police, Harry Jackson, avait coupé les angles d'une tôle carrée et ajouté le mot STOP.

Les résistances tombées, les panneaux de signalisation colonisèrent rapidement les villes. Ils se propagèrent d'ailleurs à tel point que l'on en vint à parler, vers la fin du XXe siècle, de surpopulation. Le promeneur peut observer aux alentours du parc des Bastions un éventail remarquable de formes, de couleurs et de matières qui se prêtent à leurs multiples usages.

fig. 12, fig. 13

LE FEU DE SIGNALISATION

Le premier appareil régulant la circulation fut implanté en 1868 devant la House of Parliament à Londres, permettant aux députés une traversée aisée de la rue. Dérivé d'un signal de chemin de fer, il était constitué de deux bras articulés et pourvu d'un feu rouge et vert. Actionnée manuellement, cette espèce singulière ne remplaçait pas l'agent de circulation, mais amplifiait ses mouvements.

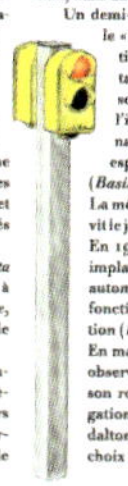

Un demi-siècle plus tard, en 1912, apparut à Paris le « Kiosque signal » : une variété hybride constituée d'une guérite élevée où couverte, abritant un agent qui actionnait des lampes et une sonnerie. Après cinq mois de service difficile, l'installation fut abandonnée. Elle donna cependant naissance, dans sa forme simplifiée, à une nouvelle espèce cultivée à l'étranger, la guérite de carrefour (*Basis gubernatoris deambulationis*).

C'est d'abord en Angleterre, au début du XXe siècle, que l'espèce du lampadaire (*Lumen erectum*, *fig. 14*) s'imposa grâce à sa capacité de se connecter à un réseau : dès 1807, Londres cultiva l'éclairage au gaz provenant de la distillation du charbon cokéfiable. Paris, déjà « Ville lumière », s'illumina d'autant plus entre 1840 et 1860, lorsque le prix du gaz devint abordable pour les municipalités. Ainsi, une variété de lampe à incandescence étaient traversés à distance des façades, tous les cinquante mètres à cause des voitures. Le gaz d'éclairage mit en valeur une nouvelle forme esthétique, crépusculaire et nocturne, par l'harmonisation des puissances lumineuses et des couleurs.

À partir de la seconde moitié du XIXe siècle, on expérimenta la splendeur de la lampe à incandescence. Ces nouveaux lampadaires étaient en général réservés aux artères principales, et accompagnés de colonnes porteuses de lampes. En 1930, à Detroit, l'agent de police William Potts implanta les premiers feux tricolores, variété qui devint automatique l'année suivante. Ayant trouvé son mode de fonctionnement et sa forme définitive, le feu de signalisation (*Lumen regulans, fig. 13*) conquit le monde. En marge de la circulation automobile, le feu peut toutefois observer aux alentours du parc des Bastions d'autres lampadaires des nouveaux sanitaires publics payants, à l'extérieur. Certains, comme les « cabines de nécessité », une variété typique du Paris de Haussmann, étaient payants et confiés aux soins de gardiens chargés de leur entretien. D'autres, comme les « chalets de nécessité », étaient gratuits (*Latrina omnibus*) n'apparurent qu'à la fin du XIXe siècle.

Depuis, la spécialiste Decaux propose de nouveaux sanitaires publics payants, à l'extérieur. Certains, comme les « cabines de nécessité », une variété typique du Paris de Haussmann, étaient payants et confiés aux soins de gardiens chargés de leur entretien. D'autres, comme les « chalets de nécessité », étaient gratuits (*Latrina omnibus automatica*).

fig. 14

LE BANC PUBLIC

On peut constater la présence de bancs publics dans les villes du Moyen Age, directement intégrés aux bâtiments. Les premiers exemplaires solitaires de cette espèce (*Subsellium omnibus*, *fig. 15*), en bois, apparurent à Paris entre 1605 et 1612, sur la Place Royale. Parallèlement, cet élément noble du mobilier privé abdiqua ses formes majestueuses pour se répandre dans les jardins publics, laissant par la population des chaises de location (*Sella pensione*), très appréciées dans les jardins publics.

Le banc fut introduit massivement dans la ville au XIXe siècle, dans le cadre de l'aménagement des espaces verts. Sous la Restauration, dès 1830, de nombreuses voies furent plantées à Paris ; le préfet Claude-Philibert Barthelot de Rambuteau y disposa des bancs et des bornes-fontaines. Depuis lors, le banc est devenu l'équipement incontournable des avenues, des voies piétonnes, des parcs et des places.

Le banc flâneur, coupé des accoudoirs, prolifère en Europe à partir des années 1980. Des variétés rares, comme le banc-affiche et le banc-abri lumineux, ont été cultivées avec un succès moindre. De nos jours, des bancs à borne Wi-Fi intégrée représentent une variété très prisée dans les villes à vocation de « cité globale ».

fig. 15

L'AUBETTE OU ABRIBUS

Au cours du XIXe siècle, le développement des transports publics entraîna également celui de nouvelles espèces, cultivées pour satisfaire les besoins collectifs naissants. Les arrêtés les plus importants furent équipés d'un édicule destiné aux passagers en attente ; parfois y étaient intégrés des locaux réservés aux inspecteurs de la ligne ainsi que des points de vente de billets.

Dans les années 1930, une variété plus légère proliféra dans la capitale française : une structure métallique rectangulaire, permettant d'émettre quelques rampants, mais aussi d'accès à toutes les humeurs du tramway. Ces barrières métalliques canalisaient les voyageurs qui attendaient leur tour. Cet abri peine en vert foncé constituait, plus encore que la barrière, un indicateur, le signal visuel de l'arrêt.

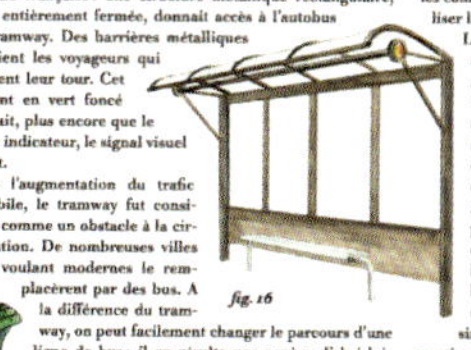

Avec l'augmentation du trafic automobile, le tramway fut considéré comme un obstacle à la circulation. De nombreuses villes qu'après avoir été oblitérées par un autre dispositif. Simple d'usage, cette pratique s'est répandue dans nombre de systèmes de transport à accès contrôlé.

Le progrès dans le domaine de l'électrotechnique permit de concevoir des distributeurs capables d'émettre plusieurs types de billet et d'y ajouter lieu et date de l'émission. Dans les années 1960, le distributeur implanté aux arrêts de transport urbain (*Largitor reservum*, *fig. 17*) apparut simultanément dans plusieurs villes et en Europe continentale.

Aujourd'hui, l'espèce a considérablement évolué, ayant acquis notamment la capacité de parler et de rendre la monnaie. L'autre est fermée et appartient payante. Deux sont actuellement menacées par une nouvelle génération de caissettes groupées, plus performantes et conformes aux exigences du mobilier urbain contemporain.

fig. 16

LE DISTRIBUTEUR DE TITRES DE TRANSPORT PUBLIC

Bien que la vente automatique ait des racines très anciennes, le véritable développement du distributeur commença à la fin du XIXe siècle : dans les années 1880, des distributeurs automatiques de cartes postales apparurent à Londres, ainsi que des automates à chewing-gum sur les quais de gares aux Etats-Unis.

À Paris, à l'époque de Haussmann, naquirent les premiers kiosques à journaux. Manifestant le passage de la vente ambulante à un système de points de vente fixes, cette espèce (*Aedicula acturum-diurnorum*) colonisa rapidement la capitale française, et par la suite le monde entier.

En ce qui concerne le distributeur automatique de journaux (*Largitor acrorum-diurnorum*, *fig. 18*), les documents démontrent l'existence d'une population isolée, cultivée à Lyon autour de 1887. Cependant, l'espèce ne s'imposa qu'à partir de 1964, lorsque plusieurs journaux nord-américains, de la côte Est et à Chicago, adoptèrent la « News-paper Vending Machine », remplaçant ainsi des milliers de vendeurs humains.

Quant aux caissettes observées aux alentours du parc des Bastions, il s'agit de deux variétés cultivées de façon désordonnée : l'une est ouverte, distribuant des quotidiens gratuits ; l'autre est fermée et appartient payante. Deux sont actuellement menacées par une nouvelle génération de caissettes groupées, plus performantes et conformes aux exigences du mobilier urbain contemporain.

fig. 17

LA CAISSETTE À JOURNAUX

La vente de journaux dans l'espace public peut prendre trois formes différentes : par criée, dans un kiosque ou par distributeur automatique. Parmi les nombreux vendeurs ambulants qui avaient l'habitude d'annoncer leur présence par un son de cloche, un chant ou une mélodie, les criés de journaux marquèrent l'environnement sonore de la ville jusqu'au début du XXe siècle.

Dans les pays industrialisés du monde occidental, les excréments canins se sont multipliés sur la voie publique. En 1981 à Thoune, le menuisier et inventeur suisse Josef Rosenast développa le « Robidog », un distributeur de sachets destinés aux excréments canins (*Cista pargamentorum*). Son appareille est élu la cérémonie des mœurs des sociétés post-industrielles.

La première espèce standardisée d'urinoir (*Latrina viris*) fut introduite à Paris en 1834, sous l'administration du préfet Claude-Philibert Barthelot de Rambuteau. Cette vespasienne — ainsi appelée d'après l'empereur romain Vespasien qui décida de prélever sur cet équipement un droit d'usage — était constituée d'une colonne couverte d'une calotte sphérique, évidée du côté de la chaussée en forme de tulipe.

La forme et la taille des urinoirs ont connu des variantes multiples, et ont souvent servi comme support d'affiches à l'extérieur. Certains, comme les « cabines de nécessité », une variété typique du Paris de Haussmann, étaient payants et confiés aux soins de gardiens chargés de leur entretien. Les cabinets ouverts aux deux sexes (*Latrina omnibus*) n'apparurent qu'à la fin du XIXe siècle.

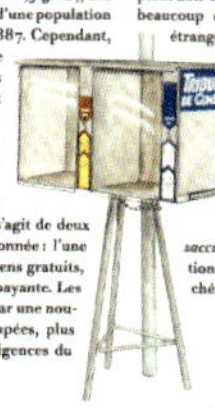

Depuis, la spécialiste Decaux propose de nouveaux sanitaires payants, à service payant est critiqué ; en 2006, les appareils du sol Parisien, par exemple, ont muté en variétés gratuites (*Latrina omnibus automatica*).

fig. 18, fig. 19

LE DISTRIBUTEUR DE SACHETS POUR EXCRÉMENTS CANINS

Il s'agit d'une espèce tardive du mobilier urbain qui vit souvent en symbiose avec la corbeille à déchets (*Cista pargamentorum*). Son apparition est le reflet de l'évolution des mœurs des sociétés post-industrielles.

Dans les pays industrialisés du monde occidental, les excréments canins se sont multipliés sur la voie publique. En 1981 à Thoune, le menuisier et inventeur suisse Josef Rosenast développa le « Robidog », un distributeur de sachets destinés aux excréments canins (*Cista pargamentorum*).

fig. 19

LES TOILETTES PUBLIQUES

Jusqu'à l'époque industrielle, la miction et la défécation avaient lieu dans l'espace public, faute de toilettes à l'intérieur des édifices. Les villes se dotèrent d'établissements plus ou moins sophistiqués, à l'instar des deux rangées de soixante sièges de la « House of Easement », au XVIe siècle à Londres, dont les trous donnaient sur la Tamise.

La première espèce standardisée d'urinoir (*Latrina viris*) fut introduite à Paris en 1834, sous l'administration du préfet Claude-Philibert Barthelot de Rambuteau. Cette vespasienne — ainsi appelée d'après l'empereur romain Vespasien qui décida de prélever sur cet équipement un droit d'usage — était constituée d'une colonne couverte d'une calotte sphérique, évidée du côté de la chaussée en forme de tulipe.

La forme et la taille des urinoirs ont connu des variantes multiples, et ont souvent servi comme support d'affiches à l'extérieur. Certains, comme les « cabines de nécessité », une variété typique du Paris de Haussmann, étaient payants et confiés aux soins de gardiens chargés de leur entretien. Les cabinets ouverts aux deux sexes (*Latrina omnibus*) n'apparurent qu'à la fin du XIXe siècle.

Depuis, la spécialiste Decaux propose de nouveaux sanitaires publics payants. Depuis leur apparition, le coût de modèles concurrents, ce service payant est critiqué ; en 2006, les appareils du sol Parisien, par exemple, ont muté en variétés gratuites (*Latrina omnibus automatica*).

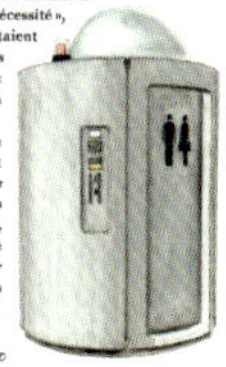

fig. 20

La présente exploration a été menée dans le cadre de *Botanique urbaine*, un projet de Legoville. www.legoville.net

Les illustrations sont de Colette Grand.

Botanique urbaine a bénéficié du soutien du Fonds d'art contemporain et du Service d'aménagement urbain et de la mobilité de la Ville de Genève.

Extracted from **Manuel de Botanique Urbaine,** *Les espèces du mobilier urbain illustrées et commentée* (Manual of Urban Botany, Species of urban furniture illustrated and annotated)

Legoville
Editions Dasein Paris, 2008

History

Though the first species of the family Mobilia urbana *appeared in the cities of Antiquity, in Mesopotamia, it wasn't until the 1960s that the term "urban furniture" came into general use. We can attribute this locution to the French entrepreneur Jean-Claude Decaux, the creator and introducer of new varieties to the French soil. In the 19th century, despite their significant expansion, objects implanted in the public space were not grouped under a generic term.*

It is very difficult to trace the origins of the first urban furniture because town planners, historians, geographers and other scientists concerned with the cultivation of urban species have never cared to document the evolution of this family. If, in the Middle Ages, certain species developed in an anarchic way, generating situations of conflict inside cities, we must place the first great expansion of this family in the modern and industrial era.

The widespread use of pavements in the 19th century was a determining factor in the birth of urban furniture, as "objects of the street". The development of these fixtures was also linked to the revolution in public transport, and to imperatives of public health – particularly following the cholera pandemics that spread through Europe in 1832 and 1849.

In Paris, the era of Georges Eugène Haussmann was fecund with new "street accessories". This prefect of the Seine département introduced protective awnings, benches, bandstands, and "chalets of necessity" along the tree-planted avenues and newly created squares. Thanks to the work of his architects Davioud, Hittorff and Baltard, a whole generation of new urban furniture appeared on the pavements of the French capital.

"An immemorial phenomenon, which plunges its roots into the memory of cities, urban furniture forms the faithful mirror of the city's decor at the same time as the most direct expression of the daily relationships which unify the city and its inhabitants."

Michel Carmona

[1]
Species that are already extinct, like the stocks, the gallows, the scaffold and the guillotine, were put up as the circumstances demanded ; this furniture, linked to the representation of power, often remained in place for years to warn those who might be tempted to disrupt public order. When they were not being used, these species thus became an urban furniture with a symbolic purpose.

[2]
Michel Carmona, *Le mobilier urbain* (Urban Furniture), p.107

[3]
Michel Carmona, op. cit., p.6

In London, concern to get traffic flowing impregnated all decisions relating to streets from the 18th century onwards. Road signage, the first rules of the road and the obligation to build pavements fertilised the ground for the arrival of new species.

In the industrial city of the beginning of the 19th century, if primitive species gradually disappeared [1], new types of fixtures grew according to criteria of rationalisation and standardisation. The increase in the number of social and individual needs brought about their global expansion. Thus the specialists are quick to admit that urban furniture has become a "major element in the development of the urban landscape". [2]

In the 1960s, in what you could call "the second coming of urban furniture", "street accessories" were given a legal status in France following the momentum given them by Decaux's works, using concepts exported all over the world ". [3]

At the end of the 20th century, urban areas from metropolises down to the smallest town seemed anxious to develop their own and varied typology. Fixtures diversified, became supports for advertising and generated legal controversy. The comfort function was mixed with that of aesthetics, the question of heritage rose up and municipal administrations were judged according to their management of urban furniture. Confronted with the problems linked to its expansion, like overpopulation and mess, the ruling bodies looked to organise the implantations by adapting them to local conditions.

According to certain observers, urban furniture is often the victim of functional mutations – hence the protests raised by certain citizens worried about the fate of their city – and it has been noticed that, these days, boundaries and railings are used by skateboarders, panels and posts as a base for stickers and public toilets as pick-up joints. Elsewhere, posts are transformed into bike racks, fire hydrants into fountains in summer, refuse containers into braziers, benches and railings in the Metro into beds for the homeless and road signs into shooting targets.

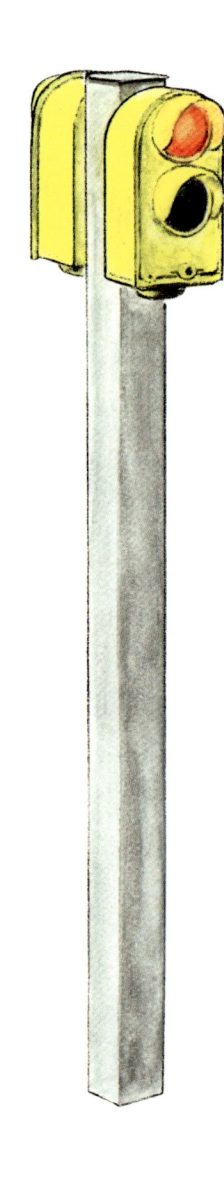

4
Quoted by Marie de Thézy,
in **Paris, la rue** (Paris, the street), p.79

Despite these hijackings, due to the conflictual character of urban life, species of urban furniture have become omnipresent in the landscape of the modern city. These days, streets and parks offer passers-by a variety of urban fixtures designed to satisfy their need for comfort, hygiene, protection and information, as well as a decorative backdrop for their daily activities. And, austere and ordinary as they may be, they seem to offer a projection screen for spirits who dream of the city of tomorrow. In 1869, an anonymous utopian described the furnishing of Parisian streets in the year 2000 thus: "they will definitively be nothing but 'beautiful shops and magnificent salons' these 'gallery-streets', entirely covered, where chairs, armchairs, gilded sofas, perfected padded and covered with rich fabrics, will offer comfortable seats for weary walkers; in the evening they will be resplendent with the thousand lights of golden candelabras and crystal chandeliers; the most modest workers, sumptuously decked out in their ballroom finery, will come here to play great ladies!" [4]

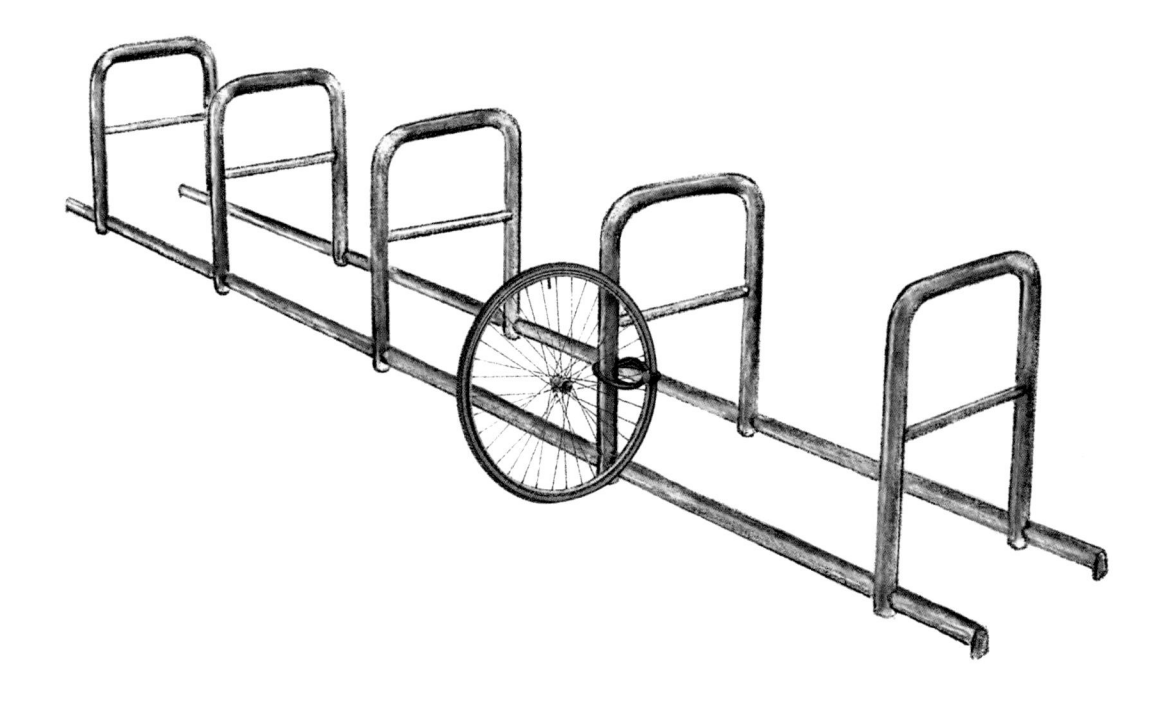

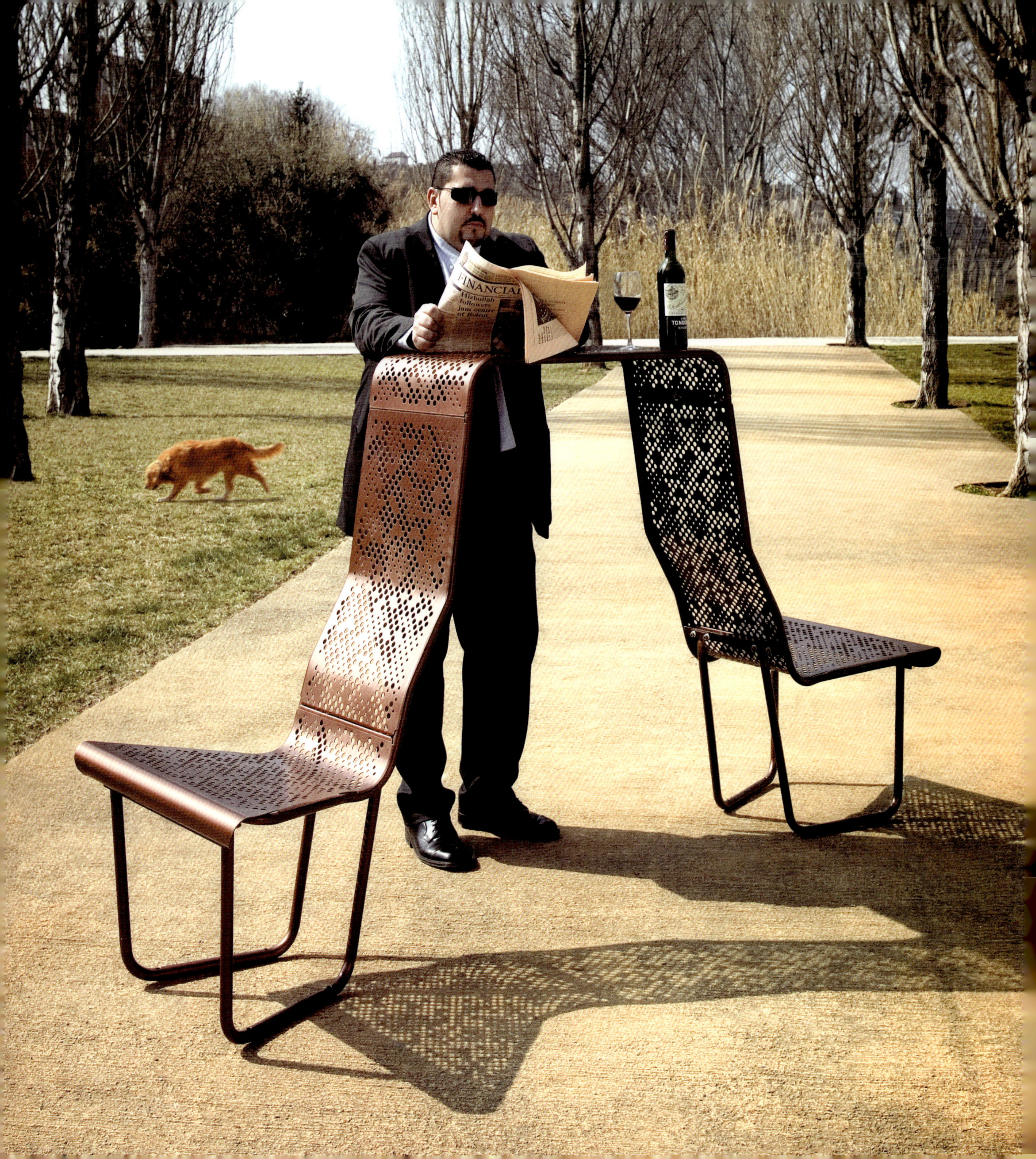
FINANCIAL
Hizbollah followers jam centre of Beirut

01

SEATS OF CONVIVIALITY

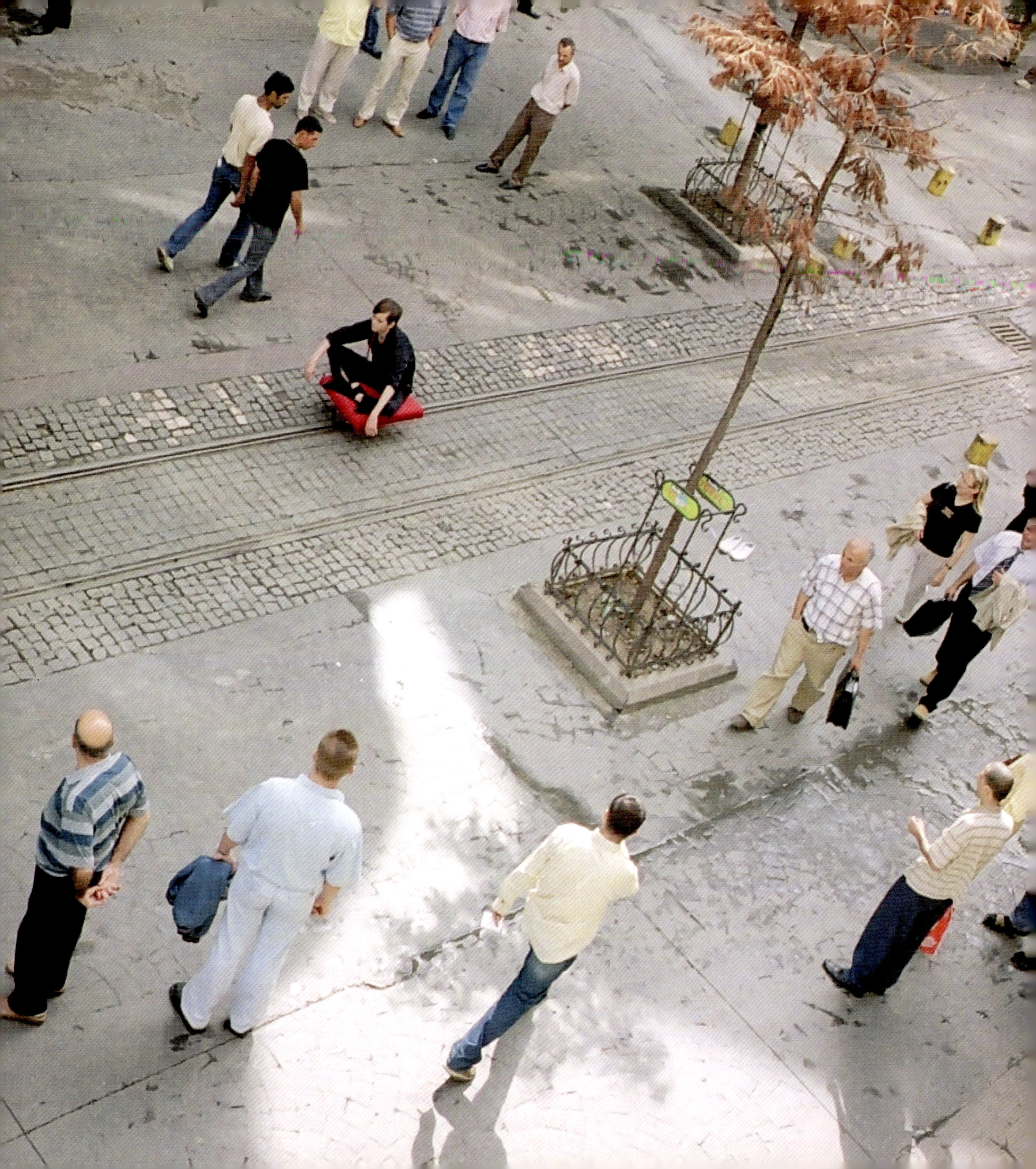

seats of conviviality

the banker - 2005
Alfredo Häberli
BD Barcelona Design
page 18 / cf. page 37

flying carpet - 2005
HeHe
Appropriating an urban element, the rails of a tramline circulating on Boulevard Istiklal, an important pedestrian and shopping street in the west of Istanbul, "Flying Carpet" creates a surprise, attracts attention and encourages exchange, allowing one to go from one encounter to another and so on in the time it takes for this individual, comfortable and strongly evocative seat to make a stop.

pages 20 & 21

Existing since Antiquity, the bench was called *scannum* in Classical Latin, meaning bench or footrest, becoming *bancus* in Vulgar Latin, under the influence of the Germanic term *bank*. From the beginning its use was collective. It was straight and could seat several people, but also came in a semicircular form which was called an exedra in Rome, signifying a meeting place where people could look at each other while talking. We find it again in the Middle Ages, this time with a back and integrated into buildings or independent. Most often it was linked to institutions: justice, for instance, was dispensed here. Over the centuries, through its form and where it was placed, it was the cultural reflection of the evolution of civilisations and societies.

In Europe in the 17th century the bench started to take its place in public spaces, and we find it again in the 18th century in the Tuileries garden in Paris, in tandem with the moveable chairs that one could rent for a moment or for the entire year. In the 19th century, along with the water fountain, it was one of the two principal pieces of furniture on the planted promenades and in the large urban parks created in this era. Becoming inseparable from streets, parks and squares, as it is today, it is one of the main actors in the spatial composition of the different sites in which it is implanted. It gives rhythm to and punctuates landscape layouts, surpassing its original role as an accessory to adopt, gradually, that of a structuring element. It also directs the gaze, offering one of several view points over the surrounding landscape.

Emblematic of urban conviviality, the bench is a place for meetings, planned or random, for pausing alone or with others, and even a rallying point or a place for discussions. Offering the pleasure of being able to sit outside, it is synonymous with a physical but also a psychic pause, a true haven in the incessant movement of the world that surrounds it. Adapting itself over several years to the evolution in how the city is used by its inhabitants, the bench has been transformed into new forms of seat: fixed standing seats; mobile chairs and armchairs or those that can change direction thanks to a pivot; chaise longues, day beds or even lounges. Combined with a table, it allows one to picnic outside or to work, even with a computer, thanks to WiFi technology. Paradoxically the bench, federator of these new alternative and shared uses, is also the symbol of exclusion. It is thus, too often, equipped with armrests or broken into segments to prevent the homeless from getting too comfortable!

il posto seats
2007
Thesevenhints
Miramondo public design
page 22

the uprooting 2006
Charles Laget
This project for the station square in Rennes evokes the uprooting inherent in each long-haul trip. The removal of the usual changes in level between the pedestrian, public transport and car spaces here reinforces the collective disorientation of the users, who are also perturbed by the structures put in place, like the seats that seem to have been torn out of the ground, a metaphor for the force of leaving.

page 23

023

deca chaise longue - 2004
Tobia Repossi
Modo

finferlo standing-seat - 2004
Mitzi Bollani
Modo

nigra seat - 1994
Màrius Quintan & Montse Periel
Escofet

024 seats of conviviality / SOLO

the poet and the loner - 2005
Alfredo Häberli
BD Barcelona Design
cf. page 37

wi-fi seat - 2009
AdrianoDesign
Colomer

025

**Biuro Projektów Lewicki Łatak
Karol Badyna, Marek Kamiński,
Marcin Augustyn, Begoña Herrera
Rodríguez, Przemek Kaczkowski,
Adam Monica, Tomasz Moskal,
Witold Opaliński, Wojciech Pawlik,
Kinga Raczak, Agnieszka Zajączkowska
City of Cracovie**

new Zgody square - Bohaterów Getta square

2005

Rebaptised Heroes of the Ghetto Square (Bohaterów Getta Square) after the Second World War, the former Concorde Square (Zgody Square) was the centre of the Jewish ghetto created in Krakow by the Third Reich. For the renovation of this space, inspiration was sought in the archives of 1943, the year that the quarter was closed by the Germans. A photograph from that year shows a young girl holding a chair with a parcel underneath it, preparing to leave, like so many Jews, with her family's most precious belongings. To evoke this tragic exodus, chairs have been installed on the square. Like the other urban objects of the site, they are in rusted metal, patinated with bronze, losing their primary use to become symbols…

026 seats of conviviality / SOLO

027

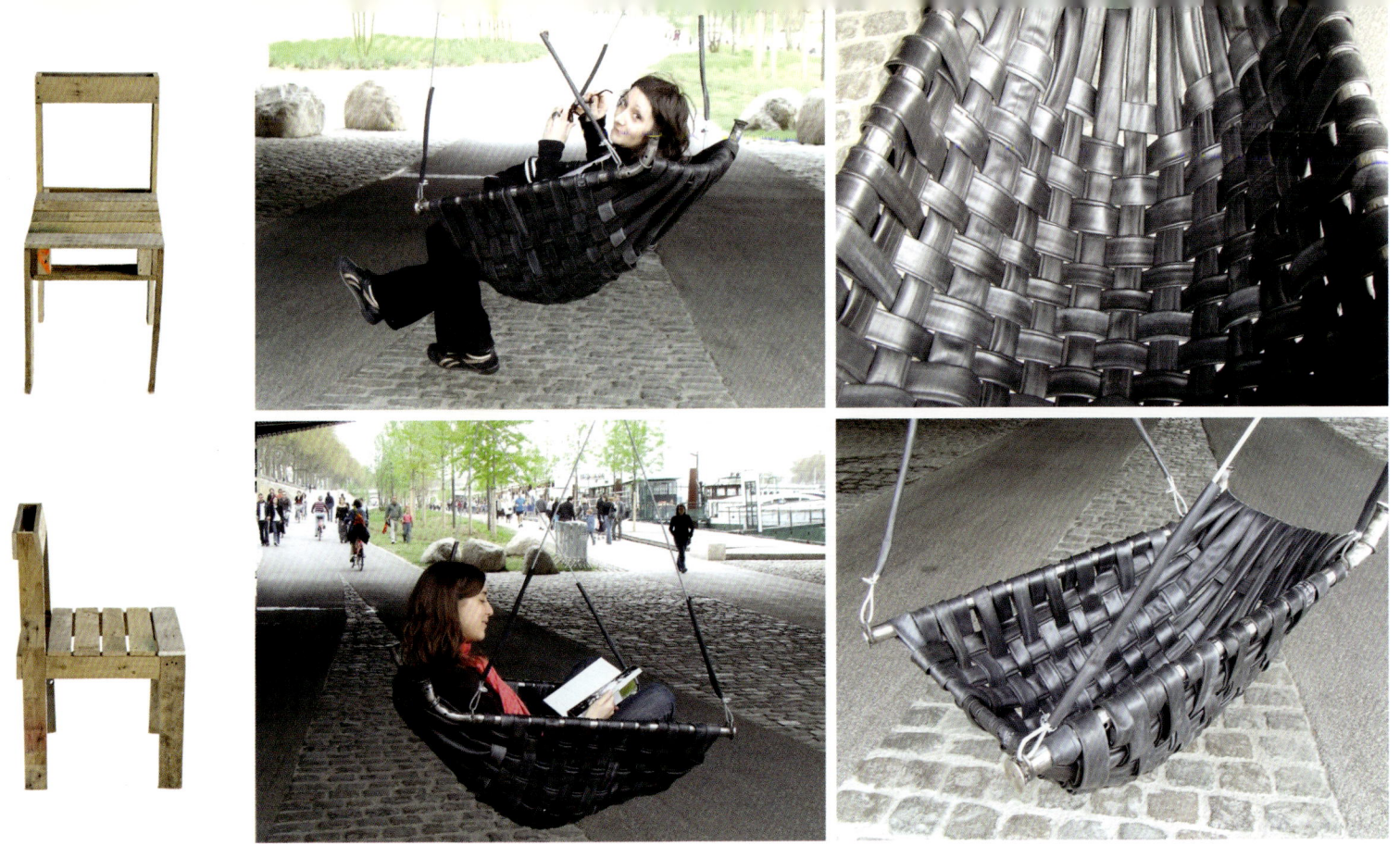

urban hammock-chair - 2009
Compagnie d'architectures Local à Louer : Julie Bernard & Amélie Feugnet

the pallet project - 2007
Nina Tolstrup
Studiorama

avio chairs - 2007
Alberto Dassasso
Vibrazioni Art-Design

028 seats of conviviality / ECO-SOLO

Alexandre Moronnoz

ccc bench

Like a large ruderal plant that grows in the interstices of the city, "Champignon Carbone Capture" ("Carbon Capture Mushroom") takes its place naturally along the lengths of walls, at the foot of tree trunks, or on pavements. Evoking the form of a tree stump or a rock that you might come across in the middle of nature, this contemporary bench offers different possible ways of sitting, its reliefs not conditioning any particular way of using it. Vacillating between geological relief and plant residue, this sculptural object, alone or in a group, is also a functional and ecological graft that captures the polluting emissions contained in the air and ensures their breakdown under ultraviolet rays. The TX Active concrete of which it is made acts as a catalyst, thus cleaning its near environment.

Luxembourg garden chairs

2003

Created in 1612 by Queen Marie de Médicis, the Luxembourg Garden extends over 23 hectares in the 6th arrondissement of Paris. Formal flowerbeds, classical statues, walks under the shade of centenarian horse chestnuts and ornamental pools form a French-style garden, surrounded by spaces landscaped in the English style. This place, which is perfect for wandering, dreaming and serenity, is also the kingdom of chairs. Today, a tradition that dates back to the 18th century is continued for the pleasure of walkers. In those days chairs, more comfortable than the existing benches, were made available for visitors to rent for an afternoon, or to reserve by the year from the chair attendants who had the concession. For more than thirty years they have been available for free at the Luxembourg Garden, one of the last Parisian parks still to have them. The linden-tree green metallic chairs and armchairs, still produced, are thus made available for everyone, forming irregular lines or improvised living rooms under the shade of the trees or, quite the opposite, under the rays of the sun.

Frédéric Sofia
Fermob
Le Sénat

030 seats of conviviality / MOBILE

Noel Blakeman

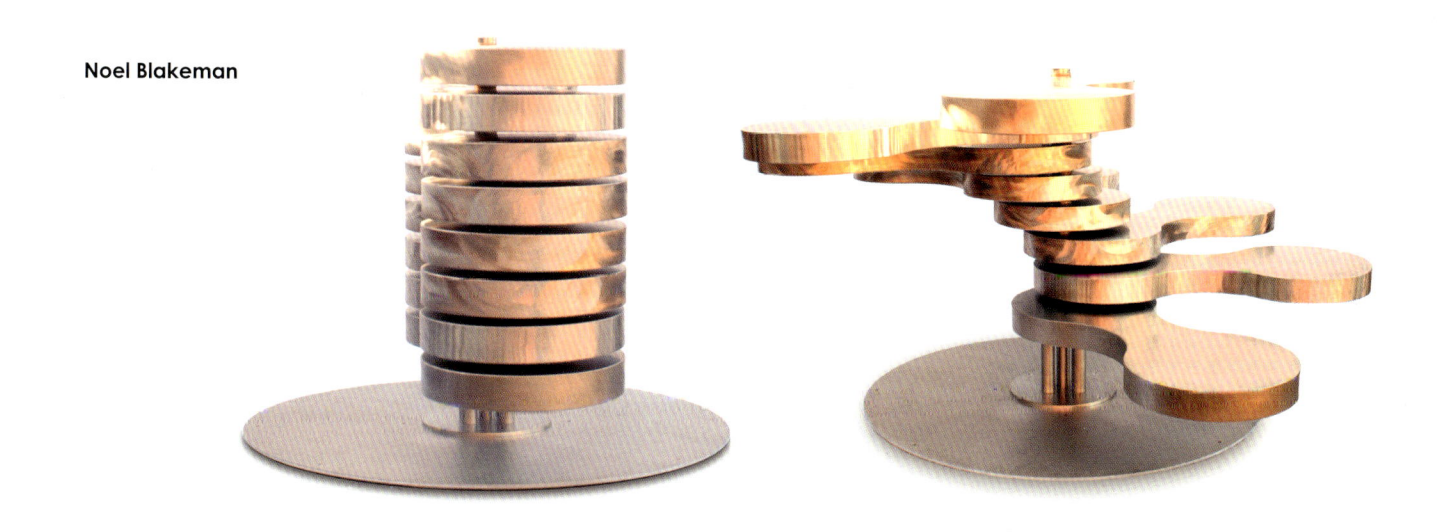

spinning seats

Eight pullout sections can be deployed at will, all of them swivelling on the same 360° central axis. In this way they form a changeable and mobile sculpture that decorates urban spaces such as public gardens. Seats or tables are thus born from the necessities of the moment and the wish to share – or not – a moment of rest, eating or conversation... Like the petals of a flower, its seats open and close, playing with the sun and the different shadows that it creates, or with the nighttime lights of the city.

Sebastian Campion
Festival Ingravid de Figueres

urban cursor

2004

Taking the outsize form of a cursor arrow, normally guided by a computer mouse, Urban Cursor is a mobile bench created to generate new kinds of exchanges by making the public space playful and interactive. Though it is installed on the square of a Catalan town, it makes the link between physical and digital words thanks to a GPS that transmits the seat's geographical coordinates and movements to an internet site. It is then mapped by Google Maps and illustrated by the self-portraits that the users send in voluntarily.

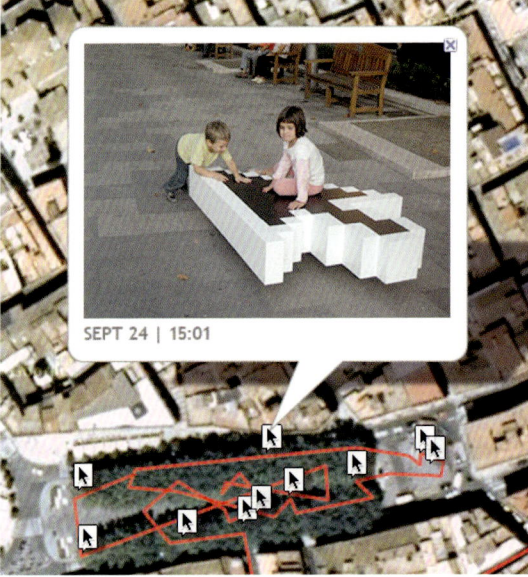

032 seats of conviviality / MOBILE

mobile chairs

In 1983, the Swiss-born French architect Bernard Tschumi won the competition to lay out the first Parisian urban cultural park on the site of La Villette in the north of the capital. Connecting with the resolutely contemporary spirit of the place, imagined as a crossroads for the past and the future, Paris and its suburbs, the city and nature, art and science, body and soul, he called on the French designer Philippe Starck for the exterior furniture. So the latter designed bright silver chairs with pure forms, acute whilst being comfortable, and with the peculiarity of their mobility on the single axis of their surprising and decentred foot. Punctuating the 55 hectares of the La Villette park, these 195 seats have just celebrated their 25th birthday and for the occasion have been replaced or restored, continuing to invite the walker through the shimmer of ambient light reflected on their entirely metallic structure.

Philippe Starck
EPPGHV

signchair - 2008
Ken Mori & Jenny Liang

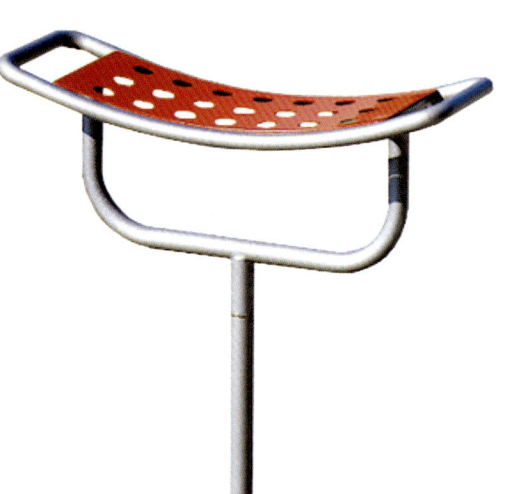

playtime stool - 1999
Frédéric Dedelley
Burri Public Elements

evolution stool - 2001
Frédéric Dedelley
Burri Public Elements

034 seats of conviviality / MOBILE

the high line

In the 1930s, an aerial railway line was put into service in the west of Manhattan, New York, The High Line. Fifty years later this line, completely disused and abandoned, has been transformed into a planted walk. Happily, the identity of this site has been kept through the preservation of a section of the rails, which interpenetrates an immense longitudinal concrete decking, accentuating the directional flow of this pedestrian pathway. They host wooden armchairs and chaise longues on runners, which can slide in order to modify the configuration, allowing to change the viewpoints over the Hudson River for the walkers.

**James Corner Field Operations
Landscape & Urbanisme
Didier Scofidio + Renfro architecture
Friends of the High Line
& City of New York**

you & me bench - 2009
Thomas de Lussac

Romeo & Juliette bench - 2009
Thomas de Lussac

chaise longue for two - 2006
Charles Laget

036 seats of conviviality / DUO

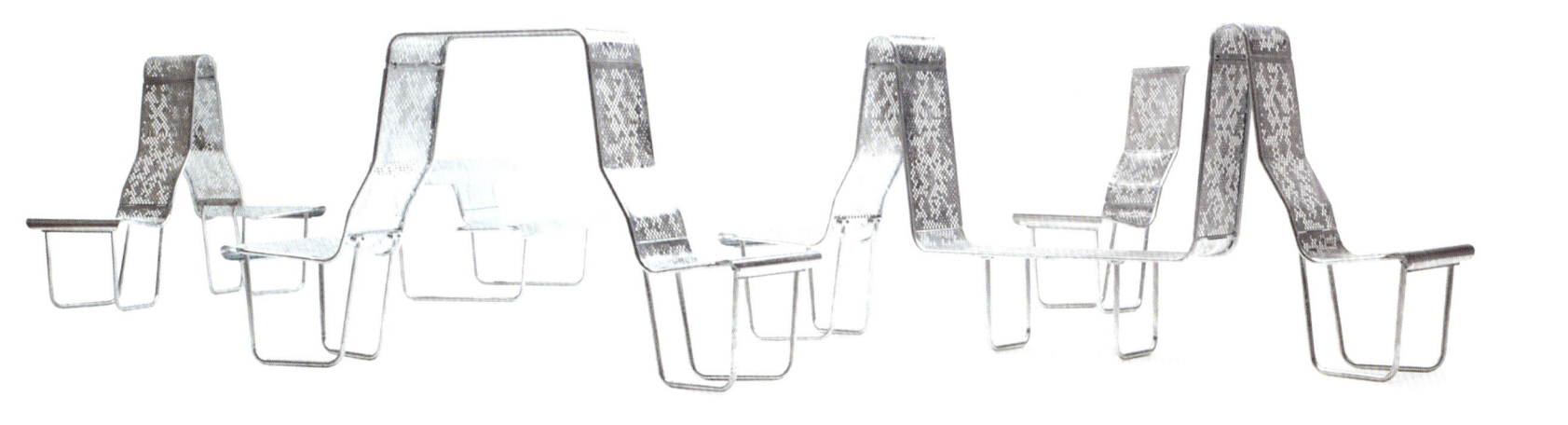

swiss benches

When designing Swiss benches the Swiss designer Alfredo Häberli was inspired by "Banco catalano" created in 1974 by Oscar Tusquets and Luis Clotet for the same manufacturer, itself conceived as a contemporary and revisited homage to the bench model that Antonio Gaudí created for the Güell park in Barcelona (1900-1914).

Here we discover the same attention to ergonomics and the use of perforated metal, giving both lightness and transparency to the different seats, ensuring that rain water does not stagnate and maintaining coolness in summer and warmth in winter. This collection of benches expands on several complementary but unusual functions aside from that of sitting. Thus, "The poet" offers a writing table integrated into its back, allowing one to work or to eat lunch. "The banker" takes up this idea, but higher up, like a personal bar, and "The philosopher" offers a visual and physical intimacy, but also gives the choice of thinking or reading alone or in company.

Alfredo Häberli
BD Barcelona Design

banda doblada bench - 2003
Susanne Cierniak & Tran Thanh Minh Nguyen
Càtedra Blanca UPV - Cemex, Escofet

prat table and stool - 2003
Mercè Llopis
Escofet

set-square bench - 2008
Thomas Grenier

038 seats of conviviality / DUO

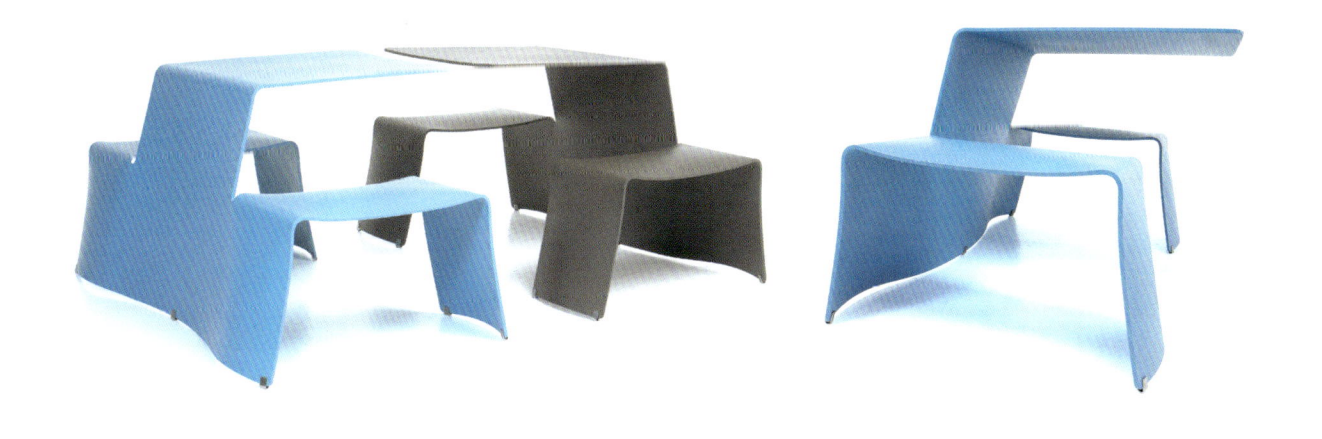

PicNik table

Created for small urban or private spaces, the PicNik table is both a functional object and a monochrome sculpture, its pure and contemporary forms accentuated by its unity of colour, seeming to stretch out naturally in space. Cut out of a standard half sheet of metal, then folded, it is also designed according to the ecological philosophy of economy of resources, offcuts being reduced to the bare minimum.

Dirk Wynants & Xavier Lust
Extremis

company bench - 2005
Olivier Chabaud et Laurent Lévêque
Compagnie

coral bench - 2009
Chris Kabatsi
Arktura

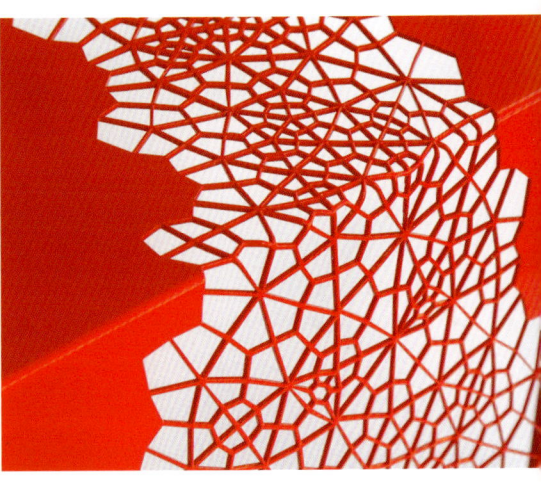

hive bench - 2009
Chris Kabatsi
Arktura

interferences bench - 2007
Alexandre Moronooz

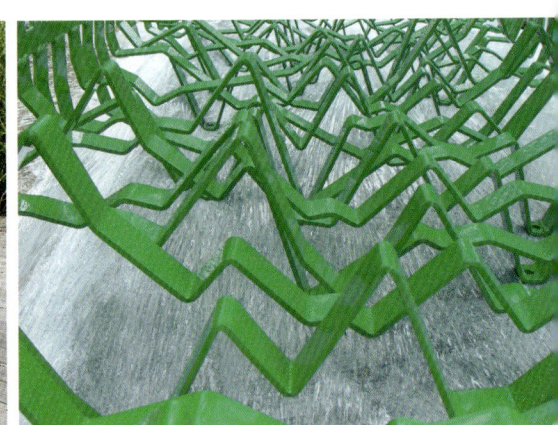

040 seats of conviviality / MESHES

Jo Meester & Marije van der Park

green oasis

From the back, it's a classic gazebo in white trellis, adorned with climbing plants offering themselves up to be admired. But, on walking round it, a funny object materialises before the astonished eyes of the walker: a mechanical digger than has become a garden factory! Associating nature and technology, Green Oasis thus has a double function. On the one hand it's a place of conviviality and intimacy such as you rarely find in the urban space, a green room in which one can enter and sit down, surrounded by the acrobatic species that symbolise the force of nature, and on the other hand it's a metallic moucharaby, letting the light filter through and muffling the sounds of the city. Through its formal incongruity, it is also an interpellation of the urban space as a permanent building site, in expansion to the detriment of a nature that is always receding.

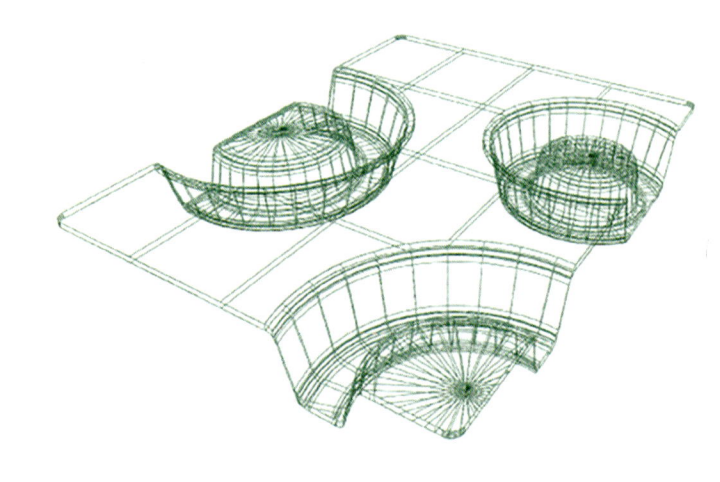

illycopresto - 2005
Gaël Le Nouëne + Marie Lang
Les Ateliers O-S architectes

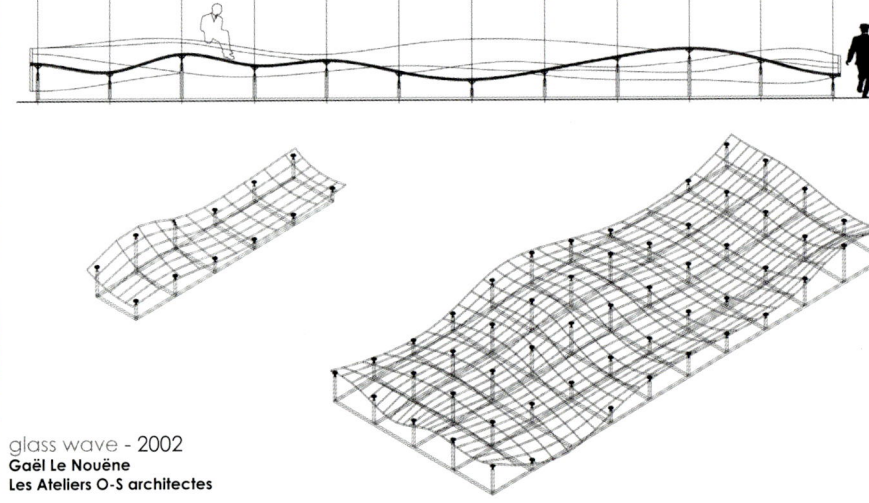

glass wave - 2002
Gaël Le Nouëne
Les Ateliers O-S architectes

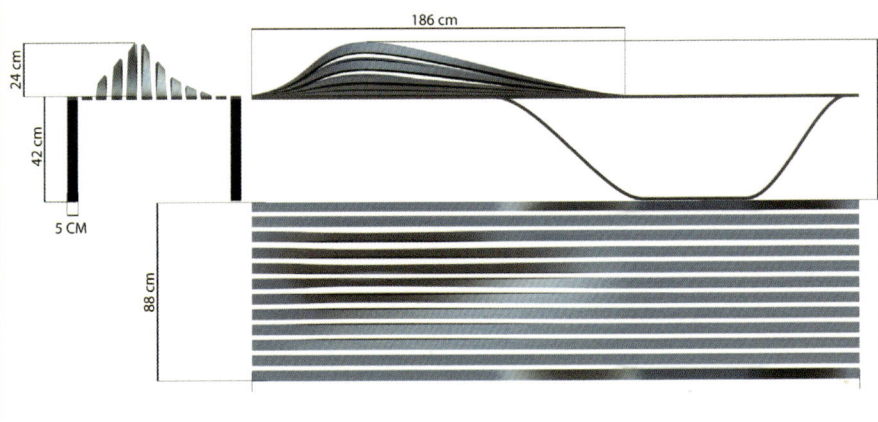

trek bench - 2009
Charles Laget

042 seats of conviviality / UNDULATIONS

burnt branches bench - 2005
Landfabrik

115 bench - 2007
Charles Laget

y bench - 2006
Alexandre Moronnoz

urban adapter bench - 2009
Rocker-Lange Architects

memory chair

The Kasumigaseki quarter of Tokyo, situated south of the Imperial Palace, is historically the site of the different ministries of the Japanese government. Progressively, their different buildings have been requalified or reconstructed, like the Central Government Building N°7, reassigned to the Ministry for Education, Culture, Sports, Science and Technology, and completed in 2007. For the creation of its new garden, special attention was paid from the outset to the memory of the site. Thus, on 11 July 2003, at one forty-seven and fifteen seconds in the afternoon, before the destruction of the old building, the shadows of its architecture and of the surrounding vegetation were recorded, and then printed on the stone benches of the future edifice. Today, they harmoniously accompany the play of the sun's rays on the structures and the leaves of the new plantings, recalling the history of the place and the passage of time.

Earthscape
Government of Japan

xurret bench - 2003
Abalos & Herreros
Escofet

045

140 325 58

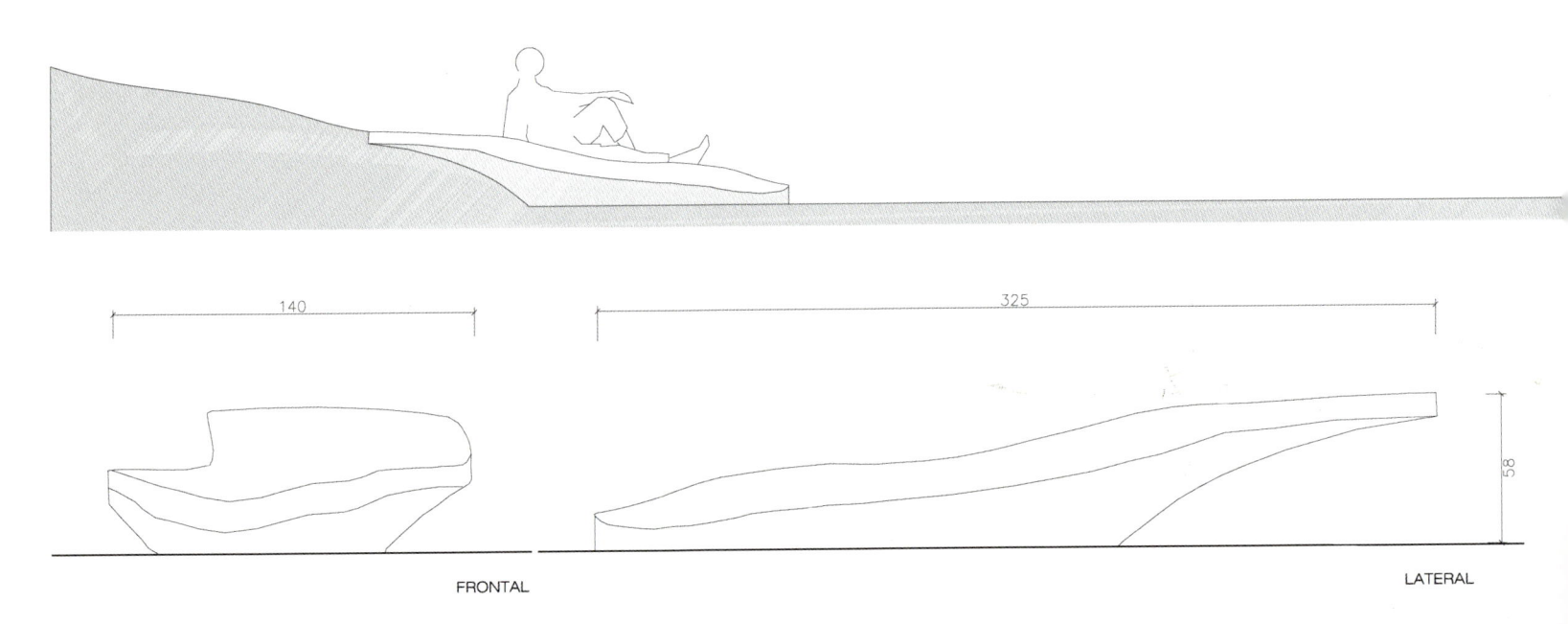

FRONTAL LATERAL

slope bench - 2000
Pich-Aguilera Arquitectos
Escofet

046 seats of conviviality / BIOMORPH

ALZADO c

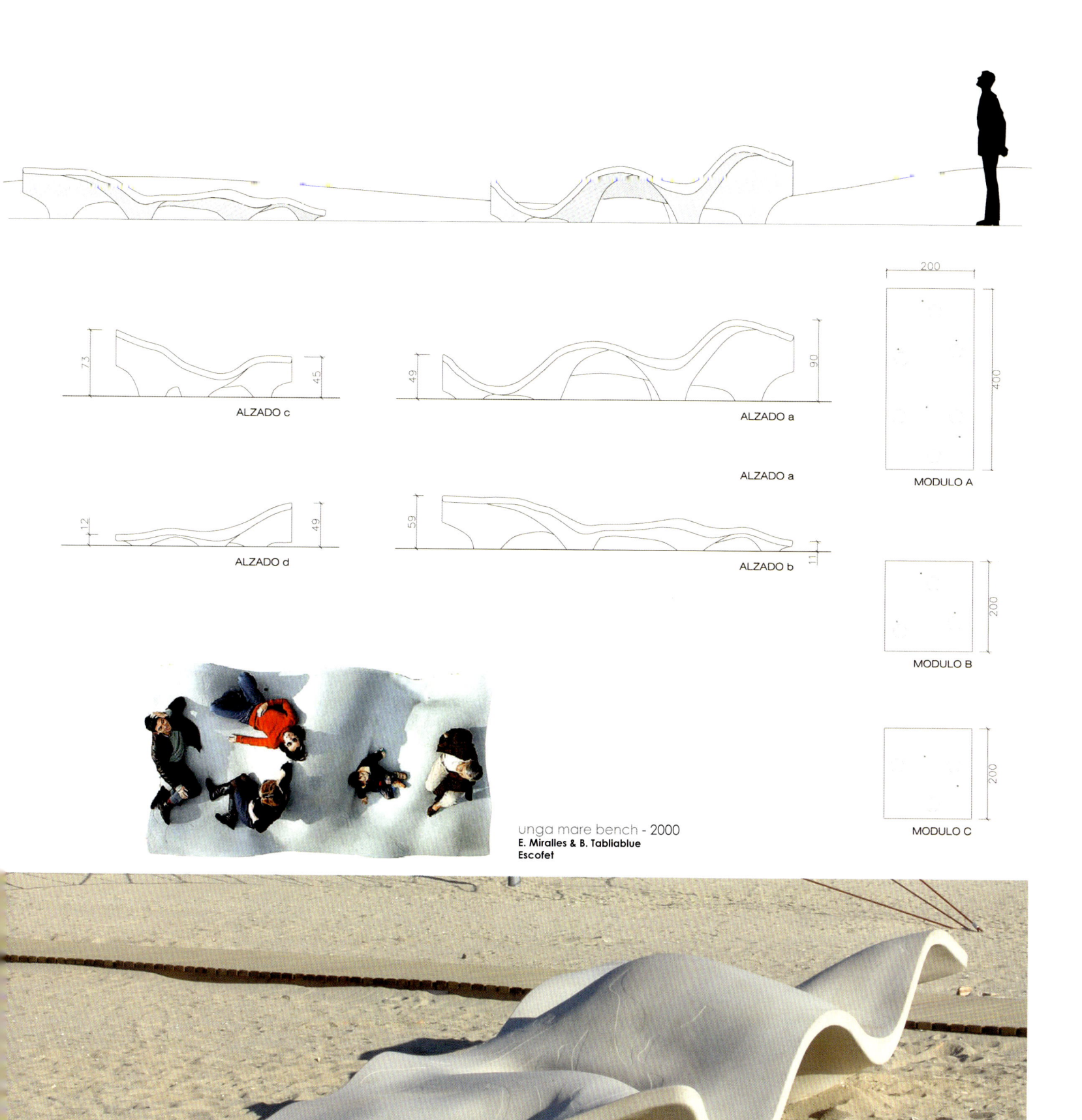

ALZADO a

ALZADO a

MODULO A

ALZADO d

ALZADO b

MODULO B

unga mare bench - 2000
E. Miralles & B. Tabliablue
Escofet

MODULO C

047

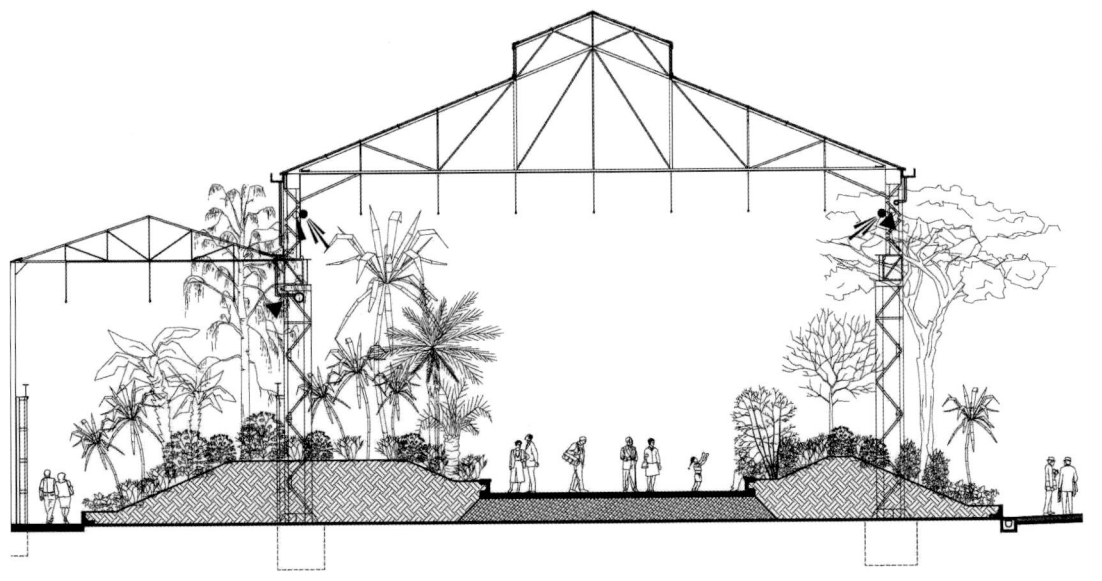

ADH / Doazan + Hirschberger
SAMOA

foundries garden

The Foundries quarter and its unusual garden forms part of the ambitious and well considered requalification project for the 337 hectares of the Île de Nantes. On the Loire, at the centre of the Nantes metropolitan area, this old industrial and river port site is on the way to a transformation, to encourage urban diversity while preserving the traces of the past.

This garden is emblematic of this approach, through its creation in the iron-framed hall of the Atlantic Foundries, where the propellers of famous ocean liners such as Le France were smelted. Entirely open to the city, it arranges in scenes, around the old ovens, a hundred or so plant species which are today very common but which arrived in Europe from the 16th to the 18th centuries via the Atlantic coast.

Both a covered passageway and a giant greenhouse, its aisles are not dotted with benches in the classic way. Instead they have been integrated into the planted spaces and invite one to relax, to rediscover and to contemplate, through immersion in the leaves and flowers of rhododendrons, azaleas, magnolias or other camellias, symbols of acclimatisation and adaptation, speaking of exile, of welcome and of lands of exchange…

049

puls bench

2007

Puls is designed to allow one to enjoy the landscape on all sides, a 360° view. Its simple but very studied form visibly offers different heights of seats and different ways of sitting. It is at the same time a bench and a chaise longue, but also a play structure that is very stable for children, and which they can climb on via its several faces and ladders. An everyday, multi-use object that requires no instructions, "made from what we recognise without even having seen it before", as their Danish designer, Martin Hartmann, says.

Martin Hartmann

Jean-Christophe Nourisson
Abbaye de Maubuisson
Conseil général du Val d'Oise
École Nationale Supérieure
d'Architecture et de Paysage de Lille
Ministère de la culture et
de la communication
& DRAC Nord Pas-de-Calais

from one place to another 5 & 7

These two projects are based in the first place on an attentive reading of the intervention sites and on a sensitive perception of what they exude through their preexisting elements. At the Cistercian abbey of Maubuisson, a heritage site that has become a centre for contemporary art, five functional abstract sculptures punctuate different parts of the enclosed park, contrasting with the grassy zones. Five benches, which are above all broken planes, created in composite concrete and painted red, thus attracting attention, invite the walker to take a siesta, read, have a conversation or simply to look at them. Using them is not obligatory, the visual apprehension of them is just as important.

At the National School of Architecture and Landscape Architecture in Lille, the context is different: it's an open space, a piece of land in a hollow, surrounded by a park, with several access roads serving three buildings from different eras, including the newly built work of the architect Nasrine Seraji. Three large horizontal planes lightly inclined take their place along the axis that crosses the site. Between a bench, a bed, a rostrum and a draftsman's table, they are indeterminate objects whose possible functions are obvious as they make a direct appeal to the body. These useable sculptures are the visual signs that allow one to create the potential for another use, another way of living…

052 seats of conviviality / PAUSE

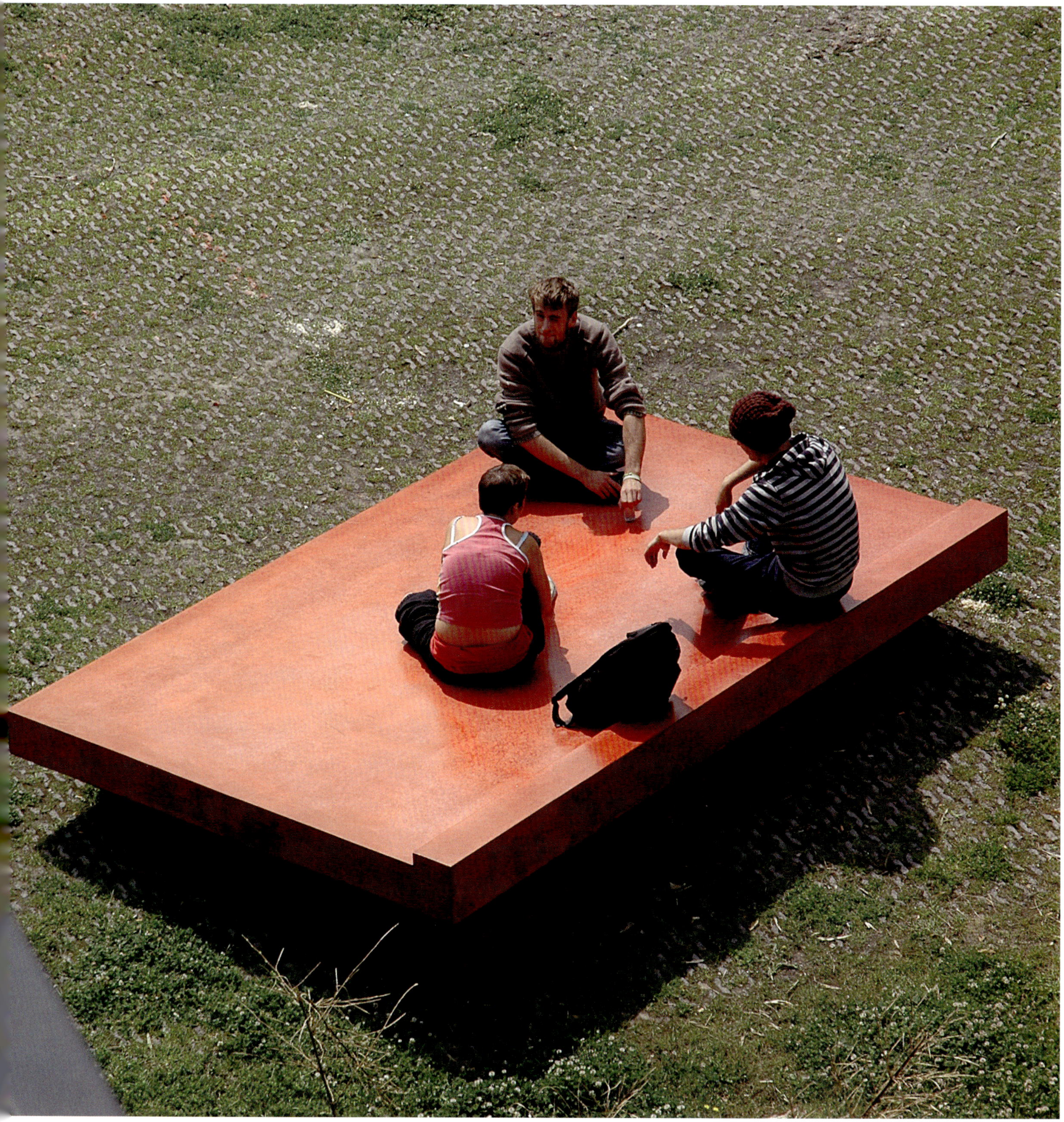

the sixth hour - 2009
Nina Dissard, Marion Vauthier & Loriane Pallatier
Workshop Vaïana Le Coustemer & Anne-Laure Puccini ; École Boule - Sophie Barbaux, Sebastien Wierinck & Sébastien Normand ; Le CENTQUATRE

054 seats of conviviality / REST

crucial collection s benches - 2005
Linde Hermans
Wolters Mabeg

collection ensemble benches - 2006
Roel Vandebeek
Wolters Mabeg

PERSON PARKING

person parking - 2009
Volker Pflüger, Giovanni Doci, John Kock
Springtime Design Team

056 seats of conviviality / PAUSE & REST

Cyrielle Duprez
Rétiwood

shrinkage

Shrinkage is designed for the intelligent rehabilitation of urban wastelands, those abandoned spaces without any precise function that are all too frequent in cities. The special feature of this Furniture/Terrace is the multiple functions it offers to city dwellers who can, thanks to it, become actors in their environment. Furniture: some of its slats can retract and be used to create seats, tables, chaise longues, armrests and footrests with unusual reliefs, to use at leisure. Terrace: when all its mobile modules are folded away, a flat surface is created that can host community events. Adaptable, this original object is also ecological as it is made from retified oak, which means it is pyrolysed at a high temperature to improve its resistance to fungi and insects naturally, and thus increase its lifespan for exterior use without using chemical products.

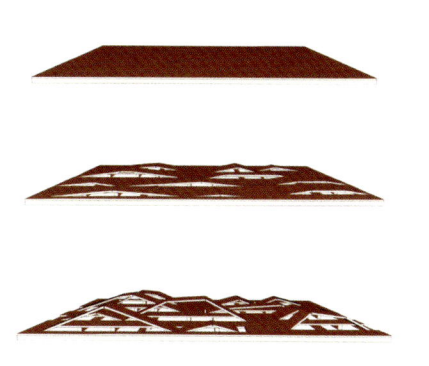

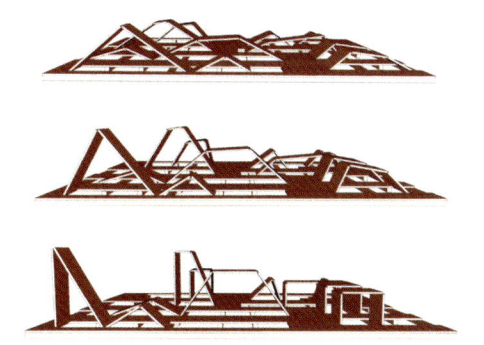

university of social sciences II campus - 2008
Kirk+Specht Landschaftsarchitekten
Campus Oberstufenzentrum Sozialwesen II

058 seats of conviviality / PAUSE & REST

riverside park south - 2008
Thomas Balsley Associates
Trump / New World Holdings, Extel / Carlyle Group, City of New York Department of Parks & Recreation & Country of clients

capitol plaza - 2005
Thomas Balsley Associates
Witkoff & Adel Corporation

325th fifth avenue - 2008
Thomas Balsley Associates
Douglaston Development

060 seats of conviviality / TO THE TABLE!

the table of the 4 locks

In Dunkirk, a place where the inhabitants of the Rosendaël quarter no longer looked, at the foot of their residential tower blocks, has become "their" garden through the simple and pertinent creation of parcels of land to cultivate and convivial elements made of wood with a real economy of resources. 1x1m squares planted with kitchen garden vegetables and herbs and equipped with wooden chaise longues have been installed, punctuating the bank of the Furnes canal. And a large table 35m long, wisely cut in half to allow a small way through, has also taken its place. Its orientation and its scale, adapted to the mass of the surrounding buildings, have allowed the locals to look anew at the site of the 4 locks, which they inhabit and maintain since its creation and where all their parties now take place.

Xavier Coquelet
Mathieu Gontier
François Vadepied
Atelier 710
Ville de Dunkerque
MJC de Rosendaël

aromatic tables

2010

Part of the Cartoucherie de Vincennes theatre complex, l'Atelier de Paris (Paris workshop) is directed by the choreographer and dancer Carolyn Carlson. All year long, dance companies rehearse here and masterclasses are organised, as well as a festival, June Events. To offer students and spectators a convivial outside space, large tables have been installed under the foliage of hundred-year-old chestnut trees. They have been designed from recycled objects and materials, old sleepers made from exotic wood and five tulip-shaped bins, which form the feet and also host aromatic plants with evocative scents, there to be shared…

Colas Baillieul & Sophie Barbaux
Les Rudologistes Associés
Atelier de Paris / Carolyn Carlson
Ville de Paris / DEVE

062 seats of conviviality / TO THE TABLE!

Cabanon Vertical
Le Bruit du Frigo, Festival « Lieux Possibles »

the mobole

Over the course of the festival "Lieux possibles" ("Possible places"), the Ramparts Garden in Bordeaux is unusually open to the public. On climbing an ephemeral staircase, you arrive at the secret lawn that overlooks the quarter of Saint-Michel. A wooden structure welcomes walkers looking for an interlude that is both convivial and intimate. Made up of a unique table and the benches that go with it, one end of it transforms into a hut in raw planks, a love nest for one night for those who wish. Stretching out under the cover of the trees, it thus offers several uses throughout the day: a space in which to snack, but also an improvised chaise longue or even a place for children to play. Its forms evoke calligraphy in relief, with the physical presence of its users punctuating the poetic phrase.

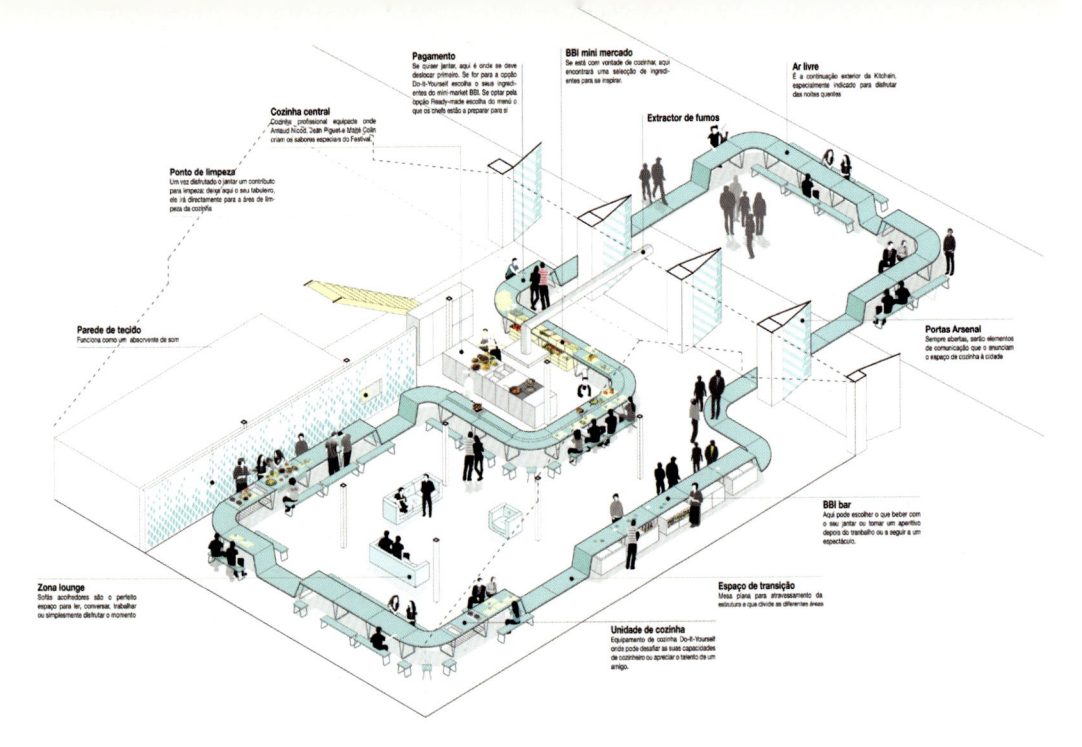

MOOV
António Louro
Benedetta Maxia
Festival Belluard Bollwerk Internacional

kitchain

In the framework of the BBI Festival in Fribourg, Kitchain was designed to unite and federate a temporary community made up of artists, visitors and the organisational team.

Inspired by camping facilities, Kitchain runs and meanders between a double space, interior and exterior. Taking the form of an immense table, it's both a convivial place in which to eat and a kitchen. Different means of storing and cooking food, such as a barbecue, are integrated into it, as well as a bar. Its forms can change according to its functions.

The festival-goers are invited to taste the dishes offered and if they wish they can also go over to the other side and cook themselves. This alternative and collective system resulted in the rediscovery and revitalisation of the founding ritual of the making and sharing of a meal.

064 seats of conviviality / TO THE TABLE!

065

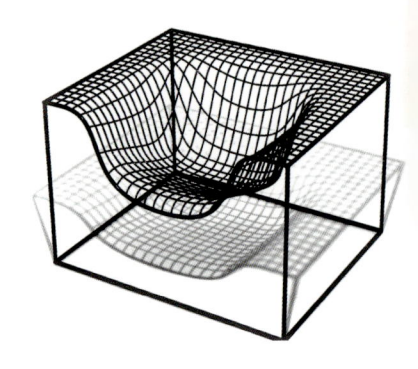

concrete things - 2008
Komplot Design
Nola

urban furniture Roppongi Hills - 2003
Andrea Branzi

b love bench - 2003
Ross Lovegrove
BD Barcelona Design

066 seats of conviviality / LOUNGE

outdoor living rooms

"Same time, same place" and "Your turn" are two lines of furniture designed for creating outdoor living rooms. They make up a body of seven elements which, through their design and the way they are used, set up a double reversal. Archetypes of domestic furniture moulded in concrete, these are therefore forms that cross over from a usual interior usage to an outdoor usage. What's more, the configurations that they allow can be adapted according to each site, modifying perception, so that each object, armchair or table forms an exception in space as a solitary object, and creates hypotheses of situations according to the direction it faces and how it is arranged in space in relation to the others. Facing each other, in a group or on their own, in the shade of trees or in an open space, these different pieces of urban and landscape furniture can make temporary private zones appear, ideal for a moment of relaxation, or for meeting other people…

Dehove & Lauro

Wagon Landscaping
Atelier Pré Carré
Coloco
Studio Basta
Festival Archstoyanie

levinets [lab]scape

For the past ten or so years, Moscovite architects and artists have set up an open-air museum of contemporary art in the village of Nikola-Lenivets, 200 km from Moscow. Starting in 2006, the Archstoyanie Festival has presented here each year the work of the collective who began the project, and invited artists. In 2009, the 710 workshop was given the task of designing the lines of the park and the maintenance of its 45 hectares of agricultural and natural spaces.

It installed a [lab]scape laboratory here to observe the natural environments and to develop via experimentation an economical form of landscaping. Here the knowledge of Russian farmers, artists and architects and that of invited French and Belgian landscape architects intersect in order to come together in this adventure. Agricultural (pasture, cereal cultivation) and forestry techniques are used to sculpt and maintain the site, the adopted rule being not to plant anything here.

Furniture elements have also been designed for setting the scene and for directing people's gaze in the immense space offered to the public. High seats, wide chaise longues and convivial terraces have been built in wood, integrating the vegetation or integrating themselves into nature.

069

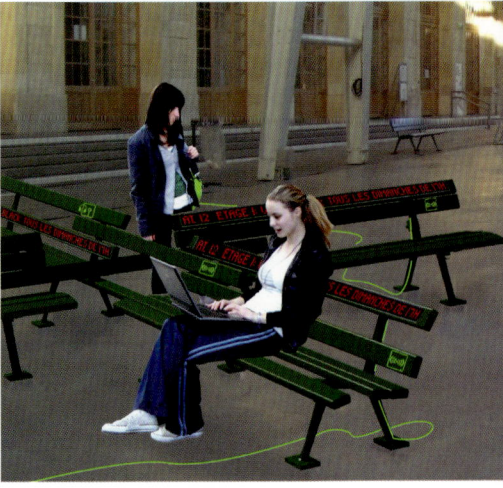

connection - 2009
Jonathan Tijou, Laura Kiritze-topor, Elise Dekens
Workshop Vaïana Le Coustemer & Anne-Laure Puccini ; École Boule - Sophie Barbaux, Sebastien Wierinck & Sébastien Normand ; Le CENTQUATRE

sonoptere, audio-solar armchair - 2008
Michel Redolfi avec Christoph Harbonnier & Marie Pierre Barbazanges
Audionaute

070 seats of conviviality / SOUND LOUNGE

Michael Schoner
Droog Design / Urban Play Event 2

boombench

Designed for the exhibition Experimenta Design Amsterdam 2008, the Boombench was installed for a month and a half on the north quay of the river IJ, in the centre of Amsterdam. An immaculate public bench, it is also a sound system: hidden in its back and its seat was Bluetooth technology that could broadcast music from a mobile telephone less than 15 m away. The high quality sound that it offered (95 dB) provided a happy alternative to the ghetto-blasters and other mobile phone speakers used by teenagers, which often have no real possibility of controlling the base and the high notes. What's more, the form of its seat appealed to comfortable and convivial gatherings. And while broadcasting music in public can attract or repel passers-by – it all depends – Boombench facilitated exchanges either way. Thus the musical offerings, from the songs of Céline Dion to the rap of Lil Wayne, followed on from each other all day long... a kind of free and democratic radio for the docks of Amsterdam!

write the sequel - 2006
Benedetto Bufalino & Victor Vieillard
Festival des architectures vives de Montpellier / Champs libre

ljubljana chair - 2008
ASOBI
MOVISI - Mdular Lightweight Furniture

aaa - 2009
A. Guillot, C. Mangin, C. Buccio, M. Levacher, C-C Jaskulski, M. Coudert, S. Mallebranche
Ecole Bleue

072　seats of conviviality / LOUNGE

Godbout Plante Associés
Ville de Montréal

the performance quarter

Montreal's Performance Quarter is a 1 km² quadrilateral in the city centre bringing together 80 cultural venues and more than 30 major festivals and artistic events. For its urban furniture, the choice went to a contemporary design project that expresses the festive and innovative character of the site. Its most emblematic element is the Festival Square armchair, which, with its pure form and flamboyant colours, evokes the idea of floodlights illuminating street theatre, day and night. The use of Ductal® concrete, a new material without aggregate that can be used to mould objects with daring forms, has enabled the development of this formal and colourful vocabulary, transcending the usual dry perception of concrete while offering attractive and extremely durable solutions. These invigorating individual seats naturally form city lounges inviting the passer-by, or the spectator, to sit down.

bushwaffle - 2008
Rebar
Droog Event 2 / Urban Play

074 seats of conviviality / LOUNGE

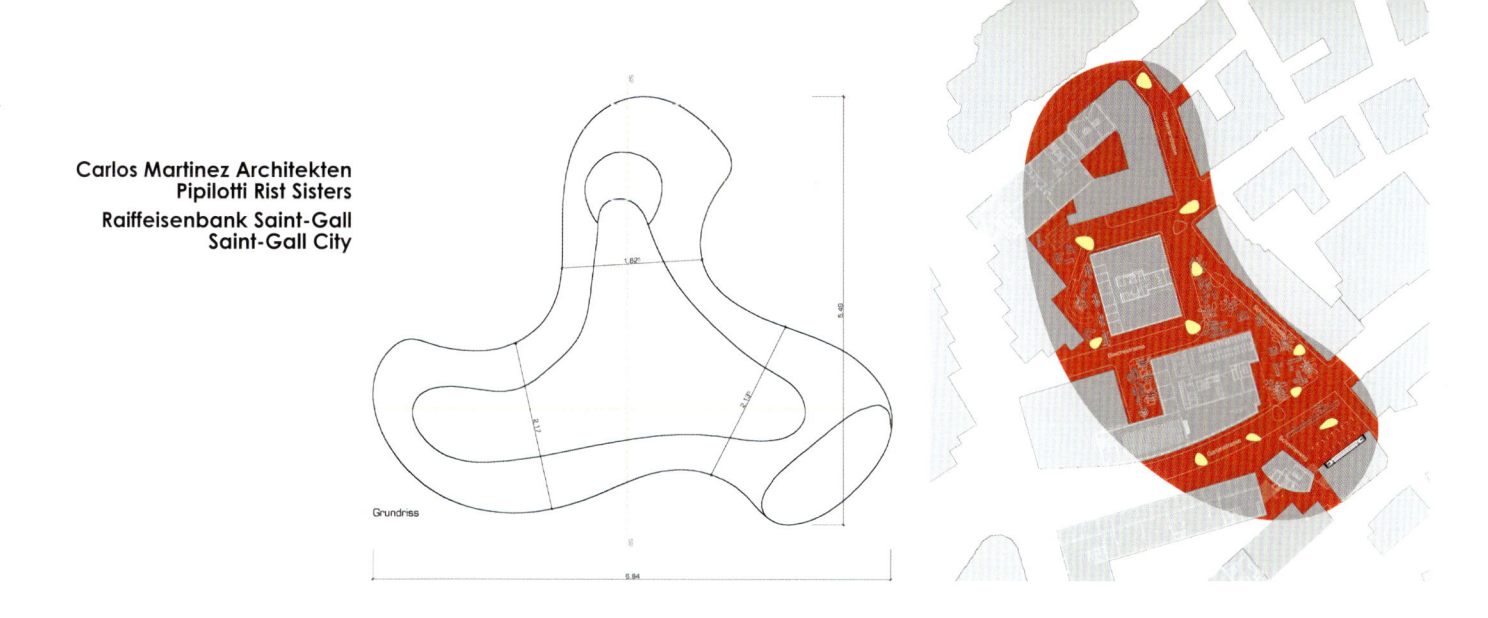

**Carlos Martinez Architekten
Pipilotti Rist Sisters
Raiffeisenbank Saint-Gall
Saint-Gall City**

urban lounge

Entering the newly requalified Raiffeisen quarter of the Swiss city of Saint-Gall, the attention of the passer-by is attracted by the flamboyant carmine colour of the ground, astonishingly supple underfoot. This giant red carpet modifies one's perception of the urban space, unifying the heterogeneous elements that make it up.

The idea is thus to create a lounge on the scale of the city and accessible to everyone, and to give this zone a new function, that of a large and convivial playground just a few steps from the town centre. The pleasant physical sensation is strengthened by the furniture, seats and tables, as well as the different curved reliefs that seem to come up out of the ground whose material – unusual and uniform, smooth and pleasant to touch – they share. They make their presence felt on the surrounding structures like a purple carpet that has become an exterior wallpaper, totally changing the atmosphere. Only four trees have been planted, Ginkgo Biloba chosen for their foliage, which is very light and more particularly golden in the autumn, contrasting elegantly with their environment. The relationship between the exterior and the interior is completely reversed, everything is calmer and even the cars that pass drive slowly in this "living room" where the individual becomes the centre once again.

076 seats of conviviality / LOUNGE

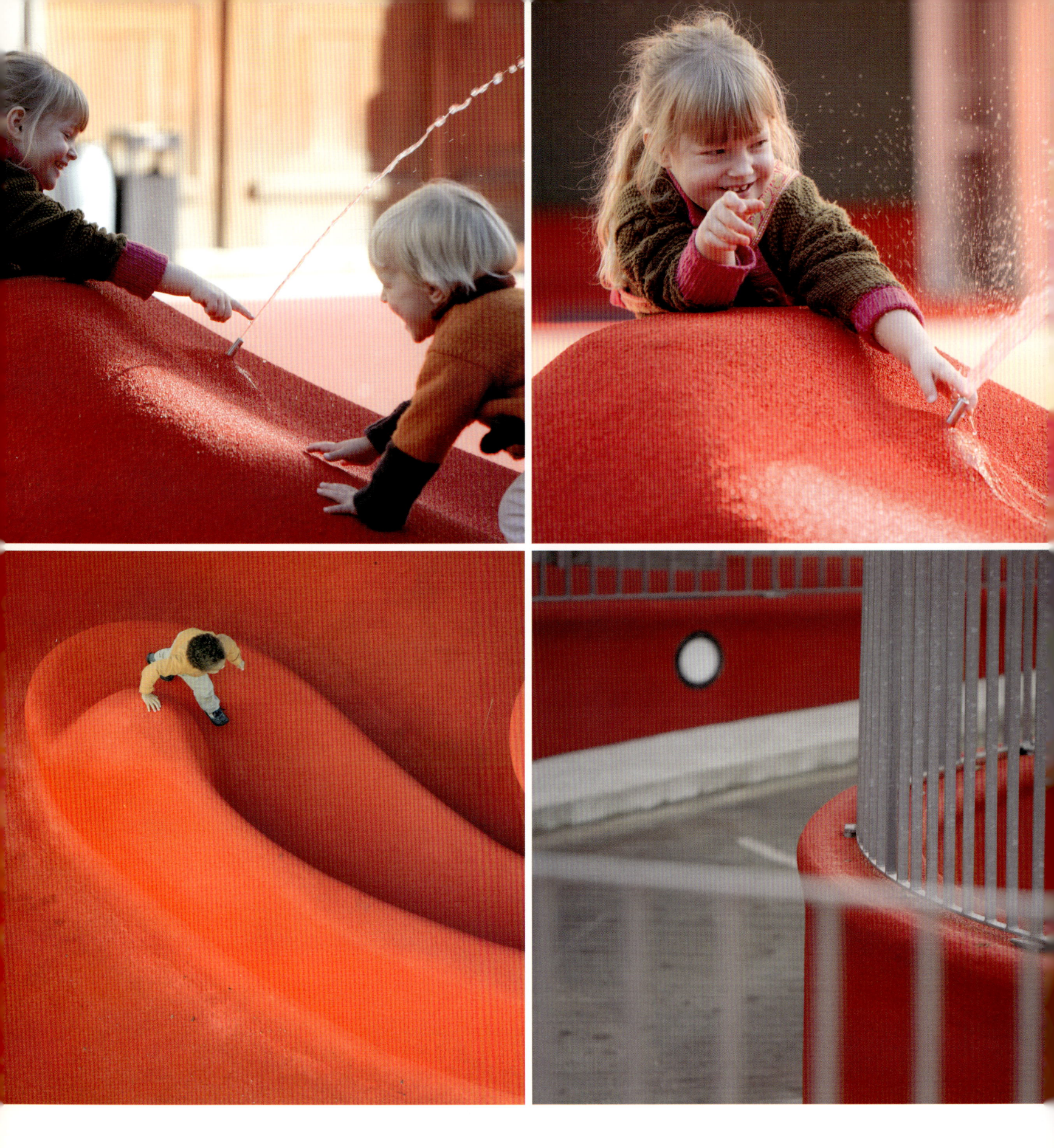

077

ge seat - 2002
Tobia Repossi
Modo

rolling through time and space
Topher Delaney - Seam Studios

078 seats of conviviality / VIEW POINTS

furniture foundation

The château of La Ferté Vidame has had a rough ride over the course of history, and today few elements of the landscaping done in the 18th and 19th centuries remain. While largescale rehabilitation and maintenance works are going on, the park is hosting works of contemporary art, created by artists who have been invited to express their personal take on the place. In 2006, strange objects thus appeared in the midst of the grassy spaces. Like nests or earths, seats sunk into the ground are offered to visitors. Only the backs of these strange structures are visible, inviting the walker to sit under the horizon line, in the middle of the daisies. The perception of one's environment is totally modified with new perspectives, different points of view, and the smells, the sounds of a whole life that one can only discover when close to the earth…

5.5 designers
Eure-et-Loire Department Council

"mirror" bench & extract from nature

The public bench is the supreme example of convivial furniture, made available for shared space, public space. It's also the ideal place for communicating and sharing with passers-by, with walkers. By transforming the whole of the object into a mirror, its back and its seat made in polished stainless steel, the bench becomes an element of the landscape and of the life of the place that it reflects, distorts and gives back in perpetual movement. When its back is painted with moments of nature from elsewhere, a poetic dialogue sets in between the object and its context. The play of reflections from other parts of the object then avoids freezing the image, which succumbs to perceptible alterations of its forms, in particular through the variations of ambient light. Ephemeral or permanent, the perception offered reminds us that everything that surrounds us is a transformation of the natural state.

Cécile Planchais
Cyria

080 seats of conviviality / VIEW POINTS

081

loco bench - 2007
Ivan Palmini
ALL +

catalano bench - 1974
Oscar Tusquets et Lluis Clotet
BD Barcolena Design

082 seats of conviviality / VIEW POINTS

Consortium Daoust Lestage Williams Asselin Ackaoui Option aménagement
Commission de capitale nationale du Québec

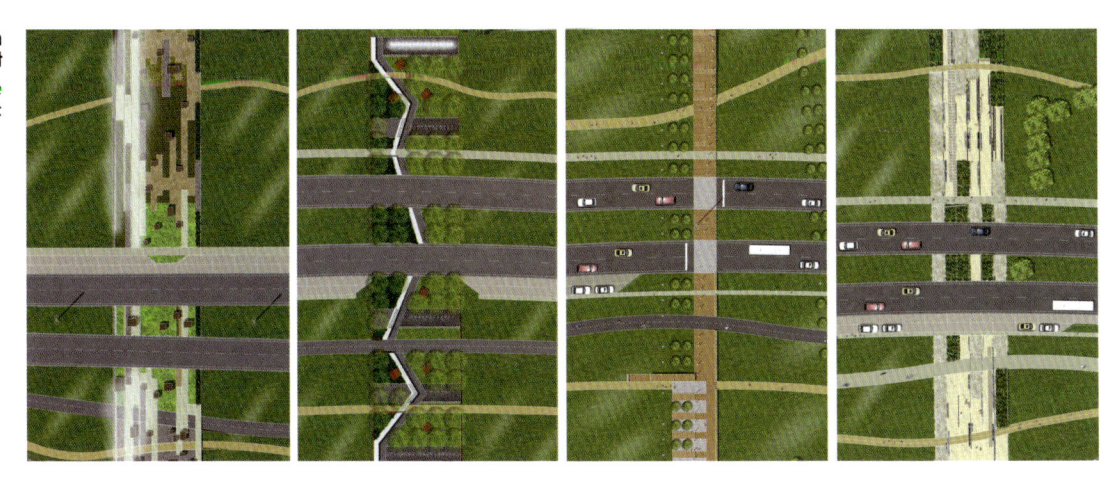

Samuel-De Champlain promenade

Samuel-De Champlain promenade was commissioned by the government of Quebec. Its objective was to give the city of Quebec back its access to the Saint-Lawrence river, while revitalising 2.5 km of coastal landscape. In order to construct a huge cycle path and a pedestrian footpath, the flagship axes of the project, they first needed to move a section of motorway that had been visually integrated towards the interior.

The spirit of the place made reference to the maritime and industrial character of the site, while creating a relationship between contemporary art and nature. Four thematic gardens or quays that make up the cultural focus of the promenade follow on from each other, with names inspired by the moods of the river. The Quay of Mists celebrates the textures and rich geometries of Quebec granite, as well as the unusual ambiances created by mist. The Quay of Tides conveys the undulation of the river, the power of water and of ice through walls and water jets and designs on the ground that evoke the cracking ice. The Quay of Men speaks of the taming of water and nature. Finally, on the Quay of Winds, light and poetic sculptures twirl around, evoking the power of the air and the flight of birds.

Each space offers a chance to stop, to sit down for a moment on different personalised seats, to enjoy the various unfolding views. You can also lie down and enjoy the "gardens of the sky" that offer themselves up at the crest.

084 seats of conviviality / VIEW POINTS

085

flow bench - 2002
Tilman Latz
Divers Cité

timber seat - 1998
West 8

086 seats of conviviality / VIEW POINTS

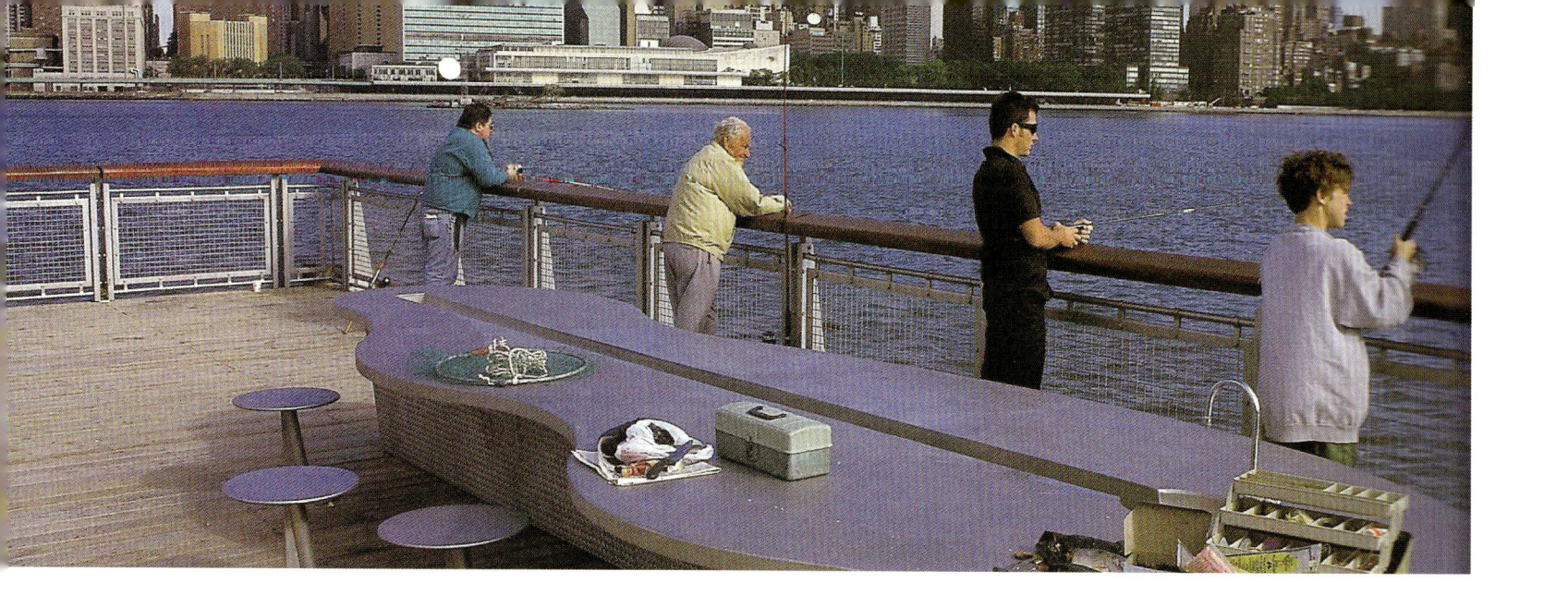

gantry plaza state park

Situated on Long Island, in the west part of the New York neighbourhood of Queens, this new park is the result of the requalification in consultation with local inhabitants of industrial spaces of the old port, whose spectacular 1920s jacks have been preserved. It offers several types of relaxation or games areas overlooking the river, zones laid to lawn or planted with willows, a mist fountain, cafes under the cover of trees, etc., but its main attraction remains the banks of the East River which have been developed as a promenade. They offer a choice of magnificent views of the United Nations building and the island of Manhattan, especially during the annual fireworks festival. A grand jetty has been laid out especially for fishermen with convivial and evocative tables awaiting them. And an immense bench whose forms evoke the undulations of the water runs from one end to the other of the pontoon, an invitation to get together and share the moment.

Thomas Balsley Landscape Architect
Lee Weintraup Landscape Architect
Laura Auerbach
Queens West Development Corporation
Empire State Development Corporation
Port Authority of New York & New Jersey
New York City
Economic Development Corporation

088 seats of conviviality / VIEW POINTS

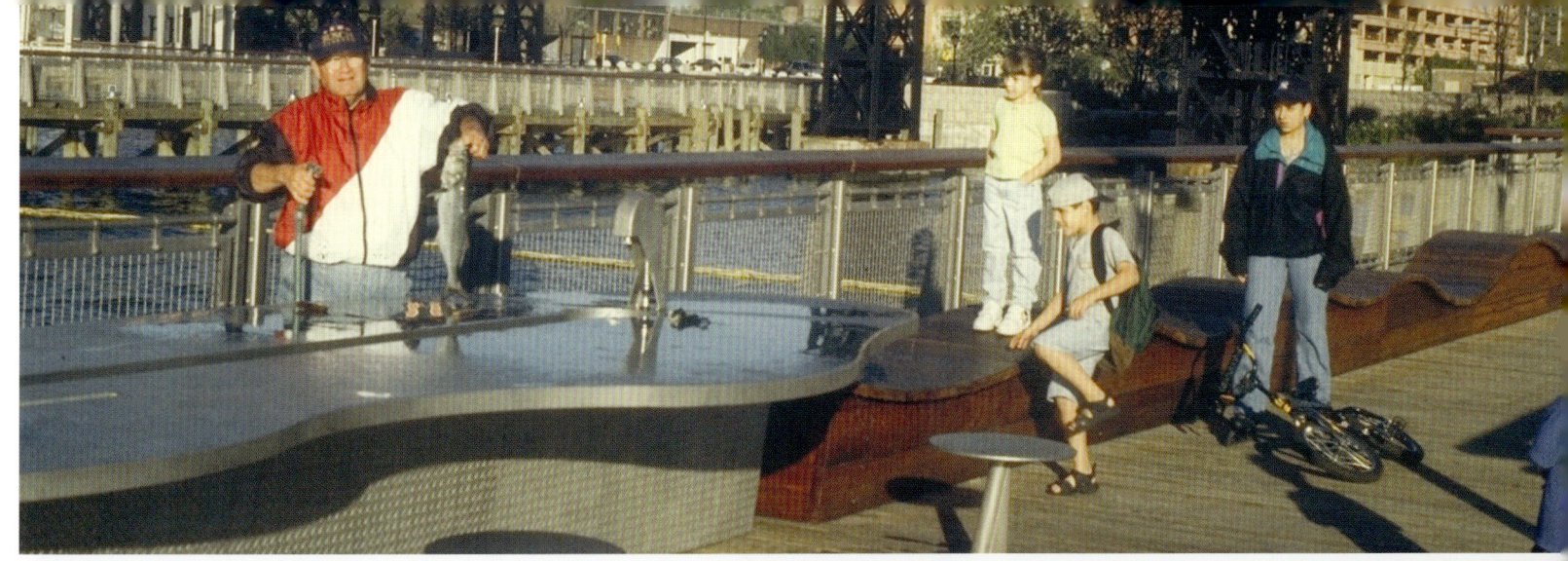

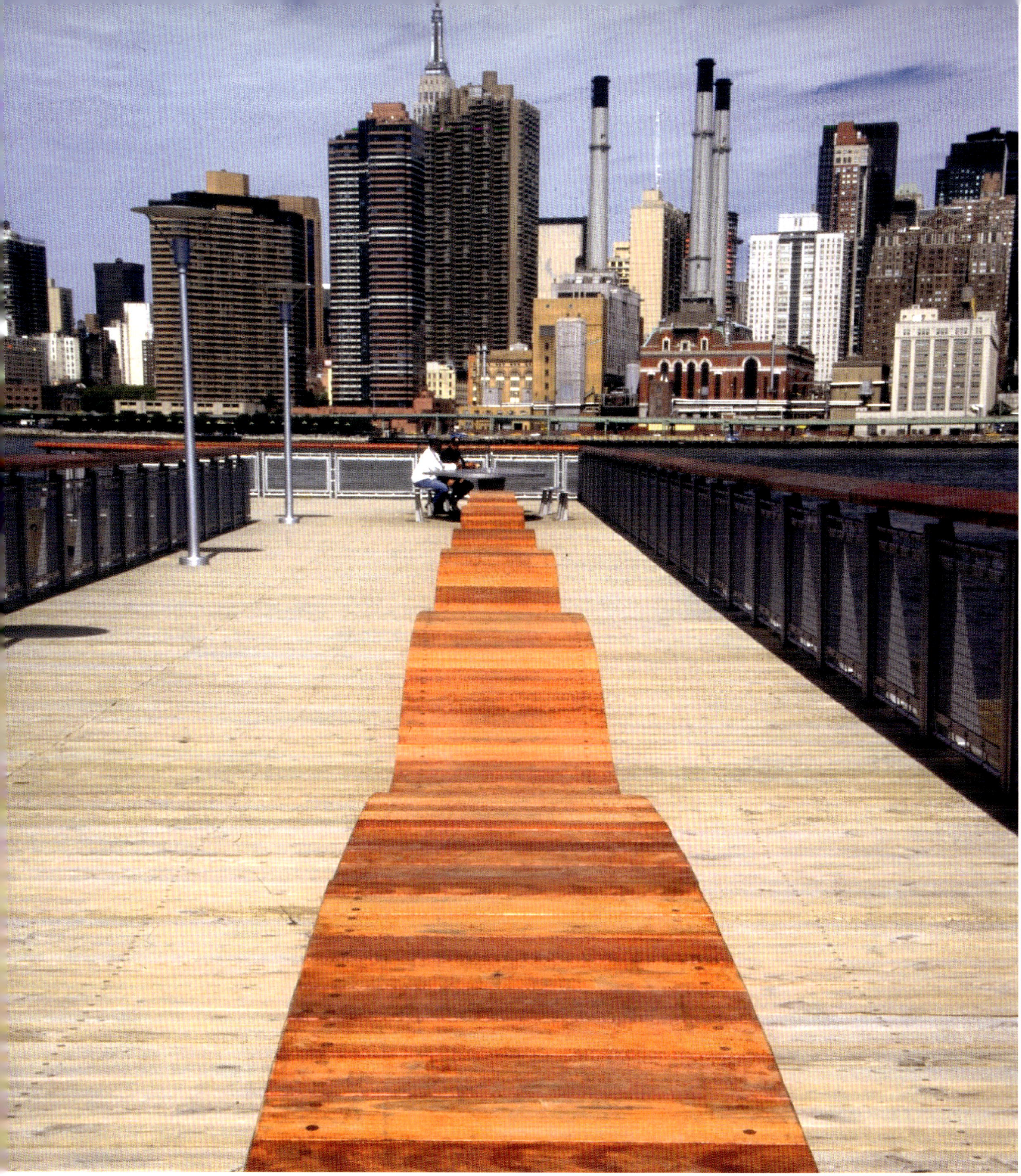

k-bench & k-baby - 2005
Charles kaisin
Vange

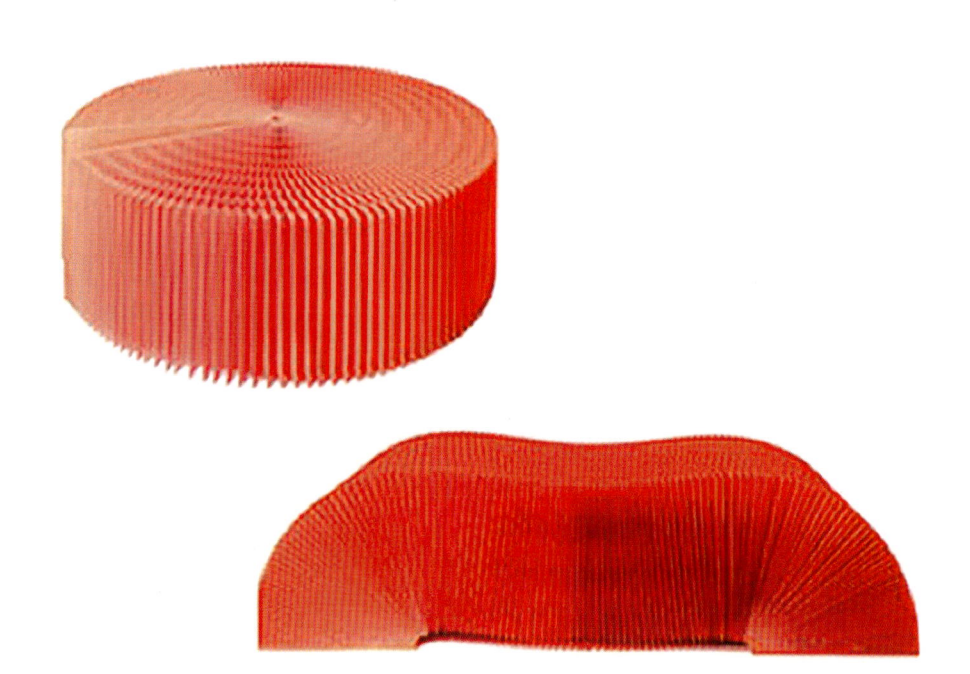

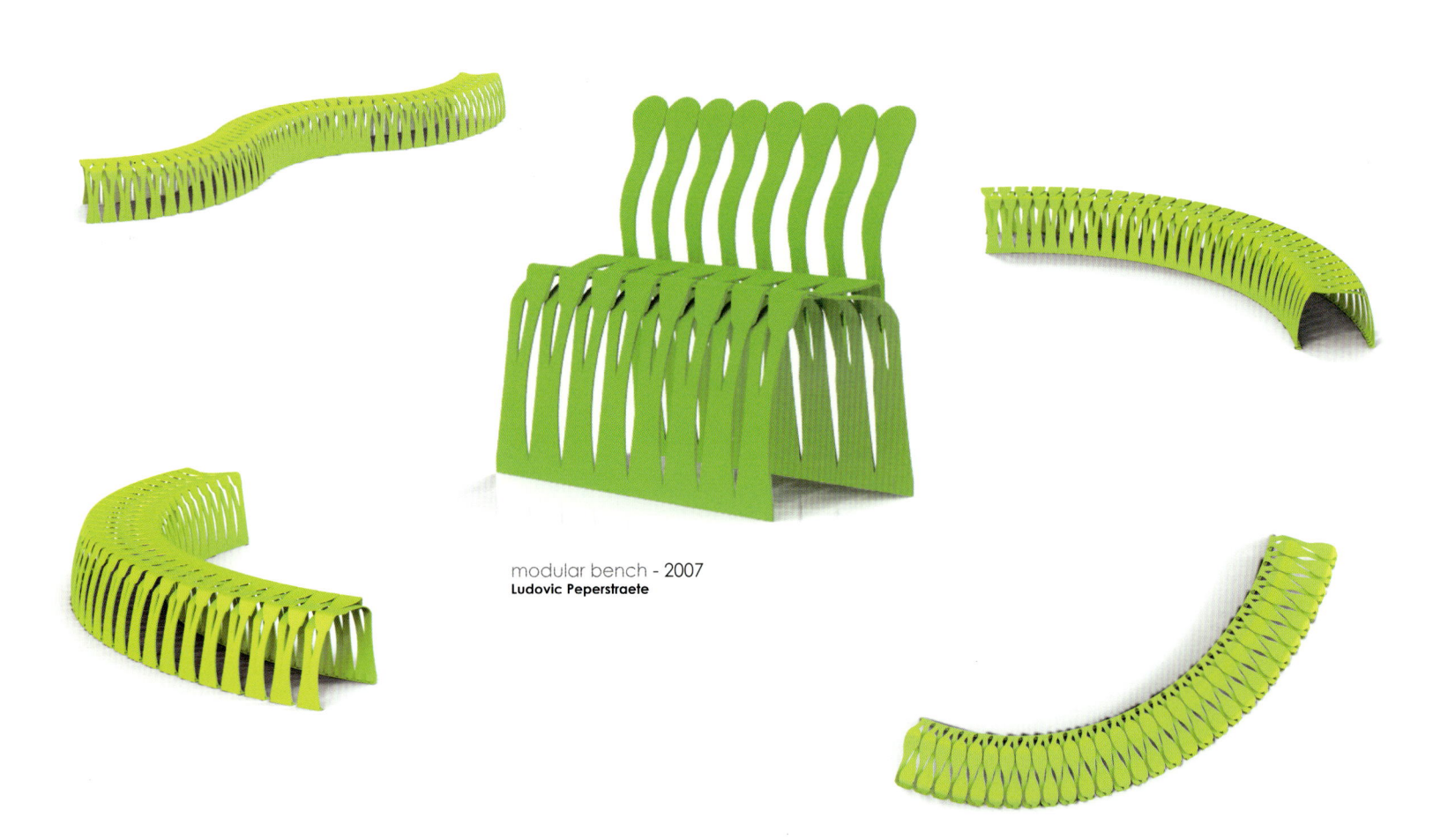

modular bench - 2007
Ludovic Peperstraete

090 seats of conviviality / STRUCTURING

Kongjian YU
The Landscape Bureau
Qinhuangdao City

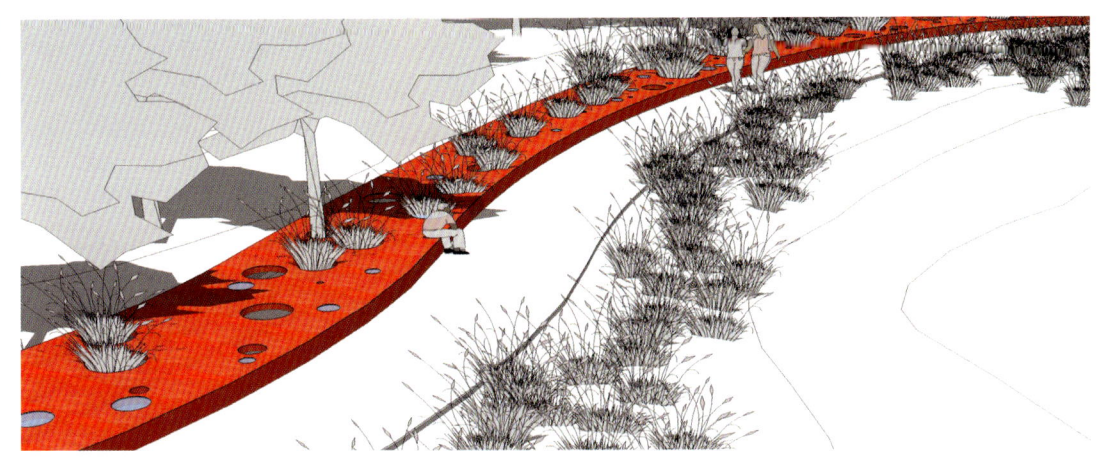

the red ribbon - Tanghe river park

The port city of Qinhuangdao is found in the province of Hebei in north-east China, 280 km from Beijing. A large park of 20 hectares has been created on the site of an old dump. It runs alongside the River Tanghe, whose name it carries, and stretches out on the two banks, one of which is equipped with a bench 500 m long. Accompanied by a walkway in wooden decking which hugs the numerous meanders of the river, this immense structure is designed for sitting, but also for lighting up the site, allowing people to come here after nightfall. It's also the main element for structuring the landscape, its presence now allowing the banks to be safeguarded definitively from uncontrolled urbanisation.

This large red ribbon, as it is called, is in steel fibre painted red, the colour of good luck in China. Four pavilions punctuate it, and the banks that it follows, previously inaccessible, have become a leisure site for the locals, equipped for fishing, watersports, bike riding and jogging. The park project also has an ecological dimension, with openings set into the bench to allow small animals to circulate freely. In addition, the lake and forest vegetation has been preserved and supplemented by flower-rich beds with a natural appearance.

092 seats of conviviality / STRUCTURING

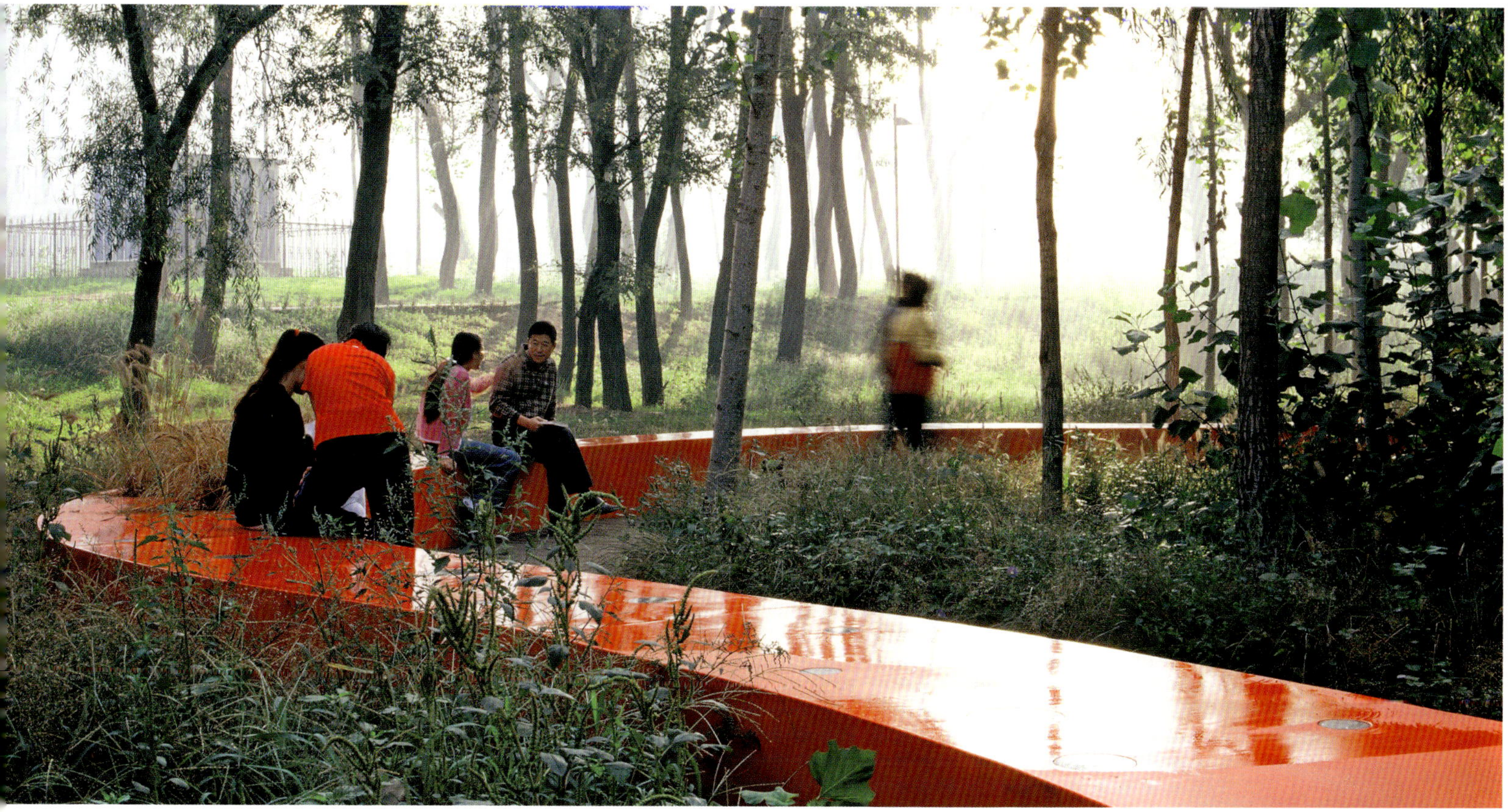

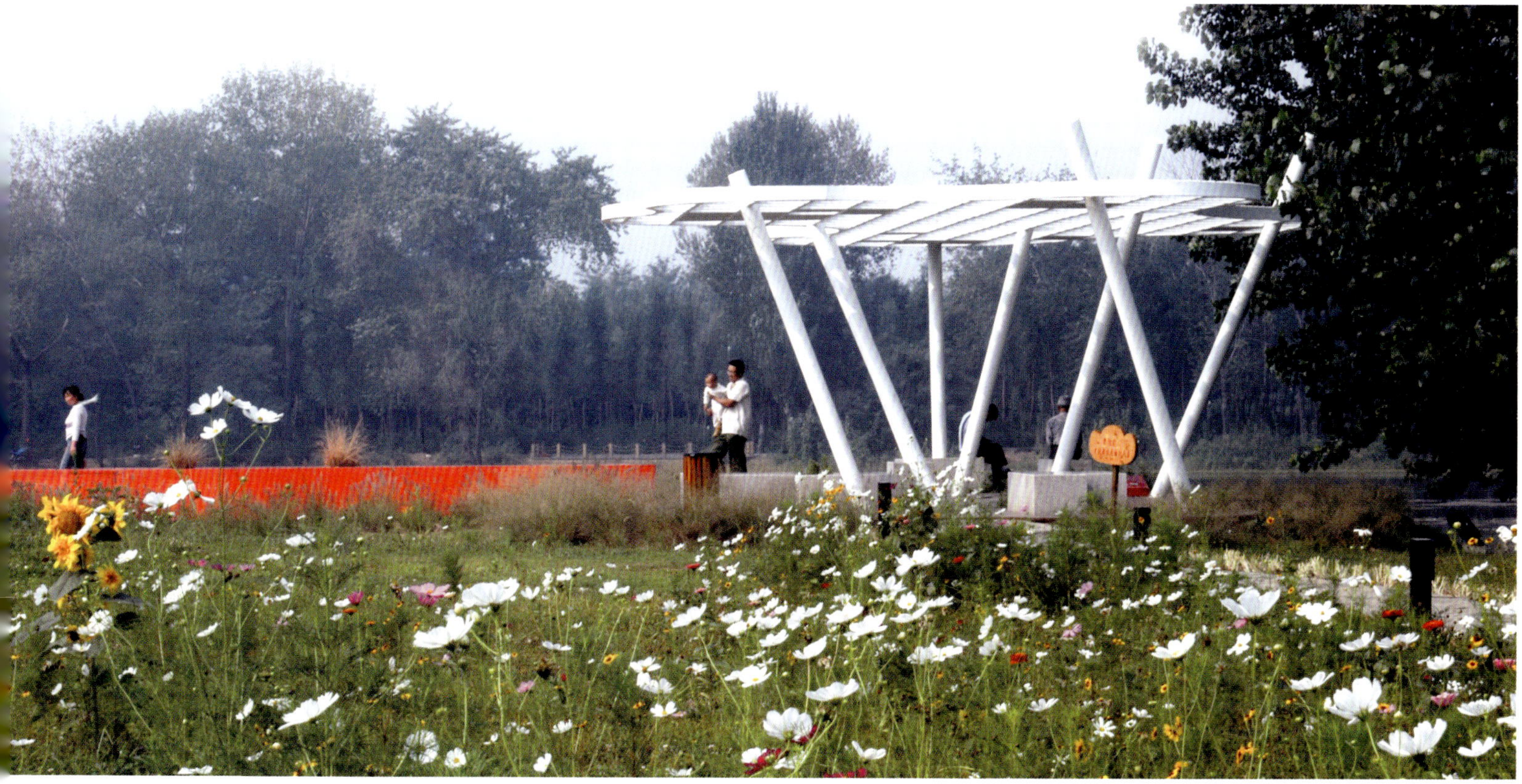

RVICES MUNICIPAUX
SPORTS ET LOISIRS
TURE ET COMMUNICATION
SYNDICAT D'INITIATIVE
P

RECYCLEZ
VOS IDEES

VOS IDEES
VOS IDEES

02

CLEAN CITY!

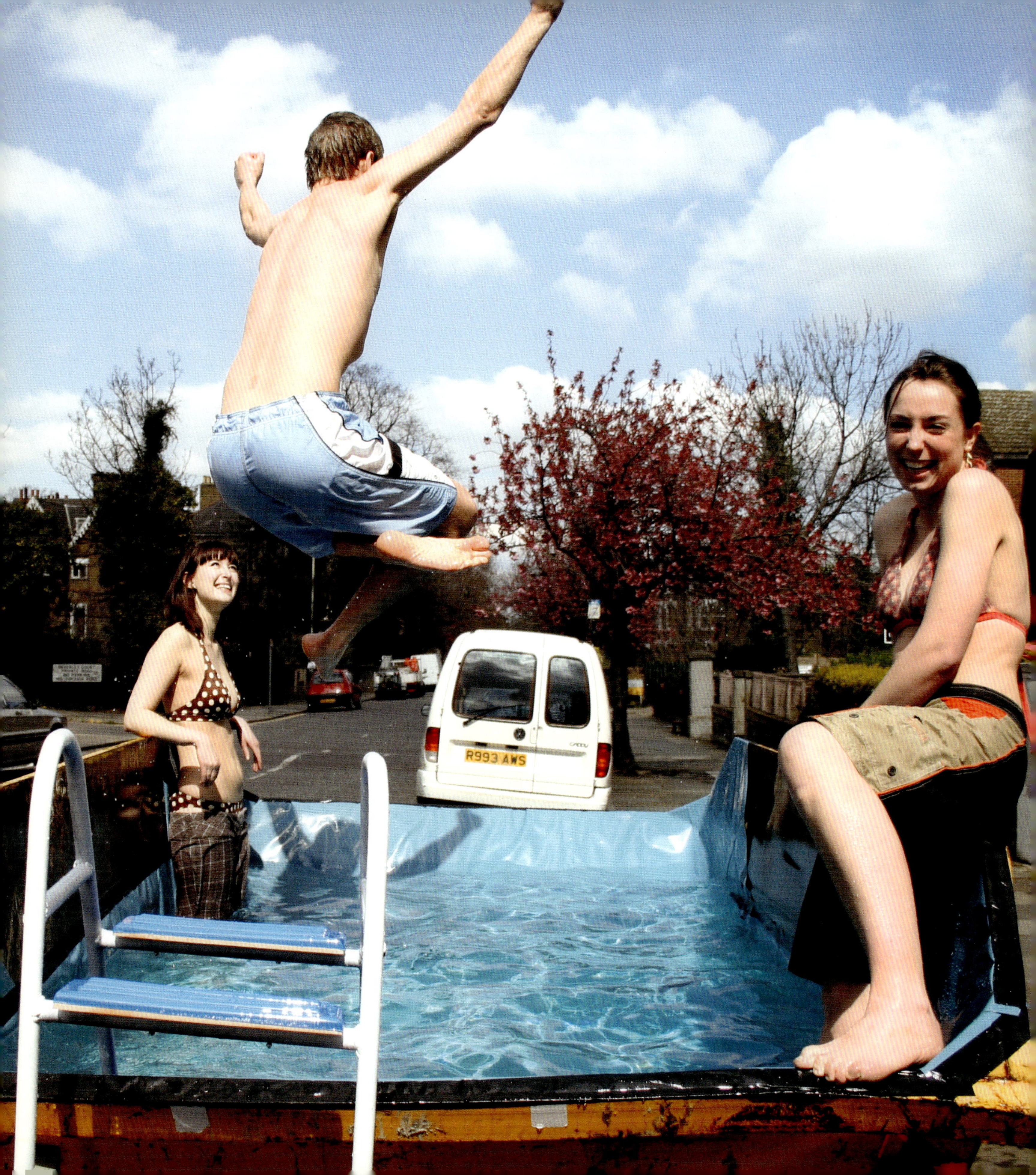
R993 AWS

clean city!

recycle your ideas!
1998
Patrick Demazeau dit : Made
Recycled containers being installed in the streets of the town of Clichy-la-Garenne, France
page 94

skip waste
2007-2008
Oliver Bishop-Young
Over two years the empty skips of London became true havens for the locals, as well as for enthusiasts who had sought out their location using the eponymous internet site. Converted on an ad hoc basis into a swimming pool, campsite, micro-garden, or even a ping-pong table or skateboard ramp, these recreational spaces offered a new way of experiencing the city, in a fun and relevant way, at the corner of the street.
pages 96 & 97

Since the creation of the first city, the management of waste has been an important preoccupation. Far more ecological than we are today, the ancients collected – albeit in fewer forms – the materials produced by different trades, like organic waste, and recycled them. In growing, cities became the deposits of raw materials and needed real organisation for collecting them.

It was, for example, in 1531 in Paris, that a first decree organised the collection of household waste, thought it did not become regular until 1667. And, still in France, it was in 1884 that Eugène Poubelle, Prefect of the Seine department, invented the refuse container to which he gave his name. At the time, he already thought of them as potentially multiple, with one bin for decayable matter, another for rags and paper and a third for glass, pottery and oyster shells!

They therefore allowed for waste to be temporarily stored before it was collected. But with the industrial era, new objects saw the day and necessitated special attention: packaging. Fixed litter bins were therefore implanted in urban centres. Despite their particular function, they followed a stylistic evolution and are today a special field of creation, which allies formal concerns with ecological and security necessities. Indeed, it was only in 1974, after the first oil crisis, that selective sorting really appeared with a colour code for each container determining the type of waste that corresponded to it. The public litter bin entered late into this process and we have only just begun to find models with several independent compartments appearing in the catalogues of urban furniture designers. Another evolution has been necessary for the past ten years or so: that of adapting these containers to standards of anti-terrorist security. Also of note is the appearance of urban ashtrays, which have become necessary following the almost worldwide ban on smoking in public places.

In parallel, in the 1950s bin bags were also developed – a new object for conditioning waste. There is very little evolution to note, except very recently where artists have given them a new graphic look, making them funny and more pleasant to look at. Their basic material has also changed. Initially in polythene, they are today made of recyclable plastic. A small form has been born in recent years, allowing for dog owners to pick up what their pets leave behind in public places. The handling of the canine species has thus become an element in the cleanliness of the city…

littershark
2002
Werner Zemp
Brüco Swiss AG, Marcel J. Strebel

This collection of bins borrows its appearance from the famous shark, with its straight profile, its body in chromed steel and its wide and slit opening, endowed with a sharp tooth that prevents household waste from being dumped inside. Tags and stickers are easily removed from this anti-vandalism metal, which is also anti-terrorism and doesn't disintegrate if an explosion occurs inside.
page 98

trash
2008
Adrian K
Art Related Product
page 99

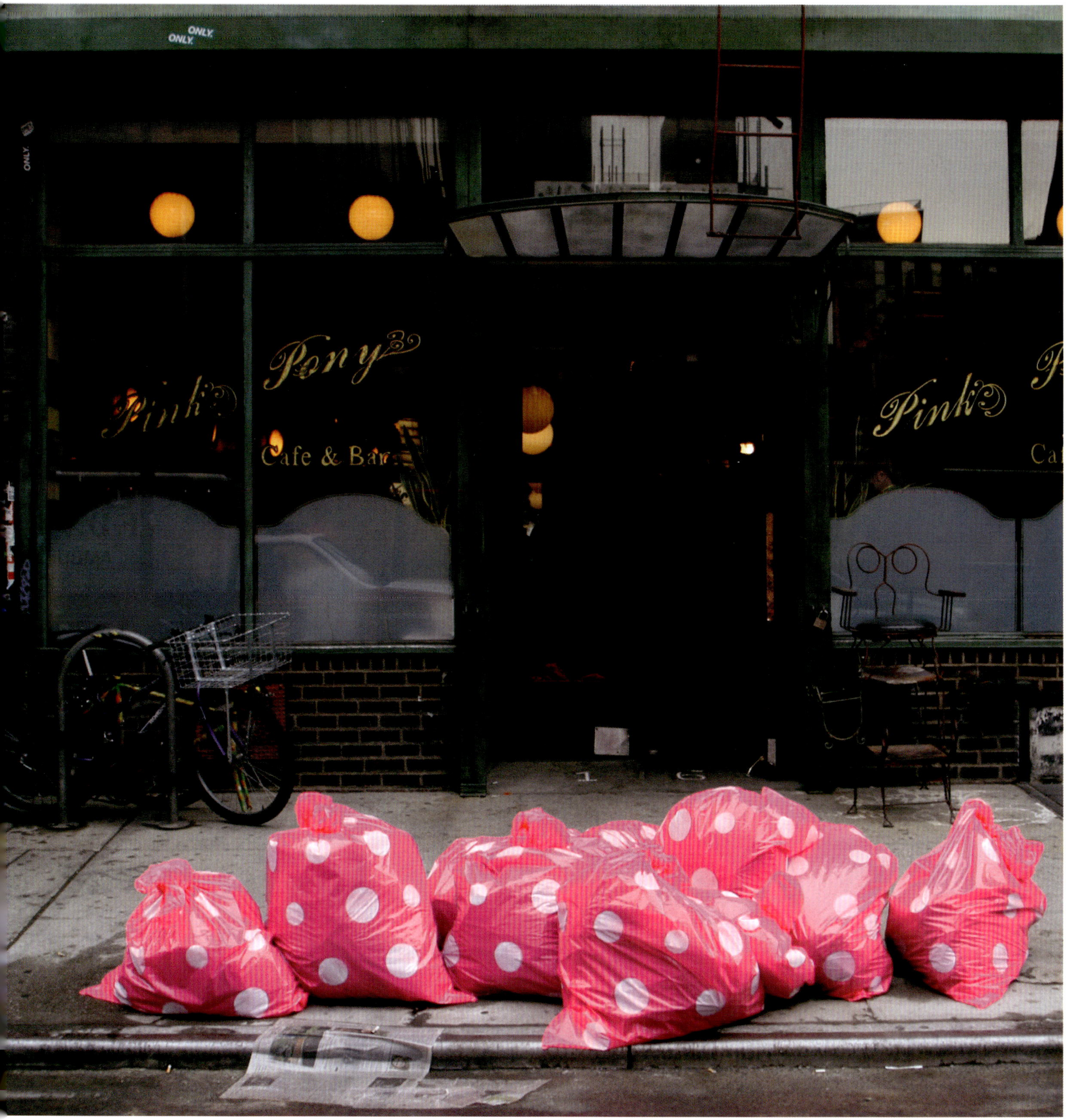
ONLY.
ONLY.
Pink
Pony
Cafe & Bar
Pink

kippe - 2008
Ferran Morgui Isanda
Onadis Barcelona Disseny

cycas - 2000
Federica Fulici
Divers Cité

missing - 2010
Franck Magné

vesuvio - 2008
Ja Design Studio / Lui Jaramillo
Manade

canasto litter bin - 2005
Diana Cabeza & Martin Wolfson
Estudio Cabeza, Urban Element

koon ashtray-bin - 2005
Karim Rashid
Casamania

100 clean city! / ASHTRAYS

fold

Taking on the appearance of a folded, creased object, its deconstructed architecture evokes its contents. This litter bin is made from a sheet of shiny inox, from recycled steel, which catches the light on its facetted contours, allowing it to be easily spotted in the urban environment. Covered with a non-solvent powder paint with anti-graffiti properties, its cleaning is thus facilitated, limiting the use of the detergents. Its lid is designed to allow for rapid collection of the bin bags and it also offers a peripheral surface for smokers to stub out their cigarettes. A finalist in the public market for the design of a cleanliness receptacle organised by Paris city hall in 2007, Pli ("Fold") is the fruit of two years of development and tests in partnership with explosions specialists in order to optimise its security in the event of a terrorist attack and to avoid ballistic effect, in other words the amplification of damage caused by the disintegration and propulsion of the different materials making up the bin. Pli has thus been officially recognised for government public security measures by INERIS (the National Institute for the Industrial Environment and Risks) and tested by Paris city hall.

Design Franck Magné
Competition of the City of Paris

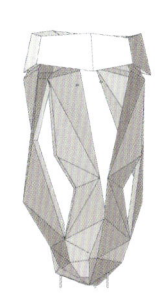

prestige litter bin - 2009
Divers Cité

degas bin - 2008
City Design / Divers Cité

green palacio litter bin - 2009
Serge Botello
Cyria

litter bin - 2004
Emmanuel Cairo (France)
Competition of the City of Paris

102 Clean city! / LITTER BINS

bonnemazou&cambus - designers
Competition of the City of Paris

cestino litter bin

In the style of the outdoor furniture that is most representative of the city of Paris, this litter bin project makes reference to nature, as much through its form as its motifs. Its design, formed by the coming together of three stems, simultaneously suggests a volume and a silhouette, and its solid and lasting material, recycled aluminium, is in harmony with both the oldest and the most recent creations of urban objects. For reasons inherent to our age (government public security measures, rapidity of collection...) the bag is visible. Today it forms part of the Parisian landscape, a reflection of a society where the treatment of waste is a major challenge. To hide it would be to deny the evidence: it is necessary to reduce the production of waste and to recycle... To communicate on this subject and on other ecological themes, the bag here becomes the medium for graphic and plastic messages, and is made more attractive visually thus going beyond its primary function.

pink!

2001 2009

In Autumn 2001, following the terrorist attacks on the World Trade Center towers in New York, the increased public security measures put in place by the French government demanded that all waste bins where a bomb could be placed and where the contents could not be visually identified be replaced. The Park of La Villette, situated in the north-east of Paris, was therefore given bin bag-holders, but chose a colour of bin bag that was deliberately different to the norm, a beautiful fuchsia. The 35 hectares of green spaces were thus punctuated by roses, and the wind happily choreographed these new urban objects. Aside from the positive reactions of the walkers, it seems that these bags had an interesting ornithological result, their lack of transparency, due in part to their colour, preventing crows from seeing what was inside them and attacking them. During 2009, the bag-holders were changed to enable selective sorting, the bags became a classic white and yellow again.

EPPGHV

104 clean city! / CONCEPTUAL

Wu Wenwen & Wang Taoran

contracdictions

Contradictions is an artistic work created from two elements that are completely opposed. On the one hand the bin bag, an everyday object, industrially made, with no interest other than to receive the waste from our consumer society. And on the other hand embroidery, an art requiring a huge investment of time and which glorifies its medium, decorates it, gives it value. Despite that, the embroidered image, here the lotus flower with its strong allegorical meaning, becomes insignificant though still attractive and unusual on this type of medium. It is not an advertisement, we don't know the message and during installations in different public spaces the object is a work of art for some, or remains simply utilitarian for others. It poses questions on its ephemeral character, which could become lasting. Should we preserve it or throw it away? And the doubt created establishes the link between the designers and their public, the questioning of the process by passers-by being much more important to them than the future of their creations.

fiore bin - 2003
Studio n'TT / Divers Cité

saturno bin
Ora Centurelli

marte bin
Ora Centurelli

poubelman - 2008
Thomas de Lussac

106 clean city! / SELECTIVE SORTING

pattumina

METALSISTEM S.p.A.
Antonello Brioso

Looking at first glance looking more like a bass drum than a bin, Pattumina completely changes one's habitual perception of this object that one has the tendency to hide or ignore. Made up of one or several modules that are easily assembled and exist in four colours, thus creating a colour code to encourage and clarify waste separation for recycling, it occupies the space in a sculptural and iridescent way. It is attractive and eye-catching, and simple for the local inhabitants to use, but also for the people with the job of maintaining them thanks to the internal bags that are easy to extract via a hinged opening system. Its permanently open lid protects the container from the rain and, when several are arranged together in a battery, gives the impression of a choir…

anti-terrorism ecocity - 2008
City Design / Ecocity
Divers Cité

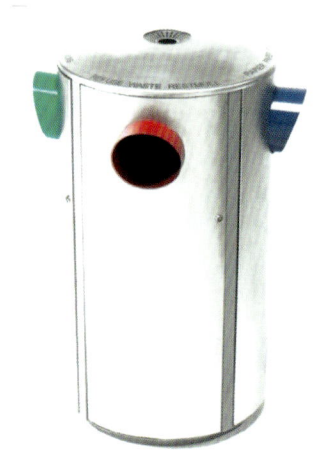

cube bin - 2007
Giuseppe Roberti
Divers Cité

quatroquarti bin - 2002
Federica Fulici
Divers Cité

bottle bank arcade, the fun theory - 2009
Simon Higby & Martin Lundgren / DDB
cf. page 183

Jack bin - 2002
Federica Fulici
Divers Cité

108 clean city! / SELECTIVE SORTING

drive-in

Gilles Belley

In France, each person produces an average of 350 kg of waste a year, almost a kilogram a day! Waste separation for recycling is rapidly increasing, and is today more popular in the rural environment than in cities, despite the different incitations. But, outside the local recycling facilities linked to places of habitation, there are numerous places with a strong density of traffic where they are also necessary, but not yet installed. The idea of the Drive-in project is to create a range of bins that would be a cross between a signage panel and a litter receptacle, to install in the motorway service areas on the Autoroutes du Sud, which are very well frequented. After drive-in cinema and fast food, here is the drive-by bin that you can use without having to leave your vehicle.

trashers - 2007
Mark Jenkins

bin bag bear - 2006
Raw Edge Design Studio

110 clean city! / BAGS

garbage bag art work

To change the negative image of rubbish, the idea of Garbage Bag Art Work is to make its favourite container, the bin bag, funny. A concept to do yourself or using the collection created to this effect. In fact, everything started with a bit of fun using a classic white carrier bag: its knotted handles became the ears of a rabbit, followed by eyes and a nose appearing with the aid of a marker pen, thus creating a nice little character and making the transportation of rubbish less depressing... The next stage was to design evocative graphics that could be printed on large bags, allowing one to compose a shoal of fish, a forest of pines or a field of flowers when several of them were seen together. Other artists have also been associated with this project, like Lily Franky and her Shiba-dog. Today these bags are manufactured, allowing anyone and everyone to become an artist by making their own extraordinary composition, while at the same time spreading the word about the necessity of Japan's very sophisticated system of waste separation for recycling.

Yoshihiko Yamasaka & Shinya Seko
Yoshihiko Yamasaka

garbage bag art work - 2006
Yoshihiko Yamasaka & Shinya Seko
Yoshihiko Yamasaka
cf. page 111

112 clean city! / BAGS

fish bag - 2009
Wieden + Kennedy
Suck UK

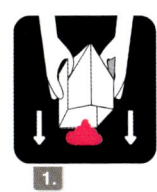

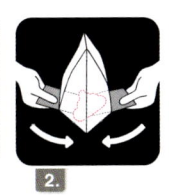

dog poo bags - 2009
Andrea Gadesmann & Nina Dautzenberg

113

whippet bench - 1998
Radi Designers

bau!haus - 2008
Gionata Gatto

114 clean city! / CYNOMORPHS

Autre Nature
Anne Sottil
Jacques Sordoillet
Biennale internationale Design
Saint-Étienne

teckel bench

The sculptural Teckel bench was born from the desire to bring together several possible uses in the same piece of furniture, to fight against the invasion of the public space by different objects, each with a single function. Resembling a hunting dog, its elongated body offers a generous seat open to conversation. The lateral back enables it to be used lying down. Its insolent head shelters a bin, the necessary receptacle for the waste discarded by passers-by. At night, integrated lighting ensures that the path is lit, without dazzling the walkers. Making reference to the film Mon Oncle, by Jacques Tati, the silhouette of this bench is a nod to Monsieur Hulot's mischievous dog, a real loose cannon slipping between the cold and dehumanised world of the Arpels and the warm and dreamy one of Monsieur Hulot. A sign that integration and functionality are not incompatible with humour and derision.

Lucien Zayan
No Longer empty & Improv Everywhere
The Invisible Dog

the invisible dog

2009

The Invisible Dog is an old factory that has recently become a New York arts centre covering 1400 m² situated in Boerum Hill in Brooklyn. Its name comes from the eponymous gadget that was made here and was all the rage in the 1970s: a rigid lead that ended in an empty collar, for surrealist walkers! So, for the inauguration of the place in Autumn 2009, 2000 people caused a sensation by walking in the surrounding streets with hundreds of these false leads, pretending to take their dogs for a walk... This new cultural centre offers artists' workshops as well as spaces for temporary exhibitions and occasional happenings. Its programming crosses over into several disciplines, from different countries including France, the native country of its conceptor and director.

116 clean city! / CYNOMORPHS

117

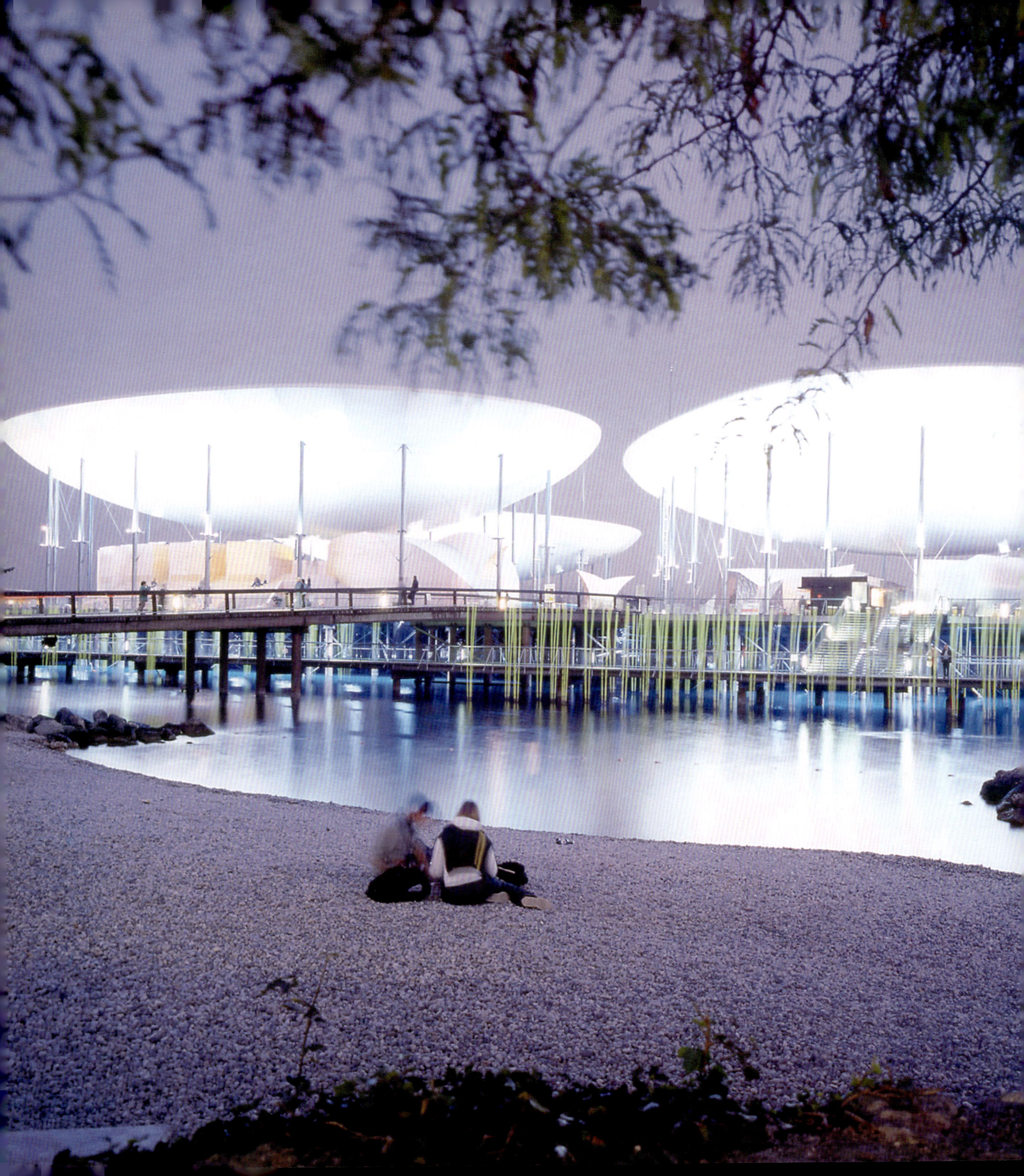

03

ENCHANTING THE CITY

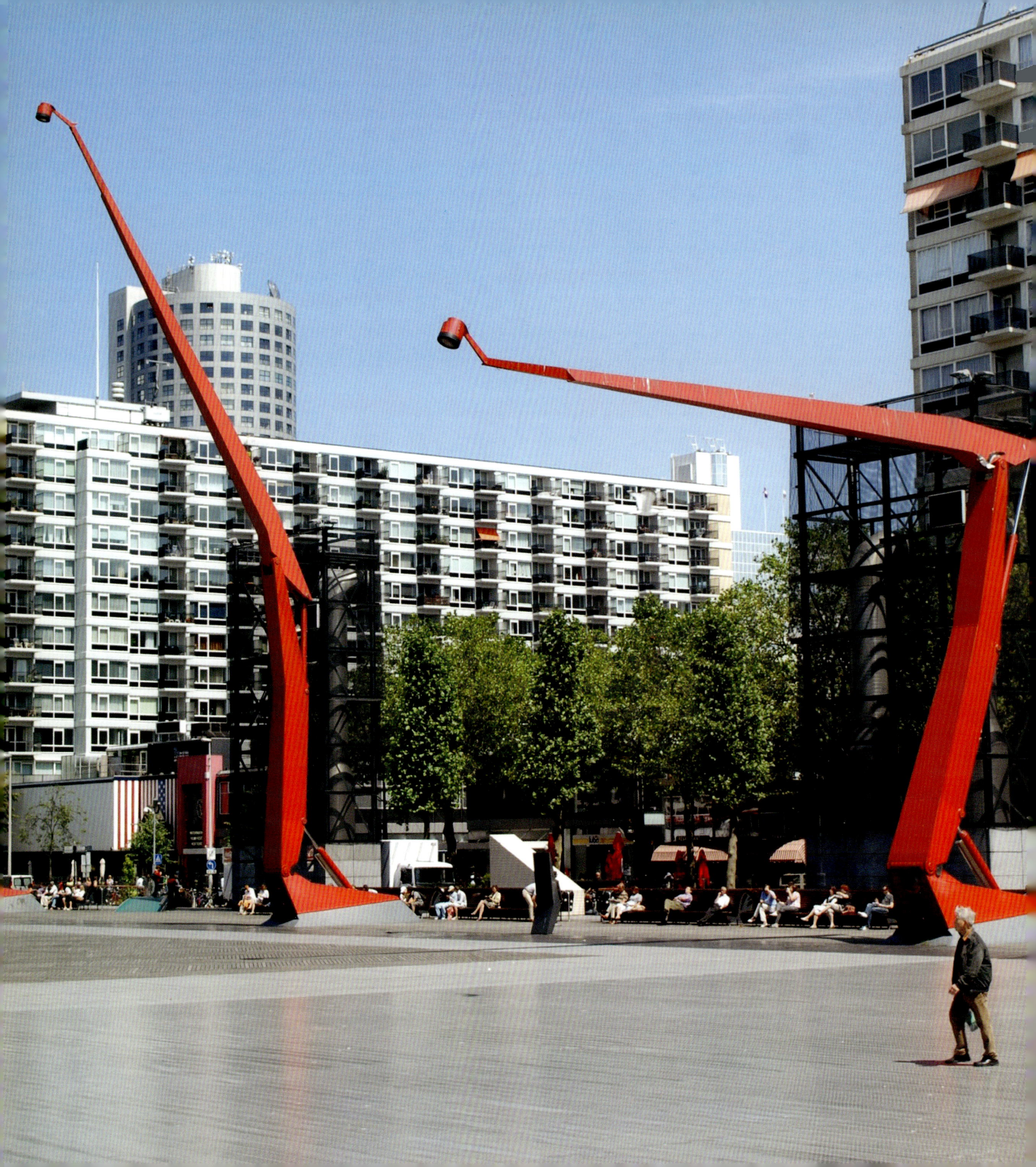

enchanting the city

artebeach
2002
Aurel(s)studio
Groupement Multipack

In the framework of the national Swiss exhibition 02 whose theme was "Nature and Artifice", the scenography of the Neuchâtel Artebeach was composed of three giant pebbles which housed the exhibition spaces, installed more than 20 m above the lake.

page 118

Schouwburg square
1996 & 2011
West 8
City of Rotterdam

Located in the heart of Rotterdam, this immense square offers an unbeatable panorama over the city. Only a few furniture elements structure it. Four huge lampposts, recalling the cranes of the neighbouring port, light up different spaces according to the needs and demands of the inhabitants.

pages 120 & 121

Sources of life, water and light accompany the city day and night. Light is offered by the sun, but when it goes down public lighting takes the baton and allows citizens to continue to enjoy the urban space in safety. In France, it was provided by candles from the Middle Ages, then lanterns at the time of Louis XIV. Thus Paris became known as the "City of Lights", with six thousand five hundred light sources illuminating it. The oil lamp was used from the 17th century in London, which was also to be the first city to adopt the gas light. The use of electricity did not become widespread until the 20th century.

Today, the street lamp remains the main source of light for the city and surrounding infrastructures. But other complementary sources are growing, such as runway lighting on the ground, spotlighting on façades and neon advertising signs, as well as small lamps giving a more localised glow. Festive and colourful, light is also the object of particular concern to diminish its energy costs, through the use of LEDs, which have a lifespan a ten times greater than classic lightbulbs, and the creation of systems capturing solar, wind or even human energy.

From Antiquity onwards, fountains marked the location of a spring, from which they collected and dispensed the precious liquid using its natural pressure. Water, the most indispensable element in the world, is a source of riches for those who possess it, and human beings spend lots of energy and time searching for it and channelling it in order to be able to use it. In Europe, it came inside several grand homes in London at the beginning of the 17th century, thanks to underground conduits. In the West, water is starting to be considered precious, which has always been the case in the rest of the world, and recycling it and saving it from pollution have become priorities again.

The fountain, a place that brought people together in the city for centuries, lost its monopoly when running water entered people's homes, remaining common only in the cities of the south and in rare northern metropolises such as Lausanne. This is to be deplored, because it performed a service for the inhabitants, visitors and tourists in summertime, recreating the conviviality of sharing it. In its decorative and architectural form, the fountain remains a fascinating and attractive element, but its place in the city is becoming reduced. And if new water features are still appearing, they are now accompanied by a concern to limit their energy needs. Ornamental pools or water tables often replace spectacular jets, their new forms making them more accessible and still a source of joy.

atlantida
1991
Enric Batlle-Joan Roig
Santa & Cole

naia
2000
Nuria Núñez
Dae

fontfosa
1995
Pep Bonet
Dae
page 122

Energy producing pavement
2008

With this innovative project, the city of Toulouse is a precursor in the field of recuperating human energy to create electricity. For the first experiment, a piece of Dutch technology, the Sustainable Dance Floor, has been appropriated. This system is normally used in a discotheque, in the form of floor slabs uplit by the movement of the dancers. It has been installed here in the urban environment and linked to a streetlight equipped with LEDs. The objective is now to improve its performance in capturing of the gravitational energy produced by the movements of pedestrians and to research a model that is economically viable, allowing for its development on the scale of the city. It could also be linked to streetlights with movement detectors, offering a significant reduction in the consumption of energy. Watch this space…

page 123

MARCHEZ, C'EST ÉCLAIRÉ...
MAIRIE DE TOULOUSE

Graf-Adolf-Square 15 - 2006
Wes & Partner Landscape Artchitects & JSK Dipl.-Ing. Architekten

Magdeleine lake - 2009
Eric Pescher
City of Gujan Mestras

princes Czartoryski square - 2004
Biuro Projektow Lewicki Latak
City of Cracovie

"starry night" atrium bench - 2008
AREA
City of Toulouse

124 enchanting the city / GUIDING LINES

Curtis Hixon waterfront park - 2010
Thomas Balsley Associates
City of Tampa

central plaza - 2009
Thomas Balsley Associates
Shigeo Kawasaki - Landscape Architect / Associate & Nihon Sekkei - Architect
Mitsui Fudosan

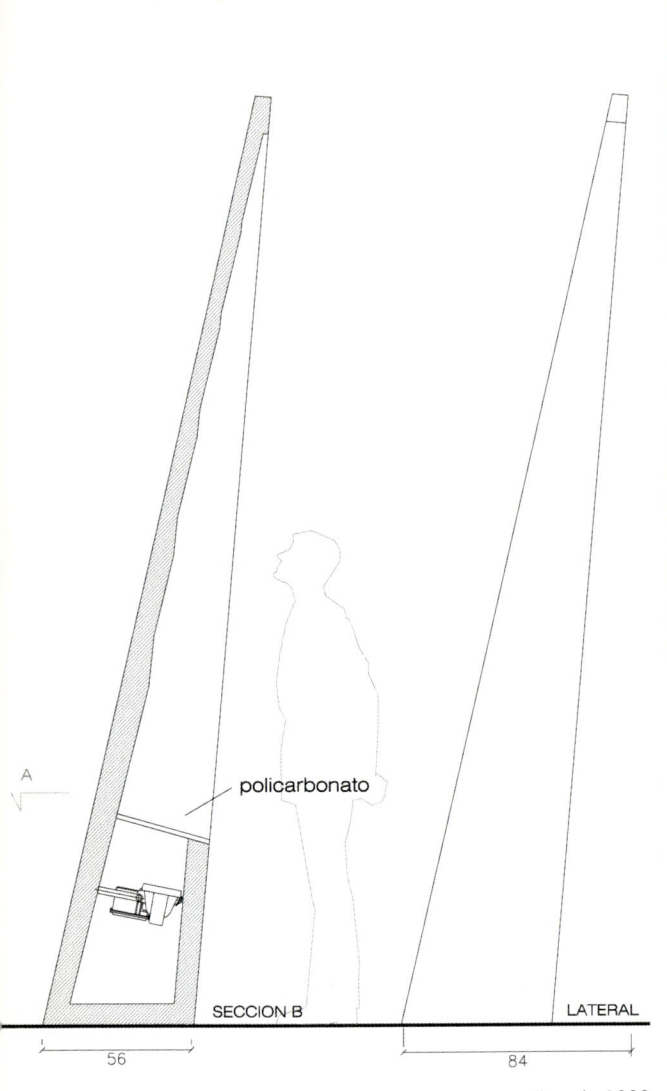

llum-i - 1988
Albert Viaplana & Helio Pinon
Escofet

light! - 2006
Nicolas Marzouanlian / Strate Collège

126 Enchanting the city / PUNCTUATIONS

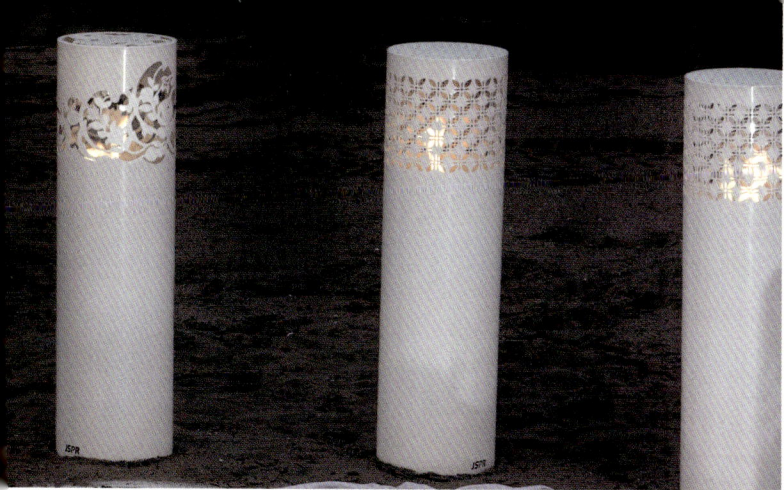

flames - 2009
JSPR / Jasper Van Grootel

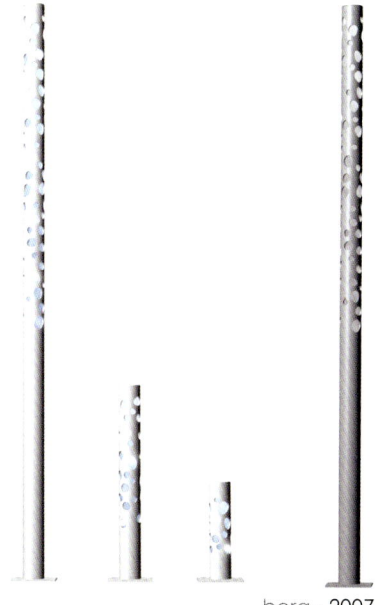

bora - 2007
**Agence Michel Tortel
Comatelec / Groupe Schreder**

live light - 2008
**Valentin Monfort
ParckDesign / Bruxelles Environnement**

127

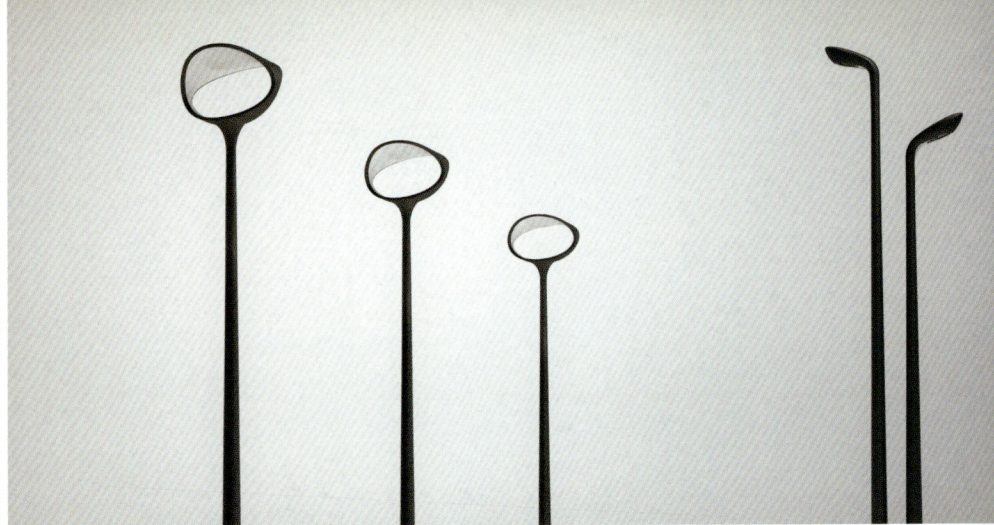

indalux range - 2005-2006
Aurel(s)stutio
3EI Indalux

cristella light - 2004-2006
Aurel(s)studio
Eclatec

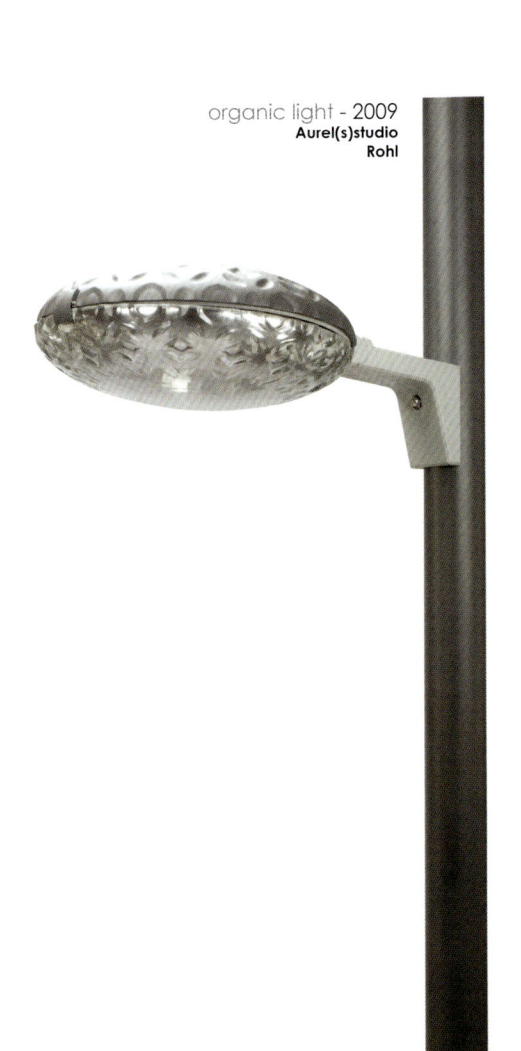

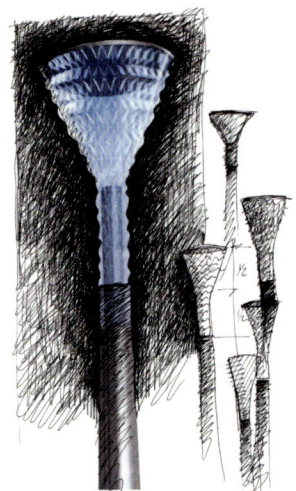

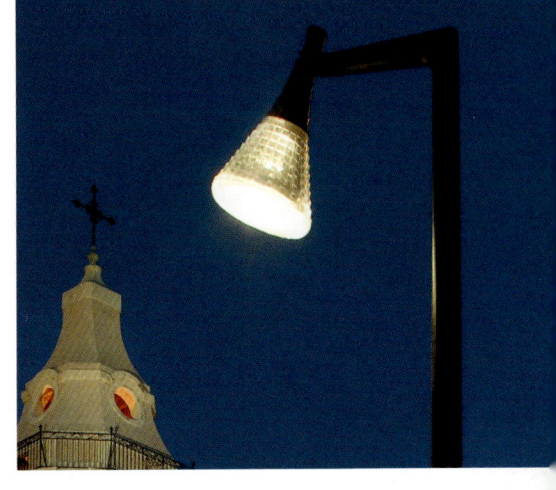

organic light - 2009
Aurel(s)studio
Rohl

perla light - 2008
Agence Michel Tortel
Comatelec / Groupe Schreder

128 enchanting the city / STREET LIGHTS

Smithfield public space - 1999
McGarry Ní Éanaigh Architects
Dublin City Council

saturno street lighting - 1998
Emilio Ambasz & Associates
Ilva Pali Dalmine

old shipyards development - 2004
Emmanuel Cairo Designer
City of La Seyne-sur-mer

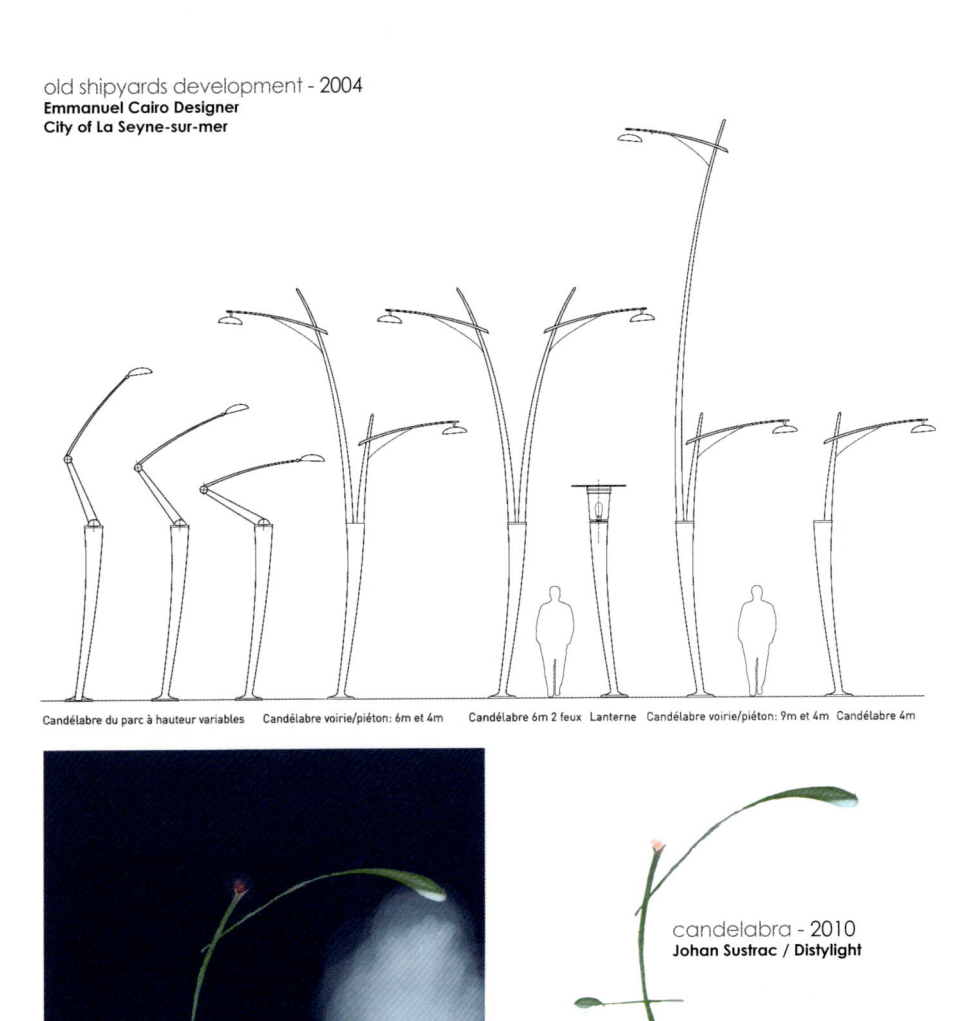

Candélabre du parc à hauteur variables   Candélabre voirie/piéton: 6m et 4m   Candélabre 6m 2 feux   Lanterne   Candélabre voirie/piéton: 9m et 4m   Candélabre 4m

candelabra - 2010
Johan Sustrac / Distylight

royal light - 2008
City design for Ecocity

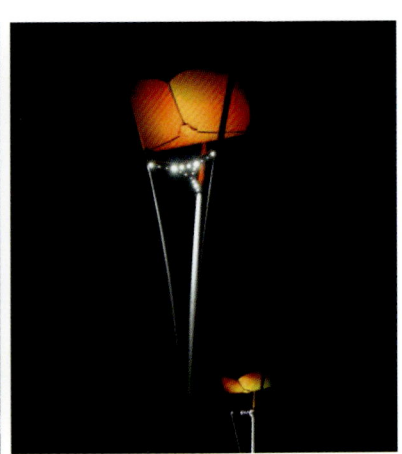

130 enchanting the city / STREET LIGHTS

Hugues Weill
designer ENSCI

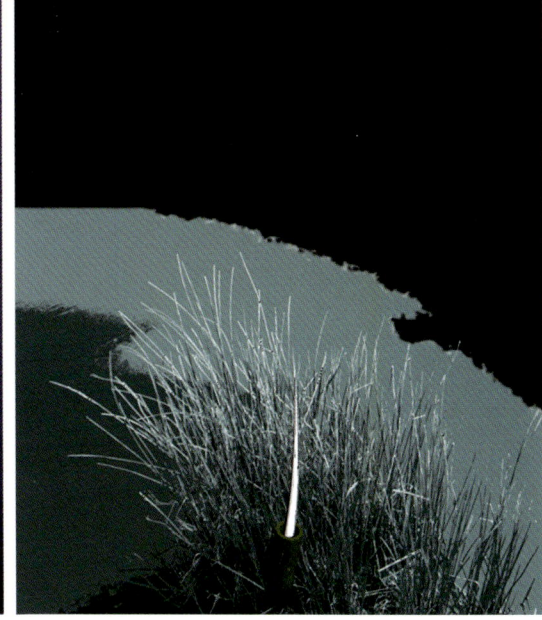

wisps of light

This lighting system, based on a low-level glow, allows one to adapt urban furniture to the real needs of cities, which are often equipped to excess with a unitary system. In most cities, reducing of the amount of light given out by half is barely perceptible, the human eye adapting perfectly to half-light and perceiving the whole of its environment a lot better this way. This range of diffusers is made up of fine luminous stems, flexible and mobile according to which way the wind blows. Whether alone or grouped together, tall or only a few dozen centimetres in height, their power can be fixed or modified thanks to a dimmer, creating a delicate, natural-looking presence.

lax - 2000
Ted Tokio Tanaka Architects
Los Angeles World Airport

132 enchanting the city / ON A GRAND SCALE

chess park, Brand boulevard passageway

In Glendale, a city near to Los Angeles, an urban landscape has become a site for chess players to gather, while conserving its function as access route. This project leaves the central space free for pedestrian circulation and organises different facilities according to the rules and strategies employed on the chess board. Two series of tables, seats and a small stage for performances follow each another at the sides, separated by five large towers of lights, made from wood and Trex, a recycled plastic. These lampposts extend upwards, like immense luminous sculptures whose forms evoke the main pieces of the game: the castle, the king, the queen, etc., recalling both the lamps of the Japanese designer Isamu Noguchi and the abstract sculptures of Constantin Brancusi.

Rios Clementi Hale Studios
City of Glendale, CA

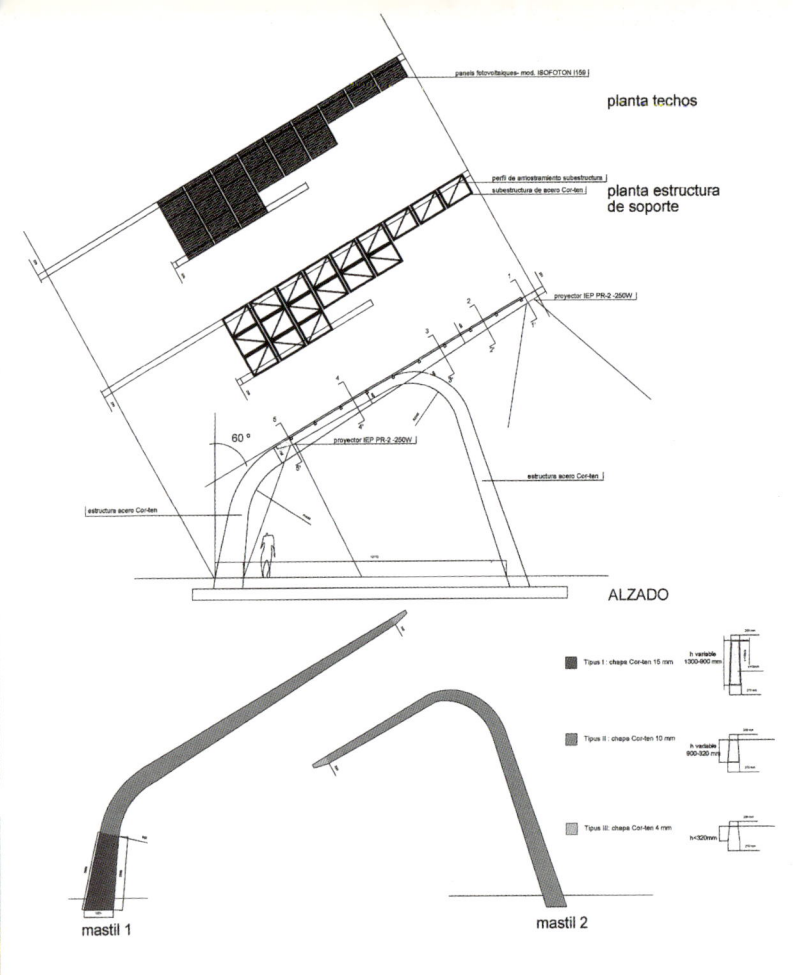

dinosaurios - 2002
Alessandro Caviasca
Siarq & Solaring, City of l'Hospitalet de Llobregat, Barcelone

totem - 2003
Alessandro Caviasca
Siarq

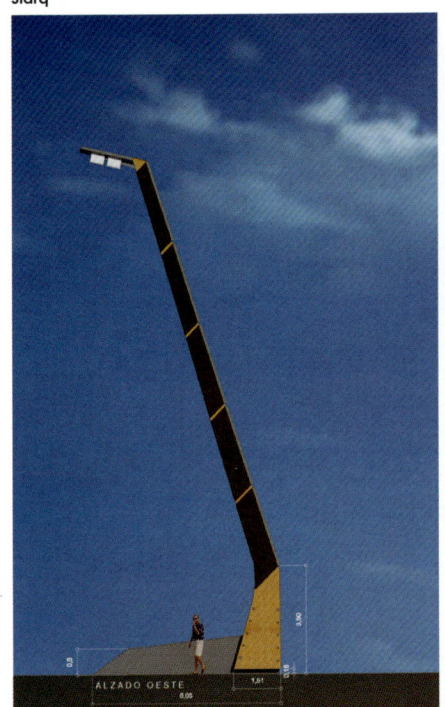

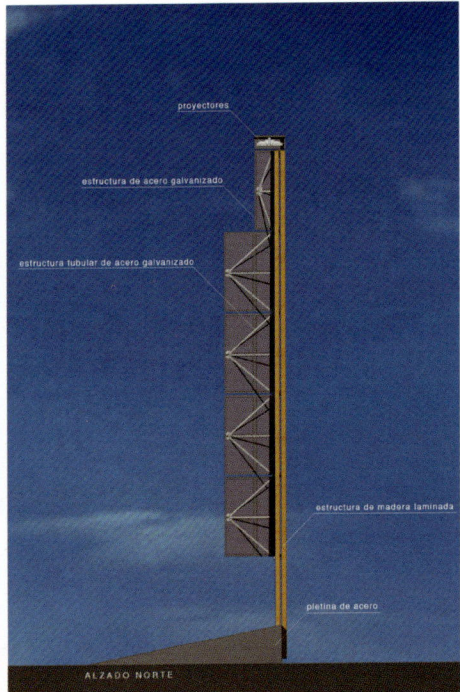

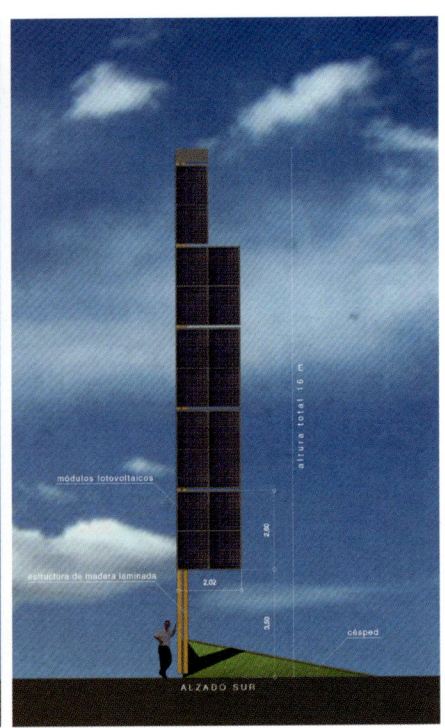

134 enchanting the city / SOLAR

solar mallee trees

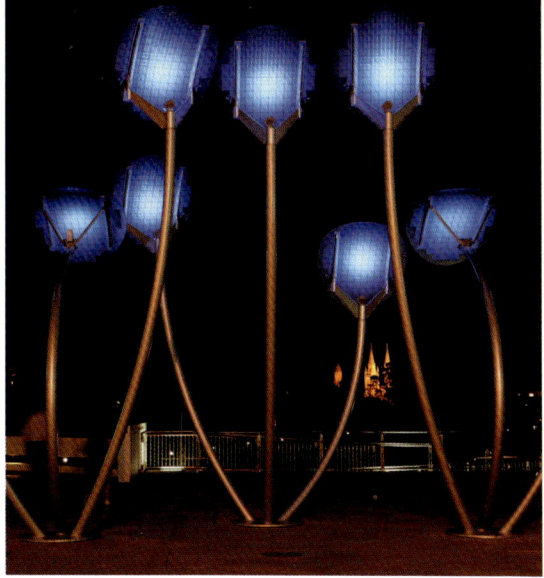

Solar Mallee Trees is the emblem of the research that the Australian government is leading into renewable energies. Its structure is inspired by that of a dwarf eucalyptus, the Coffin Bay Mallee. The suffix Mallee, of Aboriginal origin, describes the fact that tree has not got a single trunk but several forks at its base. Installed in front of the festival centre in Adelaide, it has a canopy with a new, oval, form, and cells that provide the electricity necessary for lighting based on LEDs and for the sound equipment, which continuously broadcasts the voices of schoolchildren talking about solar energy, their school being the first in the city equipped with this technology.

Street and Park Furniture PTY LTD
MPH Architects
Capital City Council

sustainable city lights - 2008
Philips Design, Eindhoven

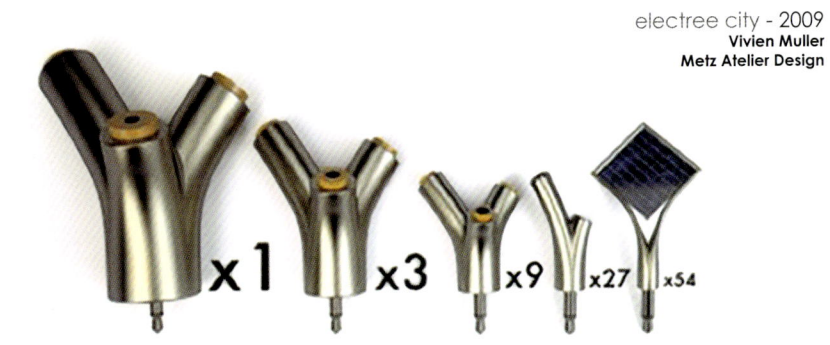

solar tree - 2007
**Ross Lovegrove
Artemide**

electree city - 2009
**Vivien Muller
Metz Atelier Design**

136 enchanting the city / SOLAR

Soren Luckins
Buro North
Victorian Eco Innovation Lab

veil solar-shade project

VEIL Solar-shade is a project designed for the Australian government, which wants to make primary school children aware of solar energy. Installed in playgrounds, structures resembling the petals of giant flowers, with a pivot that makes them moveable, carry solar panels that captivate in more ways than one. They also act as large parasols. Throughout the day, the children can reorient them towards the sun. They are informed in real time of the functioning of the energy collection through a coloured message, showing up on a part of the structures that is found in the shade. The immediate interactivity makes this teaching aid playful and relevant.

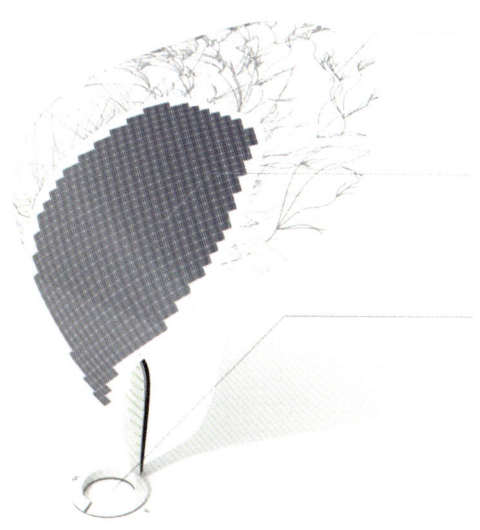

light wind lamp

2007

Inspired by the famous Dutch windmills, this wind-powered streetlight produces the electricity necessary for its own illumination. Its horizontal sails with a wingspan of more than a metre, situated 2.4 m off the ground, react to a light breeze and supply its battery. Made from stainless steel and wood, its forms, contemporary and functional at the same time, recall the storm lamps used by sailors, as well as the propellers of helicopters, and give the impression that it could soon take off… Originally designed as a mobile device for summer use in gardens, it can also be used in the urban environment fixed in the ground.

**Judith de Graauw
Studio Demakersvan
Plan B**

Alberto Vasquez
Igendesign

flow lamp

This vertical wind-powered lamp was created for the Third World and in particular for poor neighbourhoods beside the sea, where the wind can be a rich resource if harnessed without using costly technical means. Its mast is in bamboo, as are its several sails which form a spiral, allowing one to capture the slightest breeze, whichever direction it blows. A dynamo is on the main axis and the luminous sources, LEDs, are fixed at the extremities of the blades and produce a continuous or variable light according to the speed of their rotation. This ecological streetlamp was designed at a workshop at the Budapest University of Art and Design, which carries the name of an illustrious Hungarian designer, László Moholy-Nagy. And it's not for nothing that the different luminous forms that this lamppost creates recall those of this artist's photograms.

Quincy court - 2009
Rios Clementi Hale Studios
US General Services Administration

Nou Barris central park - 2007
Arriola & Fiol Arquitects
ProNouBarris S.A.

140 enchanting the city / SCULPTURAL

public light via làctea - 1990
Enric Batlle - Joan Roig
Santa & Cole

dr jekyll & mr mouse - 2008
Berger&Berger
Le CentQuatre & Archipel Ephémère

141

Marin central plaza - 2002
Topher Delaney
Rawson, Blum & Leon

supernature - 2007
Vincent Leroy / Art Entreprise
Unibail-Rodamco / Rivétoile - Strasbourg

142 enchanting the city / POETIC

Kjellgren Kaminsky
Architecture AB
The Architectural
(ASC)
(TUPB)

silent city

A commemorative landscape monument is in the course of being built in Tangshan, in memory of the earthquake that struck China in 1976, whose epicentre was this industrial city in the east of the country. This park of around 100 hectares mixes green spaces and circulation paths, creating a real living space, surrounding the ruins of the seism. A huge number of black stones are made available to visitors, who can write a message in chalk and place them symbolically where they wish. Lanterns complete this layout, inspired by traditional rice paper lamps. Also acting as protective seats, they allow one to spend a moment alone or to get together with others. These different elements, strengthened by the chromatic opposition of black and white, form several levels of reading and perception, evoking distress and hope, the past and the future.

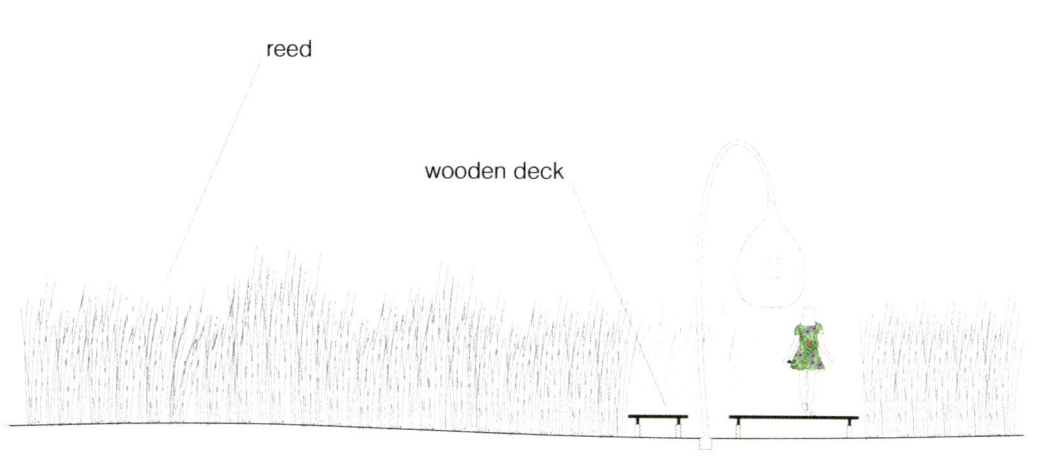

reed

wooden deck

Rousseau garden

2007

In Geneva, this luminous installation has taken over Rousseau Island, which is situated on the Rhône, facing Lake Leman. Fourteen hybrid volumes, from nursery hothouses to maritime containers, punctuate the landscape space, containing artificial plants in plastic pots enveloped in tulle. They echo the naval shipyard that previously occupied the site, which has become a place for walking, and evoke the passion for botany and immersion in nature of the famous philosopher whose bronze statue stands here. Saturated by coloured neon lights, they create a laboratory ambiance. All around, the trees and their networks of branches are lit up with a garish, synthetic green. The whole forms an incongruous and multicoloured garden where the organic is adorned with the improbable, and the artificial competes with the biological.

Maro Avrabou & Dimitri Xenakis
Trees and Lights Festival, Geneva

Fabrice Peltier
DesignPack Gallery

recycling, a luminous idea

It was a wish to familiarise the public with selective sorting and recycling, good ecological gestures that can make one optimistic about the future of the planet, that motivated this project. Plastic bottles were chosen as an emblematic object, recalling that only one in two is currently collected after its first use... Thus, in 2009 during the New Year's Eve festivities, an ideal collective and federating moment, they formed the basis for the creation of luminous decorations and Christmas trees. Punctuated with lights, they decorated the rue de Richelieu and André Malraux square in the first arrondissement of Paris, as part of the operation Paris illuminates Paris. A citizen-based initiative that aims to leave the blame-laying approach behind and offer constructive and artistic alternatives.

lighthouse -2004
Cornelia Erdmann

color design hotel - 2008
Carole Picard
Jean-Marc Galabert / A7 Management

impression - 2009
Michiel van Kempen, Brent Cazemier, Martin Bruining, Marieke Vromans & Peter van Kempen

146 enchanting the city / WINDOWS

Sylvie Fajfrowska 2005
Anne Brégeaut 2006
Virginie Barré 2007
Henri Cueco 2008
Julian Opie 2009
Glen Baxter 2010
Abbaye Saint-André
Centre d'art contemporain de Meymac

advent calendar

Advent (from the Latin adventus which means arrival) is the period of four weeks leading up to Christmas, when both children and adults await and prepare for the big day. The eponymous calendar is a German tradition started to make children wait more patiently. It often takes the form of a piece of card with 24 pre-cut windows that can be opened day after day. Inside you can read a phrase from the Gospels or find a treat. Since 2005, the Meymac contemporary art centre in Corrèze has upheld this tradition by inviting an artist to create a monumental calendar on the façade of the Abbey of Saint-André. Each day, from the first of December to Epiphany, a new window lights up, revealing the image of the day and eventually forming an exhibition of contemporary art, urbain and stimulating in the heart of the hard winters of the Limousin.

147

N building

2009

Near the train station of Tachikawa, a town in the Tokyo metropolis, a strange building attracts the attention of passers-by. Its façade is entirely covered in QR codes, the two-dimensional bar codes that allow one to access digital content by photographing them with a mobile phone. The building is thus a huge source of multimedia information, diffusing for example a message in the form of an SMS in real time, videos, shopping information, or virtual poster campaigns. The advantage of this new form of communication is its neutral graphic form which avoids an additional visual pollution of the urban space which is already invaded by different signs, information systems, brand names and other traditional or digital display panels.

Terada Design architects
Qosmo & Izumi Okayasu Lighting Design

148 enchanting the city / INTERACTIVE

Moment Factory
La Vitrine Culturelle, Montréal

the cultural shop window

Like London, New York and Boston, Montreal has been given a structure that unites the functions of information desk and ticket office, where tickets for all the city's cultural events can be bought. Baptised the Cultural Shop Window, it is situated in the new Theatre Neighbourhood and its frontage has been the object of particular attention. This permanent installation is made up of movement detectors and 35,000 LEDs which can change colour according to the movements of passers-by. Its luminous architecture is therefore continuously changing in a random way, and it also becomes a place of interactive and artistic creation for those who stop here and deliberately experiment.

Hérault Arnod Architectes
Chris Younés
Inex
Michel Forgue
Cité de l'Architecture et du Patrimoine
Exposition « Habiter écologique »

2008

vertical housing scheme

Allowing one to live in the city ecologically and to make it viable and desirable while 80% of the population dreams of having their own house is the theme of an ideas competition launched to design a residential building in Boulogne-Billancourt, in the west of Paris. One of the solutions proposed is the creation of vertical housing, which is portrayed as an alternative to individual above-ground territories, coupled with large exterior spaces that make up a landscape expanding upwards. Another particularity of this eco-project is its south façade, which is covered in Grow2, a new American technology created by SMIT. This "voltaic ivy" provides a hybrid energy from the rays of the sun and the force of the wind, while reflecting the light.

150 enchanting the city / INTERACTIVE

twists and turns

Mader Stublic Wiermann
Uniqa

In Vienna, Austria, the exterior structure of the Uniqa tower, belonging to a large European insurance group, has been equipped in its entirety with a long aluminium shell carrying 45 000 LEDs. These form a huge network that can transmit video images with a 3D program and a sequence entitled "Twists and turns". Even if the logo of the firm is displayed from time to time, the interaction between the architecture and the images created exceeds the simple effect of an advertising screen or panel, the façade becoming progressively an abstract form in perpetual transformation. It is also a new component in the landscape, on which it imprints its variations, multiplying at its feet in the Danube's flow.

the altoviseur - 2004
Julien Berthier

resonance 2 - 2005
Denis Brillet / Block & Metamobil

152 enchanting the city / MIRRORS

Earthscape
Mitsubishi Estate
Tokio Marine & Nichido Fire Insurance Co.

Minato-Mirai business square

Yokohama, Japan's second largest city, has developed thanks to its maritime façade, becoming a large commercial port. Today, it is growing vertically through the construction of ever-taller towers. The ornamental pond in Minato Mirai business square evokes this double filiation through an optical game. When it is filled with water, words relating to the sky appear very readable. In brief, those concerning the sea become the most visible. It thus raises questions about existence, reminding the inhabitants of their origins, born of the oceans to grow up on land…

decoys - 2005
Mark Jenkins

ecorafts - 2010
Paule Kingleur
Exposition « Regards sur la biodivresité », Bagatelle Parc
Paris City Council

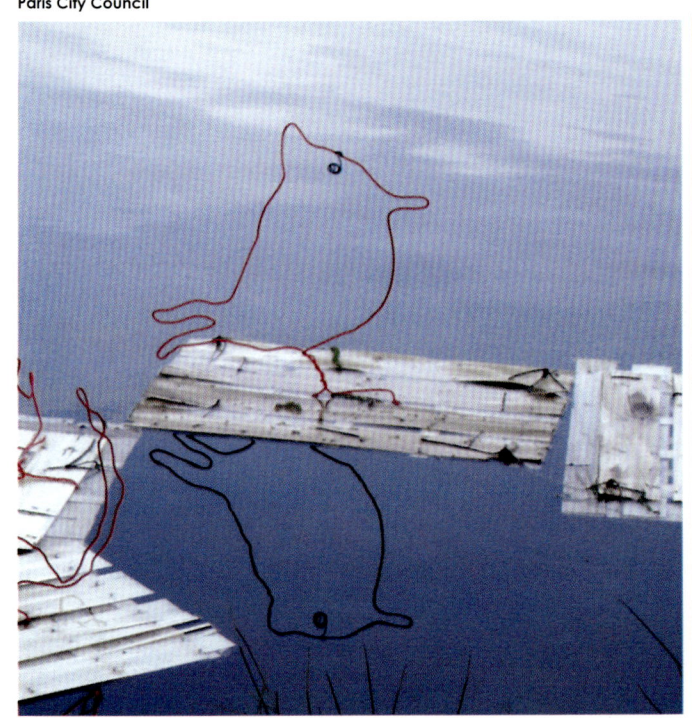

154 enchanting the city / WATER AS MIRROR

**Atelier Dreiseitl
City of Portland**

Tanner Springs park

Pearl district, a neighbourhood in Portland, was historically a marsh, cut in two by the River Tanner. First of all industrialised and crossed by railways, it has progressively becomes a residential and commercial zone. To accompany this evolution, a park with an ecological purpose has replaced the industrial wastelands all around. In the first place the ground was rid of pollution and the aquatic habitats recreated, allowing for flood prevention by collecting heavy rainfall. The memory of the site has been preserved by recreating a pathway on an old railway track. A large wall has also been created using old rails where artistic pieces of glass enclosing natural elements have been integrated, and play with the light like the different surfaces of the surrounding water.

Jaume Plensa
Kruek & Sexton
Crystal Fountains Toronto
Jean Max Llorca
US Equities
Henri Crown and company

Crown fountain

Located on the old railway site of the Illinois Central Railroad company, Millennium Park unfolds over 24 hectares in the centre of Chicago. Marrying art, architecture and landscape design, it incorporates several cultural facilities, as well as three works of art: Cloud Gate, Jay Pritzker Pavillion and Crown Fountain. The latter is situated in the south-east of the park, and is made up of two fountains in black granite, fifteen or so metres high, rising up at the extremities of a large rectangular pool. These immense structures have a screen that broadcasts portraits of the inhabitants of the city, framed so as to give the impression that the jets of water from the fountains are spurting from their mouths… Thanks to the several millimetres of water spreading out from the feet of these two towers of images, there is a total interactivity between the reflections of the faces, which change regularly, and those of the passers-by who come here to refresh themselves. This "in situ" art offering has become one of the most popular spaces at the site, thanks to its originality and its social involvement.

156 enchanting the city / WATER AS MIRROR

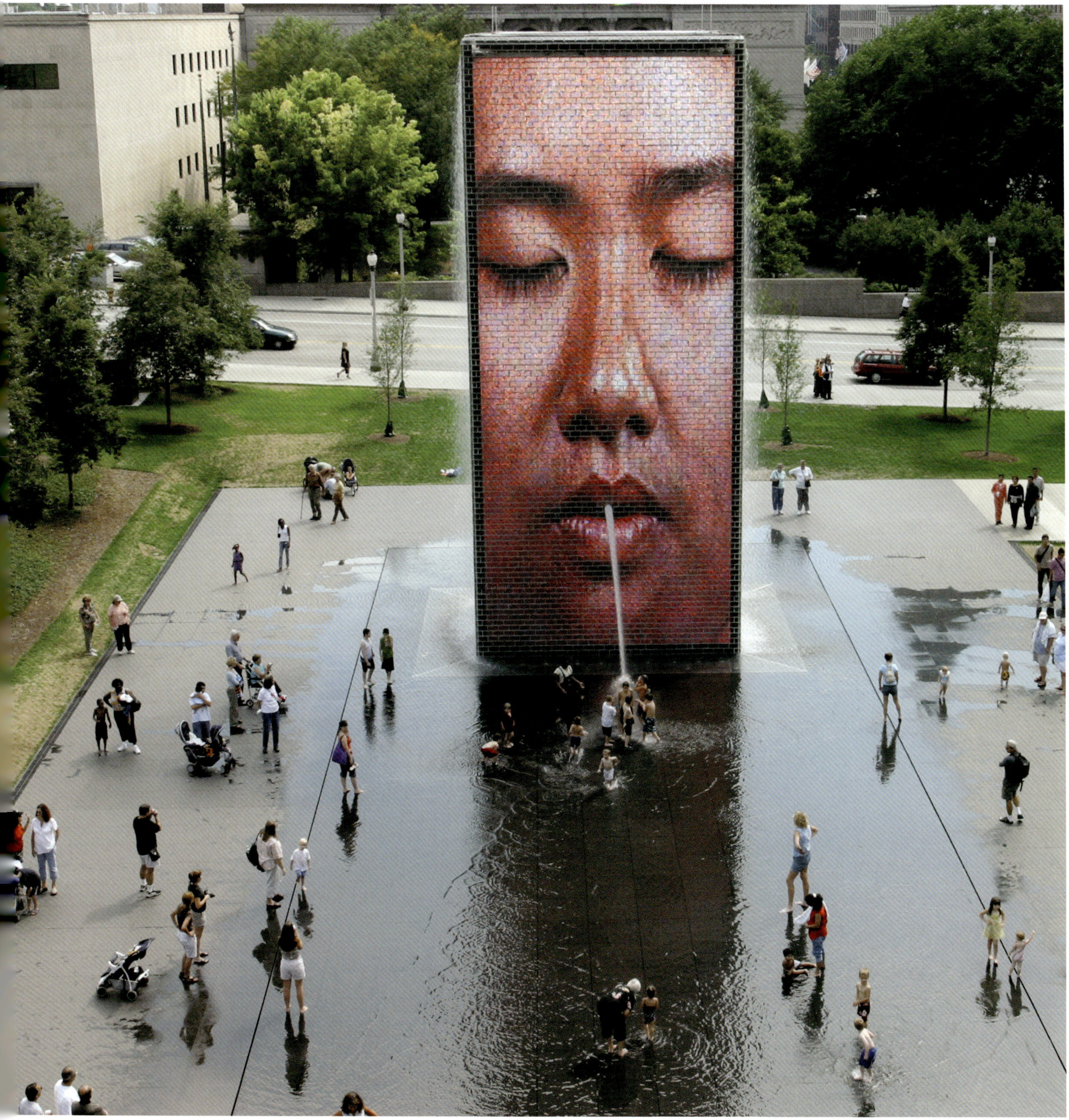

river eyelash

2005

Pittsburgh's Point State Park stretches out over 15 hectares at the western point of the city centre, nicknamed the Golden Triangle. A place of memory, it commemorates in its location the war between the French and the native American Indians, in 1754 and 1763. A large circular water feature and its huge fountain is one of the main attractions, situated at the confluence of three rivers which meet at this place. In 2005, this space was given a monumental artwork. Three thousand bouys, threaded on a pink rope like a giant necklace, stretch out towards the open water on 42 lines leaving from the quay, forming the imaginary eyelashes of the city… Pink, yellow and red, they undulate with the currents and the winds, taking different forms, like that of the waves or the arches of the neighbouring metallic bridge, artistic and playful echoes in the landscape.

Stacy Levy
Three Rivers Arts Festival, Pittsburgh PA

158 enchanting the city / WATER CIRCLES

Gustafson Porter Ltd
Department of Culture, Media and Sport
The Royal Parks

Diana, Princess of Wales Memorial Fountain

To pay homage to Diana, Princess of Wales, after her tragic death, a special fountain was built in Hyde Park, London. Set into a natural slope, it unfolds as an ovoid circuit of water with irregular curves evoking Lady Di's openness and willingness to give herself to others. The sides of this sculptural granite ring offer natural seats where one can sit with one's feet in the cool water watch and listen to the different water effects that punctuate it. The sound effects created are as varied as the "Chadar cascade" evoking India or "Rock and Roll"... All come together to compose a score as convivial and radiant as the princess herself was known to be.

François Mitterrand square

Located in Burgundy, the French commune of Le Creusot is historically linked to the metallurgical industry. Over the past decades its economy has been transformed, basing its development on tourism and leisure, as well as education with, in particular, its University Institute of Technology. This development project was designed to create a link between the town hall and the town centre. Water was chosen as the medium, present in different forms and variations. Thus, a geyser shoots up in front of the Town Hall, and then becomes a small stream of water which runs up to Place François Mitterrand. Every now and then mist effects rise up from the ground, temporarily changing the perception of the urban landscape. These aquatic scenes follow on from each other, finishing in a dry fountain with jets, forming as many micro-events on the esplanade.

François Tribel
Jean Max Llorca
Communauté Urbaine Le Creusot Montceau

160 enchanting the city / WATER FEATURES

**B. Huet, O. Bressach,
JB. Huet, L. Canazares
Jean Max Llorca
City of Albi**

Vigan Square

To reappropriate its historic centre, which had been invaded by cars, and make it harmonious and convivial, the town of Albi, in the south-west of France, has transformed Vigan Square into an open space, without changes in level. With no furniture cluttering it up, it is available for walking and for festive uses or occasional events. This deliberately empty space is enlivened every now and then by the well-chosen adornment of a dry fountain made up of 81 jets. Thanks to five hydraulic systems, controlled by a computer program, the height and the rhythm of the water jets vary, creating alternating pyramid figures.

Rakvere central square

Rakvere is the capital of the region of west Virumaa, in Estonia. A central square has just been laid out, punctuated by five different sized circular zones, concave, convex or flat, with different functions. A marquetry of paving stones draws these spaces out on the ground and surrounds them with a wide grey and black zigzag motif. Several facilities are installed here, a large fountain, a playground for children and curved series of benches, as well as large yellow lanterns which lean over each of the circles, like immense shower heads. Taking on the form and the colours of a playground for adults, this site, which looks like a throwback to the comic books of the 1950s, calls to and attracts passers-by in a city where places to walk were until now almost nonexistent.

Kosmos
Rakvere City Department of Development and Planning

**Lodewijk Baljon
landscape architects
Combination Infra Forumpark (CIF)
City of Apeldoorn
BAM project development
Heijmans project development**

Apeldoorn station square

Located in Apeldoorn, facing the historic train station of the same name, this square reflects the rural identity of this region of Gelderland, in the east of Holland. Because of its situation, as a gateway to the city, it is also a very pleasant open-air waiting room for rail transport users, including numerous cyclists, and of relaxation for the inhabitants. A granite water table, which uses little of the precious liquid, is one element in the layout that shows the ecological approach of the project. In the same way, the ground is entirely made up of cobbles with the colours of the local sand, criss-crossed with irregular cracks that act as drains leading the water to the foot of the pines, thus evoking the neighbouring landscapes of dunes modelled by the wind.

Agence Faragou
Department Council of Alpes-Maritimes

watering as the wind blows

In the laying out of the RD 6202 bis road in the Alpes-Maritimes département, in the south-east of France, particular attention has been paid to its relationship with the environment. The driver sees alternate sequences of 300 m visual openings and planted walls succeed each other, integrating this piece of engineering into the territory rather than making it a scar on the landscape, as is too often the case.

In order to ensure the natural irrigation of the different plantations on either side of the road, seven windmills collect the energy necessary to operate an automatic watering system. They are equipped with an aerogenerator with a propeller and rudder, orienting them according to the direction of the winds and thermal currents to capture the slightest breath of air. Each one supplies more than a thousand square metres of gardens, thus making the site entirely autonomous from an energy point of view, with the water provided by existing ground water. This idea, which truly corresponds to High Environmental Quality standards, makes the most of the richness of Mediterranean species.

164 enchanting the city / WINDMILLS

165

urban bocage

2008

Bocage, the rural landscape of the west of France, is made up of ditches bordering ridges of earth planted with trees, which mark the limits of the parcels of land. In danger of disappearing following the regrouping of land necessary for industrial agriculture, bocage has an undeniable ecological function. It collects rainwater, which is filtered and rid of pollution by a natural aquatic vegetation, while irrigating the roots of the trees planted on the embankments. Taking up this exemplary process, Urban Bocage proposes to connect city drainpipes to planted moats, adorning the pavements with greenery and filtering the rainwater thanks to specific plants, in order to give back a liquid suitable for making the dead ground of the cities live again.

Elodie Stephan

166 enchanting the city / RECYCLED

topic-eau

This autonomous object is disconnected from the urban hydraulic network, but connected to the environment in which it is implanted. It grafts itself to existing objects, a tree, a lamppost or a building, to capture rainwater thanks to a stainless steel funnel. A flexible pocket provides its storage place, before the precious liquid passes through a series of filters (from 50 to 0.2 microns + active carbon) allowing for the elimination of bacteria and viruses. Beneath, a ceramic tap redistributes what has now become drinking water. This ecological fountain is an alternative to the normal way in which rainwater and domestic used water is collected, which in places such as Paris is combined, necessitating far more purification treatments than if it was done in a more selective way.

Isabelle Daeron

spruzzi d'acqua water spray - 2004
Tobia Repossi
Modo

street fountain - 2002
Helmut Smits

radi millennium fountain - 2000
Radi Designers
SAGEP, Paris

o'claire drinking fountain - 2005
Cécile Planchais
Eau de Paris

aqua fountain - 2004
Gemma Bernal & Associats
Urbes 21, S.A.

estadio fountain - 2008
Ramos & Bassols
Urbes 21, S.A.

by-pass fountain - 2001
Gemma Bernal & Associats
Urbes 21, S.A.

lilla fountain - 2004
Tobia Repossi
Modo

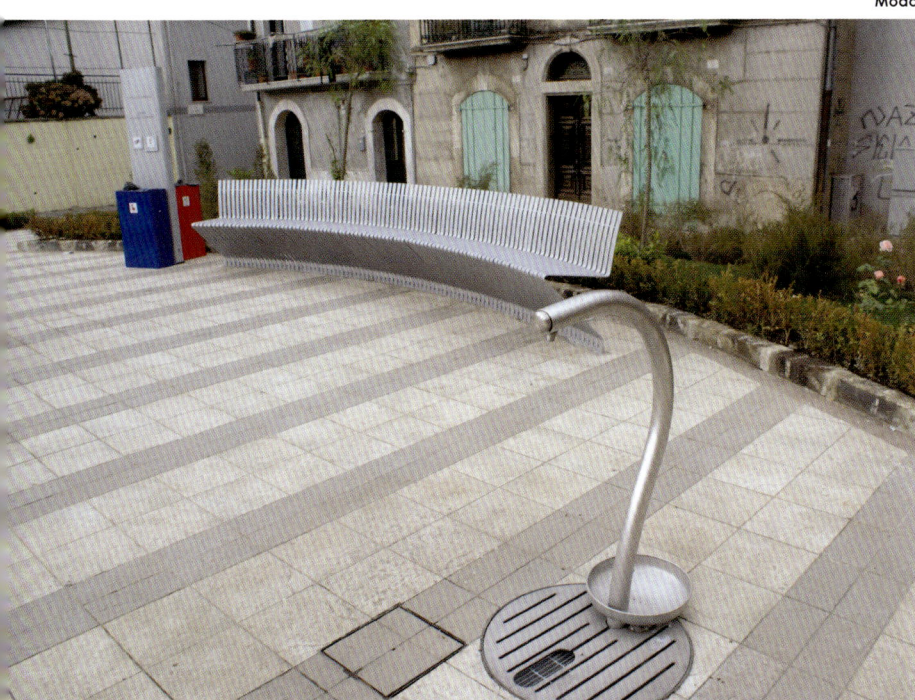

tana fountain - 2000
Francisco J. Mangado
Dae

169

ACCES POMPIERS

ACCES POMPIERS

04

URBAN EXPRESSIONS

m-city

urban expressions

prohibited!
2009
Sophie Barbaux
Le CENTQUATRE, Paris
page 170

La Kommune garden
2009
Teurk, Atlas
La Kommune Belleville Zoo

First famous for the huge mural that overlooks it and for the workshops that hide behind, the wasteland located at 23-25 rue Ramponeau in Paris's 20th arrondissement changed its bearing in 2009. An intergenerational and multicultural shared garden has sprung up here without warning, born of the urgency to create a new neighbourhood space that is ecological, fun, artist and utopic. A few undisciplined flowerbeds were installed, plants grow here and there, play areas have been organised, peopled with poetic objects created from reclaimed materials, like the "Umpire's chair".

pages 172 & 173

Historically the first urban messages were road signs, with the mileage posts of the Roman era. Then signs appeared from the Middle Ages, directing the traveller at crossroads. Street names started to become widespread during the reign of Louis XIV. Road signs were formalised for the first time by the French State which, in 1835, created a code for destinations, then for the state of the roads, and a colour code governing their presentation. In 1909 in Paris, the first four international symbols were born: Dip (or humpback), Bend, Crossroad and Level Crossing. Inspired by railway use, the first red and green traffic lights were installed in London in 1868. Then in Detroit, in 1914, the first traffic-controlling information appeared, notably the Stop sign.

From the Middle Ages onwards shop signs flourished in cities, early forms of advertising. It was only at the end of the 19th century that they were supplanted by posters, which also served to spread information about laws. In time, numerous supports for advertising fixed to walls developed, and in 1971, in France, a new form of urban furniture called Mupi appeared: a structure in the form of a lollipop, with two faces lit from inside, which one now finds all over the world.

This forest of signs is starting to provoke radical reactions. Thus, in 2007, with the support of the population, the city council of São Paolo, the largest city in South America, prohibited any outside advertising in an unprecedented law. An end to visual pollution! The 15,000 advertising hoardings, flashing neon lights, campaigns on buses and taxis, electronic information with flowing texts, even the distribution of flyers… have been suppressed and the city is breathing in a new way!

In parallel, and since the second half of the 20th century, designers have been working on new, relevant types of convivial systems of signage and of spreading information with an ecological aim. And the ground, like the walls, of cities, is invested with artistic creation, whether or not it has been sollicited. Interventions and hijackings physically metamorphose pedestrian crossings, car parks or traffic routes, gables or façades. The inhabitants "speak" to the inhabitants…

heads or tails
2007
Legoville
page 174

resident's park
2006
Osa
B-side tuning of the KunstWerk building, Cologne
page 175

174 urban expressions

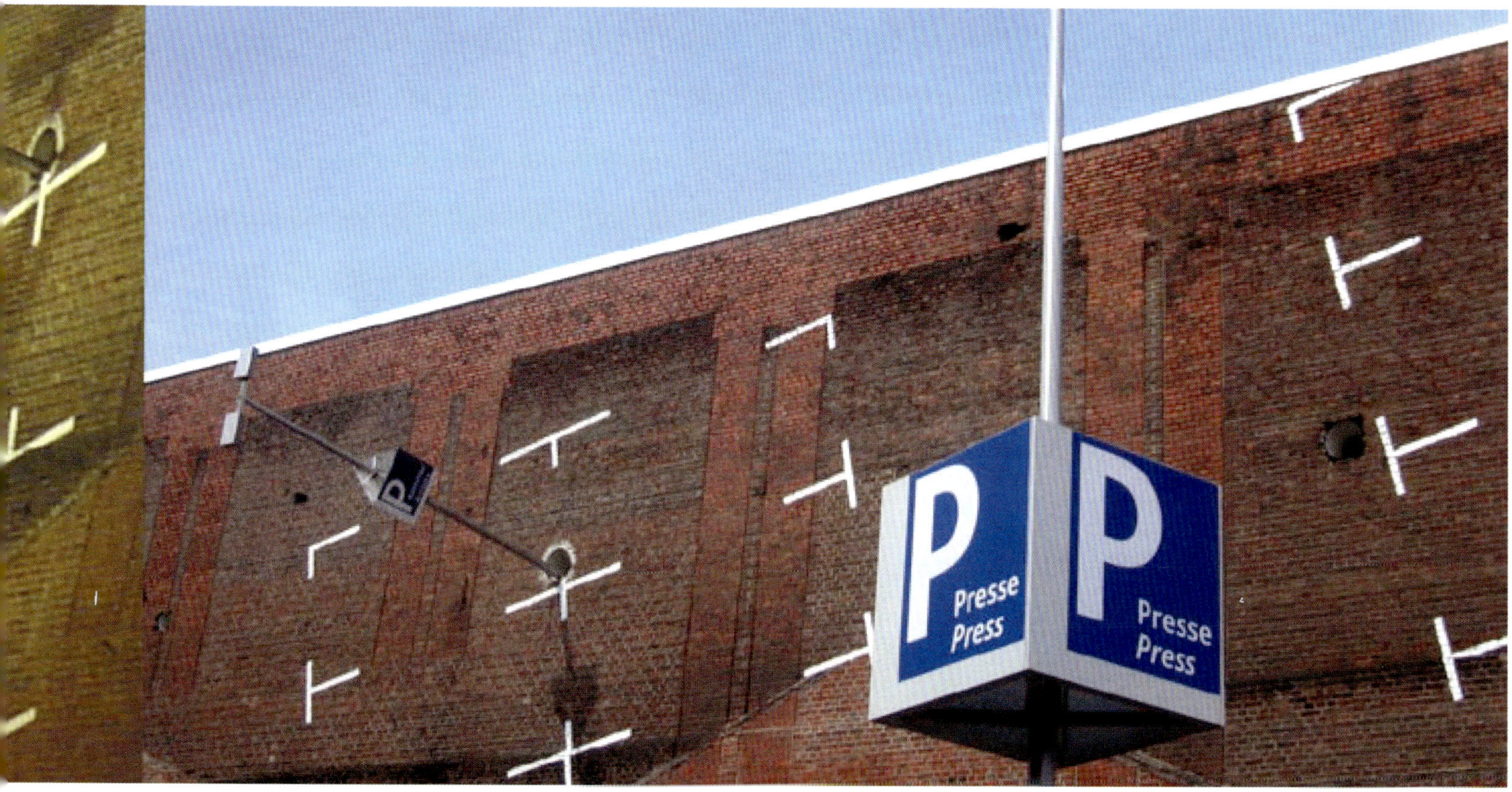
P
Presse
Press
P
Presse
Press

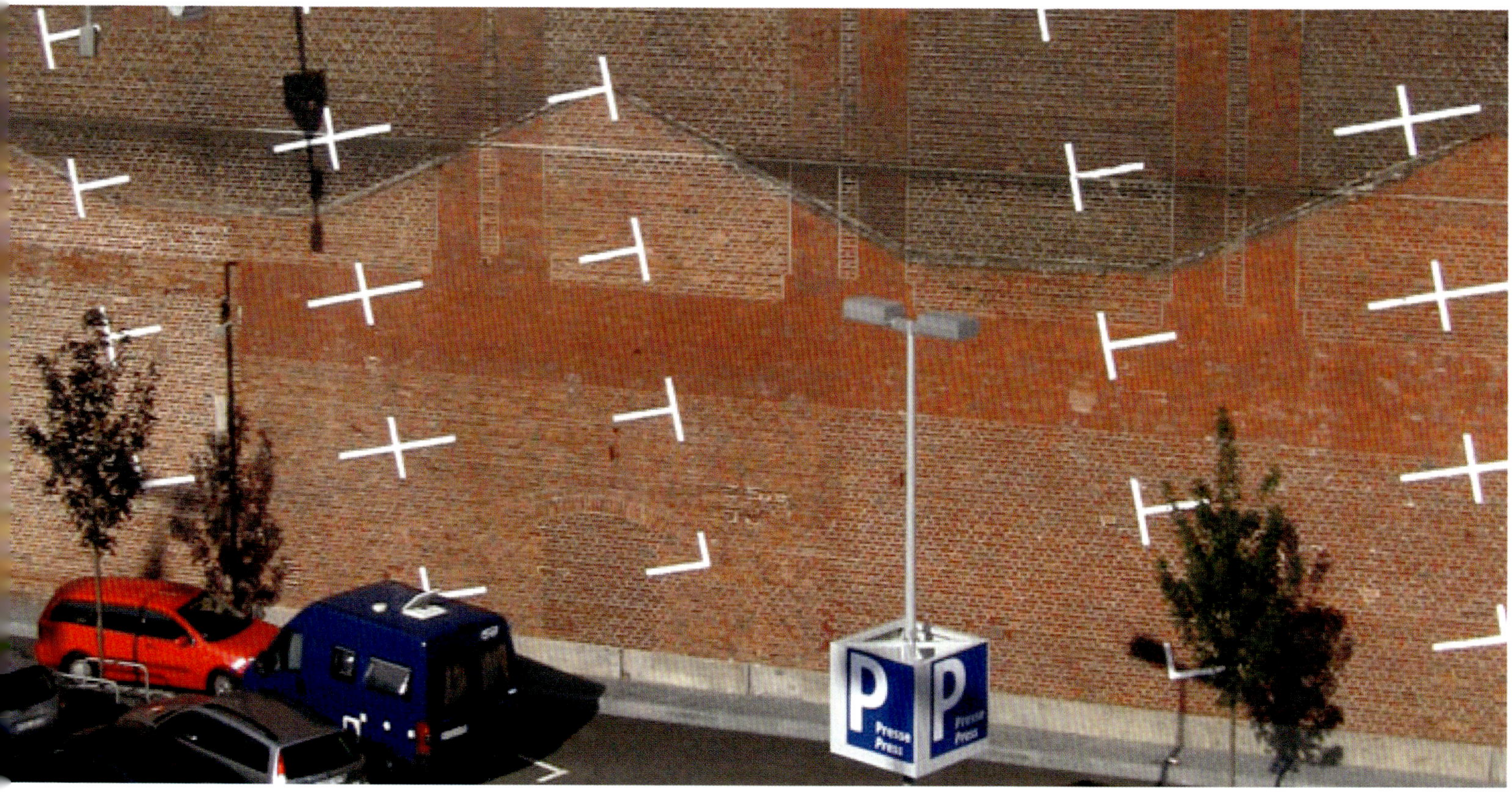

nails! - 2009
collectif Fichtre
Competition for the 1% artistic budget of the Vauban Junior High School in Maubeuge

176 urban expressions / CROSSINGS

AdrianoDesign

urban ways

Pedestrian crossings are well known to city users, allowing them to cross the road in a space that is visible to drivers, grouped together and in security. They are both simple and efficient, with their universal stripes, regular and parallel to the axis of the road. But, while keeping their primary function, they can also adopt original motifs cut out of the ground markings and change the appearance of the city, making it more convivial and communicative. Thus, each quarter can have its own specific and personalised decor, expressing its identity, its history… Their users, as well as cyclists, have the time to notice them, then to read and finally appreciate them. This isn't the case for drivers, whose rapid circulation doesn't allow them to notice that the zebra stripes are not the same as usual, and thus is doesn't present any danger. They can be used as an advertising medium. But their vocation seems more interesting if they provide cities with new urban paths, which can be take to know the city better, followed to get your bearings or as a game of educational or fictional routes.

Johnny B. - 2008
Legoville
Place Neuve, Geneva

extraordinary meeting - 2008
Legoville & Christian Gräser
Oberbottigen, Berne

178 urban expressions / PARKING PLACES

**Irb Zurich
Ruedi Baur
Axel Steinberger
Chantal Grossen
Jürgen X. Albrecht & Eva Simonsen**
Schweizerische Gesellschaft
für Immobilien Sgi.

media campus

Media Campus, a new multimedia business centre, is situated in the western quarter of Zurich, in a renovated former printworks. It offers an attractive work environment spread over 28,000 m^2, which can host up to 500 people. In order to lay out the car park, it was necessary to redefine a physical and graphic identity for the territory which would correspond to its new functions. Contrary to the old site which had only one entrance, with a doorman, we are now in a space with multiple access. Large luminous information panels, from which white lines depart leading to the parking spaces and different offices, create a continuous stream of information. This signage on the ground, which seems to go off in every direction and to cancel itself out, is in fact very structured. With its large arrows, it guides the visitor and the user simply and also points out the small gardens made up of large planted tubs and seats, which modify the impression given by the site, making it convivial.

Biuro Projektów Lewicki Łatak
City of Cracovie

new Nowy square

Nowy Square was created in 1929 in Krakow, Poland. Numerous photos testify to its past life, with its ritual abattoir, its public toilets, the surrounding building... Today, stalls, hawkers, kiosques and bins have taken possession of the place.

The rehabilitation project proposes to recall the past, and to give back to this site its specific identity, based on its forms, its materials and its initial perspectives, as well as the sounds, the smells and the different people that gave it a daily history: the metalworker that lived in house N°7 and died before the War, Mr Francis, the garlic seller...

As in the commemorative panels of the synagogues and the ex-votos of the church that are its neighbours, collective memory establishes itself. At first by breaking up the existing ground and reusing this material to create a new surface, which also diminishes the production costs.

Then, by engraving the emblematic names of the neighbourhood, like those of important municipal counsellors and legendary personalities of the local demi-monde, as well as the logos of business and institutions that have disappeared. Not all the space has been marked, but some places have been preserved to pursue this obligation to memory.

Osa
Anja Ohliger
Stephan Goerner
Ulrich Beckefeld
Rica Kaiser
Plan 09 Köln

assimilation

In the south of Cologne, in Germany, newly constructed road junctions have roundabouts in their centre, just drawn out on the ground in paving stones. They are unoccupied, like voids! The idea is to give them character and a soul, even if it is ephemeral. Thus one of them is decorated with motifs forming a white lace, like a paper doily. Creating an improbable and incongruous island, this intervention personalises the site, recalling the sculptured architecture of façades from the "Gruenderzeit" (era of the founders) of the second half of the 19th century and beginning of the 20th. It thus pits form and function against and other and questions the coherence between design and site.

chronological steps - 2007
The Central Government Building n°7, Tokyo
Earthscape
Government of Japan
cf. page 44

182 urban expressions / STAIRS

the piano stairs case

In the framework of an unusual advertising campaign by Volkswagen, three short films entitled "Fun theory" were shot "live", inciting citizens to live the city in a new way. One made the waste bins of a park speak when you put something in them, and followed the reactions of the surprised walkers. The second encouraged passers-by to throw their bottles into a very special place which attributed a point to each drop, like a jukebox. The third incited users to take a staircase instead of the escalator next to it. Transformed into a piano, its steps produced a sound and by climbing you could pass from one octave to another, or come back down to really play... 66% more people than normal took the staircase, relinquishing comfort!

Simon Higby
Martin Lundgren & Patrik Sundberg
DDB Stockholm
Volkswagen

the landing

The Italian word *graffiti* comes from the Latin *graphium* (scratch), whose etymology is borrowed from the Greek *graphein*, which means to write, draw or paint. We find the first examples of it in Antiquity and all through the evolution of Man. Today, everywhere, graffiti is considered as an act of vandalism, punishable by the law, because it most often degrades the property of another. Its most frequent tools are now paint bombs and markers, but one can also envisage practicing it differently, as with The Landing.

At the crossroads of art, music and technology, this concept is a mix of "live" video painting and electronic graffiti, taking the form of nocturnal performances. Thanks to cameras, projectors and computers, video images appear progressively, as if really painted on the walls, thanks to a paint roller that applies nothing, but is made up of green LEDs. In fact, all is just an illusion in this new mode of expression, clean while remaining potentially subversive…

Sweatshoppe

184 urban expressions / GRAFFITI & CO

Invader

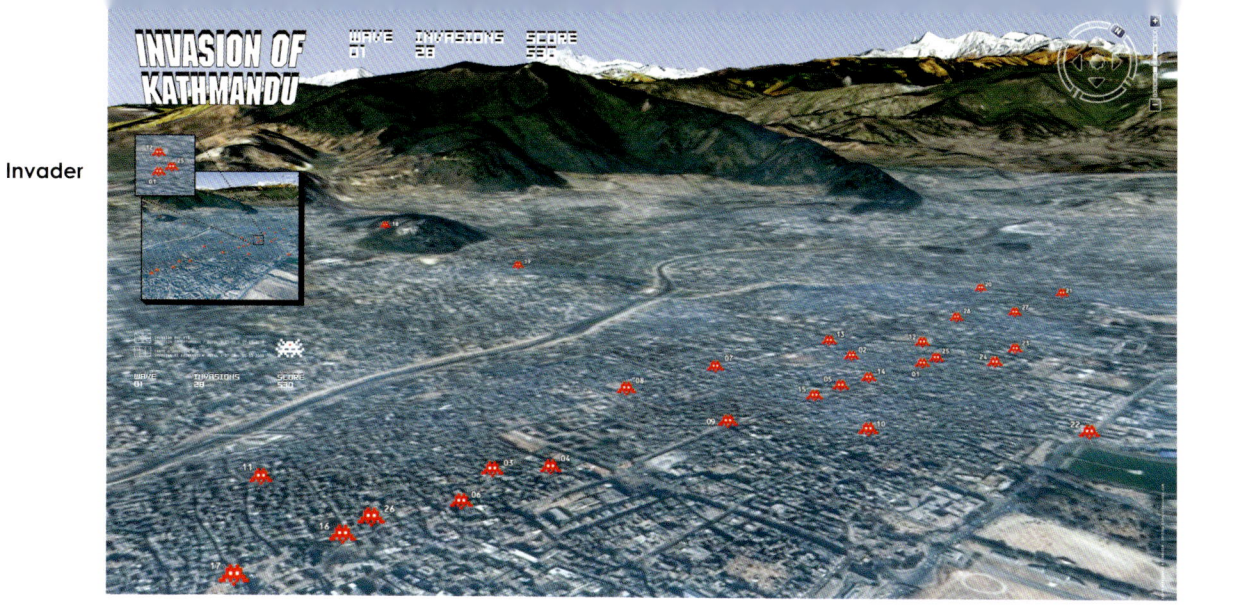

space invader

For more than 10 years, curious little characters have punctuated the international urban space. These "space invaders" seem to have come out of the eponymous video game from the end of the 1970s, which prefigured the advent of the pixel and digital technology. They materialise in the form of mosaic tiles on the walls of Paris, London, Tokyo, Mombasa or even Kathmandu. Today, more than 40 cities in the world have been "invaded". The space invaders install themselves in strategic places like the "Game over" frieze at the exit of Belleville Metro in Paris, or more confidential ones, like the little "Mario" seeming to walk out of a fire hydrant in New York. For each metropolis, a run-down of where they have implanted themselves allows acolytes to follow in their footsteps using UFO-books, "guides and maps of the invasions". Representing a particularly judicious use of a material to express a concept, the artistic invasion and its incredible geographical and temporal expansion makes it one of the major projects of the "Street art" movement.

Kanardo
Nuits sonores 2004
City of Lyon
Unchi Leisure Centre
Arty Farty

You Are Beautiful

panos, fake roadsigns

In 2004, then again in 2008, the whole city of Lyon was filled with oblique, funny or provocative road signs that seemed to have sprung up on their own in a single night. Around fifty artists, graphic designers, post-graffiti artists or illustrators from twenty or so countries had been invited to create true-false urban road signage, identical in every way to those that one finds on French roads.

All red, the colour of interdiction in the highway code, they are turned towards the pavement rather than the road so as to avoid accidents... They forbid Christmas trees from skateboarding or a hybrid animal to be created genetically, they prohibit the adverse effect of a slow life or call out with phrases like "You are beautiful" or "Thank you for your suffering"!

This incursion into the daily life of the locals cocks a snook at all the prohibitions that our society drums into us at any moment of the day. It also allows truly contemporary graphic design to be seen by everyone and provokes smiles, astonishment, even questions. This initiative, militant in all senses of the word, shows that you don't need much to make the city more joyful.

Francois Morel	Teurk	Rob Reger
Kanardo	Andrew Rae	Mike Perry
Meomi	Freak Fabric	Cody Hudson

187

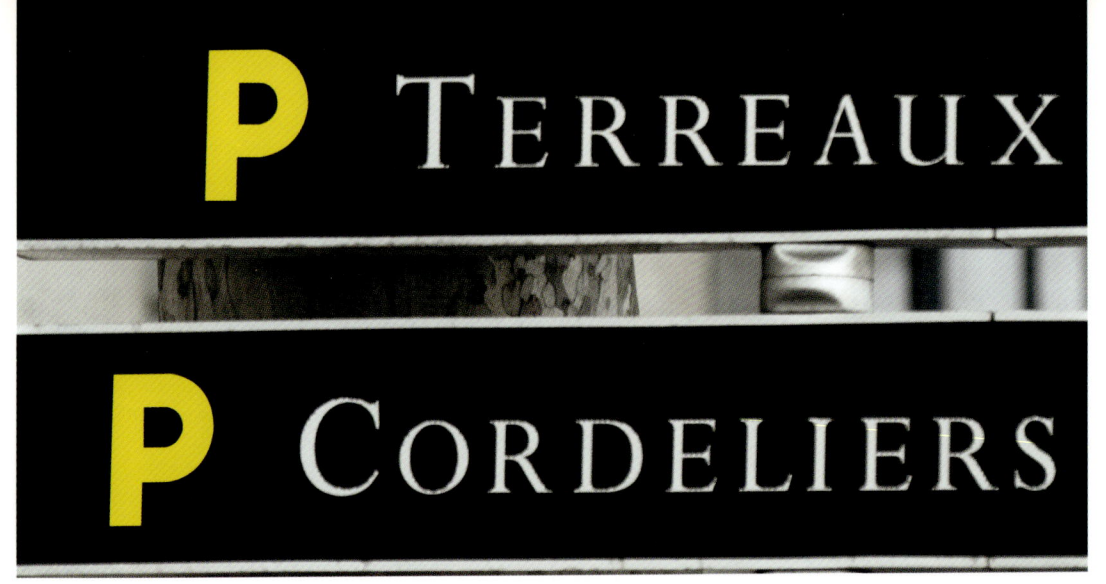

**Yan D. Pennor's
Art Entreprise
Lyon Parc Auto**

Lyon car park

For the first time, the building of car parks has been accompanied by cross-disciplinary thought, bringing the aesthetic dimension and functionality together and thus creating a dialogue between technical concerns, architecture, design, art and communication. Jean-Michel Wilmotte, who is known for his scenographic interiors, has played the harmony and conviviality card, notably through the use of indirect light and the reassuring transparency of screens, as well as through the visual emotion provoked by the installation in each site of works of art by international artists such as Daniel Buren and Joseph Kosuth.

But it's outside that the surprise begins and calls out. The graphic charter and signage have been entirely designed to create an immediately identifiable image. The shape of the signs has been redrawn, becoming oblong. The usual red and blue code has been modified by the adoption of new colours, conveying the information in a two-way fashion: in yellow on a black background for car drivers, in black on a yellow background for pedestrians. And Perpetua, a strict and elegant typeface, has been adopted. In total it offers users a specific and simple graphic identity, facilitating the use of this new generation of car parks.

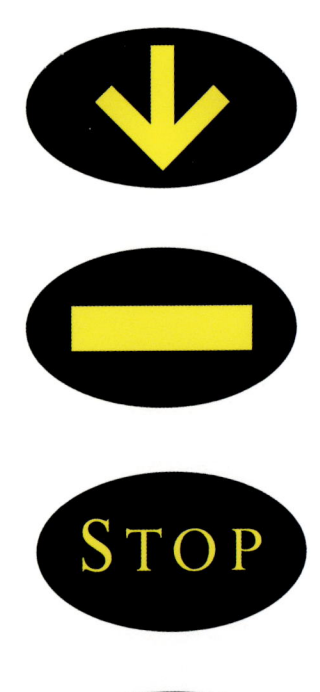

P
ENTRÉE
ENTRÉE

NIVEAU SUPERIEUR
INTERDIT AUX PIÉTONS
SORTIE

PARC ANTONIN PONCET
VEHICULES ELECTRIQUES
1,8 M

P
PARC CORDELIERS
15 Km/h
ENTRÉE
ABONNÉS
1,80m
Europa

untitled - 2006
Paris

ampelmann - 1961-2010
Berlin

190 urban expressions / TRAFFIC LIGHTS

eko - traffic light concept

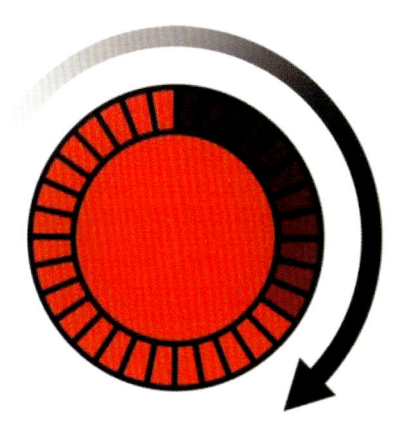

This new concept of "red" light which counts the time that remains before it turns green, allows for a true evolution in city driving, where stops are very frequent. Drivers are less stressed, they know exactly if they have time or not before setting off again and they don't need to keep their feet tense on the pedals of the vehicle, eyes riveted on the traffic lights to be able to move off at the right moment. In optimum conditions it also encourages "Stop & Go", which is still rarely used. This consists of stopping one's engine at each light, manually, or automatically if the car is equipped for it, allowing for substantial savings in fuel and reducing CO_2 emissions. With a greater traffic fluidity, pedestrians are also better informed and therefore safer.

Damjan Stankovic

ambient traffic-light

The numerous environmental phenomena that determine the state of the space in which we live are little known. Semáforo Ambiental, designed and tested in Bogota, captures different types of information on its ambient ecosystem and reproduces them in real time. The levels of air pollution, the quantity of electromagnetic waves, the atmospheric pressure, the humidity, the temperature…, are thus made available to passers-by via a structure evoking a multiple traffic light, and transmitted in parallel to researchers.

Estudio 6 Class
School of Architecture and Design
Universidad de Los Andes, Bogotá
Hernando Barragán & Felipe Mesa

Tissu à L.E.D

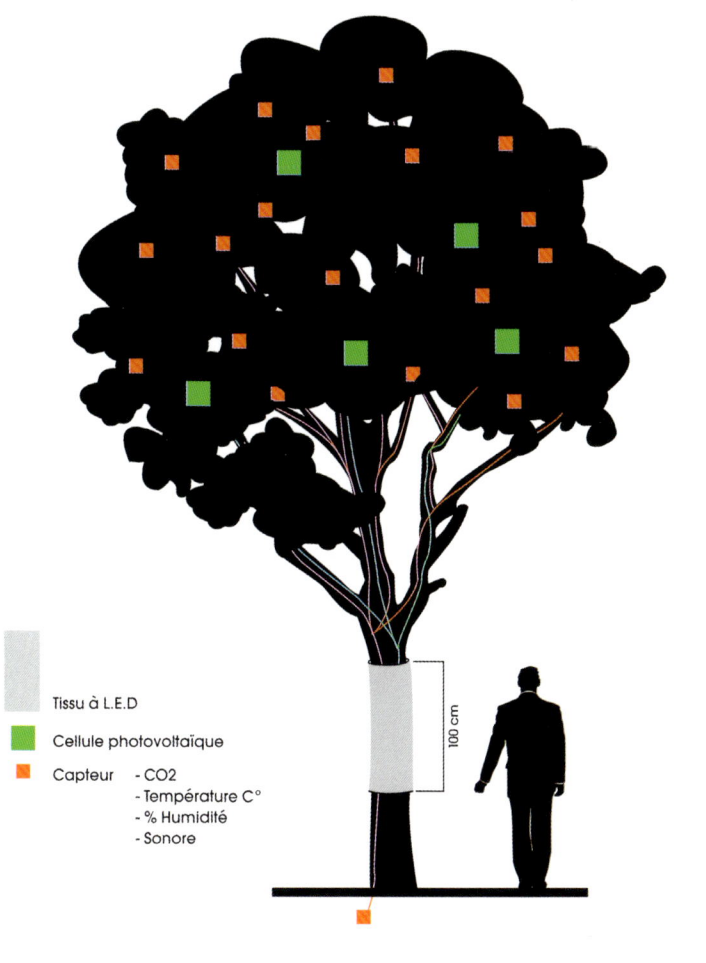

Cellule photovoltaïque

Capteur - CO2
- Température C°
- % Humidité
- Sonore

100 cm

193

118 218 - 2007
Benedetto Buffalino
Leaves Day of Lyon

nature - 2009
Sean Martindale

Paris floral park - 1969
Daniel Collin
City of Paris / DEVE

194 urban expressions / SYSTEMS OF SIGNS

Emmanuel Cairo & Thérèse Troïka
EPPGHV

signage system for the park of La Villette

In 2008, a competition was launched to define the direction of the new signage at the Park of La Villette. One proposition has developed a flamboyant project for this, on the scale of the site. It advocates the colour red as a true sign of recognition, conferring identity and readable, functioning as an ideal complement to the green of the vegetation, which is very present in the different landscape spaces, but also as a pertinent echo of the scarlet follies designed by the architect Bernard Tschumi. It maintains the importance of words, already used in the names displayed on certain emblematic places, to be taken up as a monumental commitment for the whole of the graphic charter. In counterpart, the arrow signs are both a guide and a narrative support, as these signs, understandable by everyone, don't enter into competition with the several visual codes that already exist.

Irb Zurich / Ruedi Baur, Axel Steinberger,
Tibor ARchert, Jürgen X. Albrecht,
Jan Eric Stephan, Claudia Wildermuth
Buga 2005 Gmbh.

buga 05

Every two years, a big horticultural event entitled Buga takes place in Germany, each time in a different city. In 2005 it settled in Munich, offering floral exhibitions and ephemeral gardens to the public, as each edition of the festival has done in the past. Taking into account the size of the space to be taken over, the bias for the scenography and signage was to punctuate the several parts of the site with solid volumes that could be used as the support for information printed on tarpaulins. Bales of straw provided the basis of this concept, offering the two-dimensionality necessary for the information and the possibility of a simple implantation in the site, without needing to be anchored in the ground, thanks to their size, their weight and their rectangular form. They imposed themselves visually and formally as an obvious fact, naturally evoking the limited time span of this event.

196 urban expressions / SYSTEMS OF SIGNS

PARK
TERRASSE
KLEINE GÄRTEN
PARALLELE GÄRTEN
TOILETTEN
BEHINDERTEN WC
WICKELRAUM
SEEGASTRONOMIE
BUSFAHRER TREFF
SEE
SCHÄNKE

UFERSTAUDEN
101

PARK
TERRASSE
BUGA SEE
AUSGANG OST
INFO
ZELLENGARTEN
PARALLELE
GÄRTEN

SANITÄTS
STATION WEST
TOILETTEN

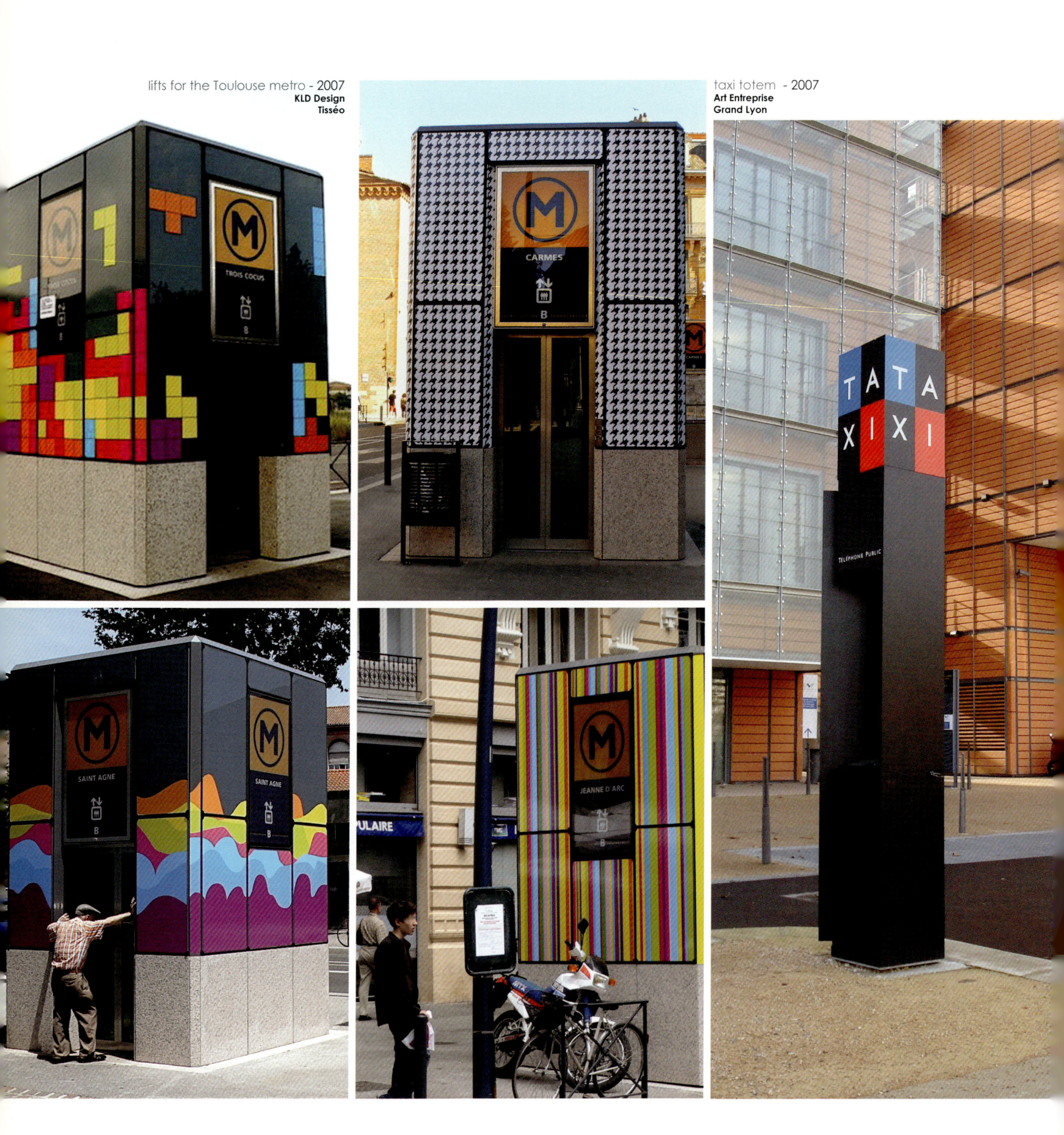

lifts for the Toulouse metro - 2007
KLD Design
Tisséo

taxi totem - 2007
Art Entreprise
Grand Lyon

198 urban expressions / SYSTEMS OF SIGNS

**Outsign
Altarea**

building site hoarding

In 2006, the town of Kremlin-Bicêtre, in the south of Paris, innovated in the field of building site hoardings, with the launch of its large project of urban renewal. Entitled Okabé, was a real focus for life that was to rise from the earth, combining all the functions of a town centre: shops, offices, housing, culture and public spaces. This new generation facility was the first French green shopping centre, certified "French Standard tertiary buildings – High Environmental Quality Approach (HQE®) – Shops". To announce this ambitious programme, the site was theatricalised thanks to an ephemeral scenography of hoardings with bright colours, accenting the long fence around the property limits like coloured commas. Their tops, cut out to form the key verbs of the future activities and uses, question the inhabitants. Okabé opened in March 2010.

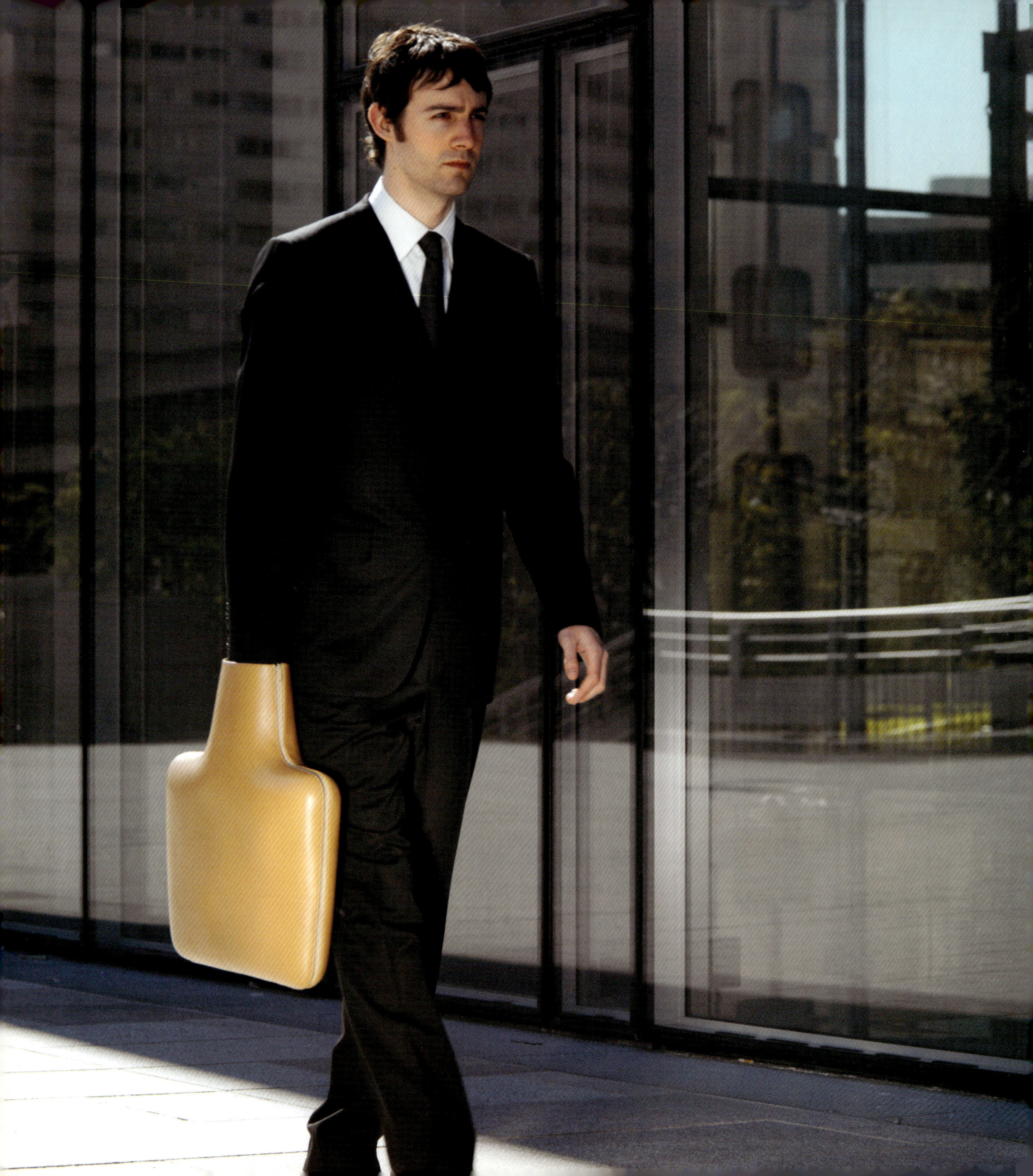

05

SHELTER

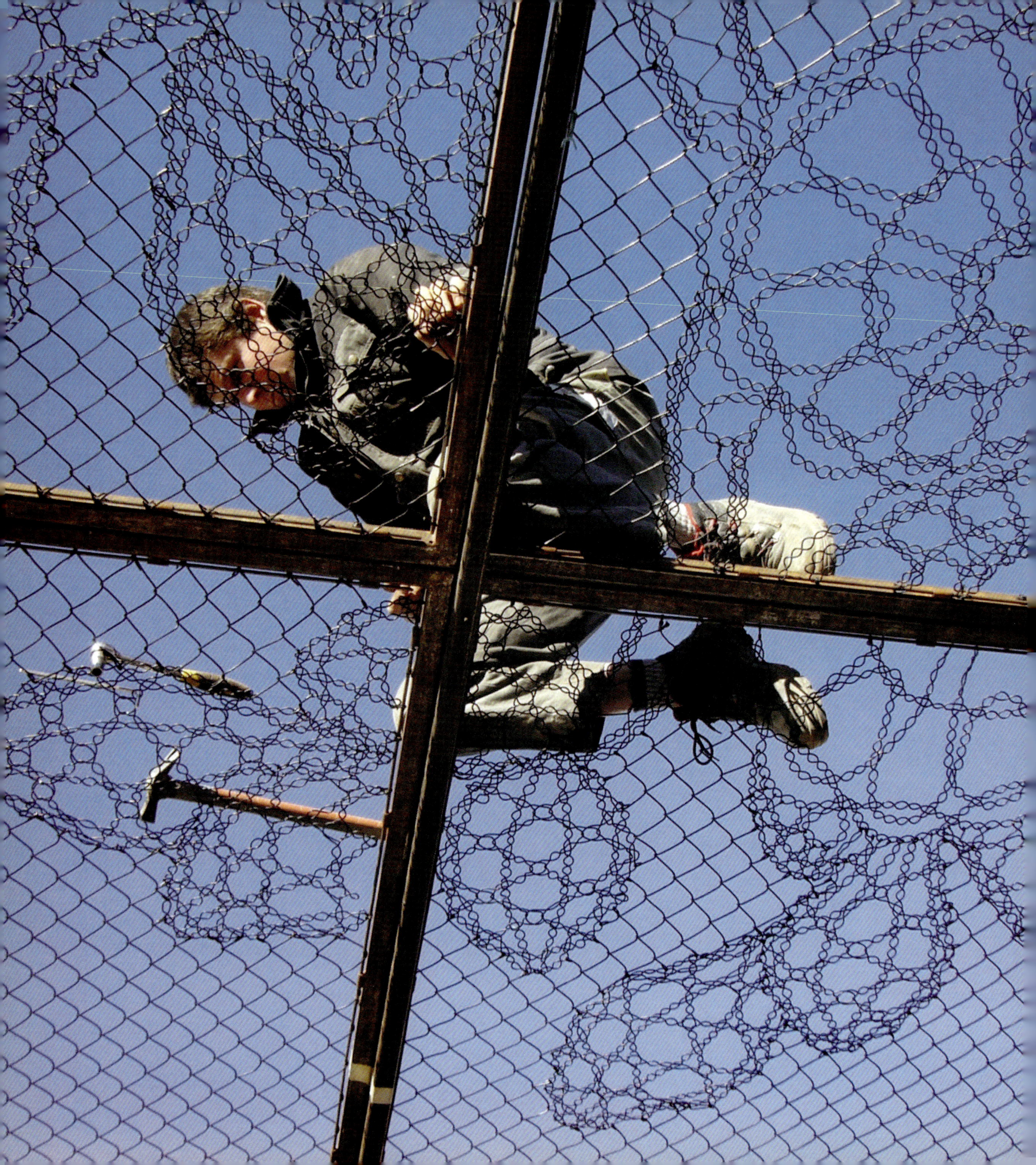

shelter

business class
1998
Radi Designers
Collection du Fond National
d'Art Contemporain
page 200

lace fence
2005
Joep Verhoeven / Studio Demakersvan
Idfence BV

Inspired by industrial production, taking chickenwire as its raw material and giving it a new twist, Lace Fence is born. This astonishing fencing, working like a contemporary lace, transforms our view of an everyday object, which is reinvented and becomes aesthetic, even artistic!

pages 202 & 203

Today, three objects are synonymous with shelter in the city: the posts that protect pedestrians from the invasive parking of cars on the pavements, the fencing that marks the boundaries between public and private space and the bus shelter that protects its users from bad weather.

Posts, the first known kind of urban furniture, marked the frontiers of Mesopotamia, then the edges of neighbourhoods in Rome, already assuring the safety of passers-by at the sides of roads. They disappeared from the end of the 18th century when raised pavements became widespread. In the 20th century, they reappeared in the form of solid blocks, stakes – with or without a chain – and retractable posts, becoming an element that is very present in the urban space. Too present and too ugly for some, anti-parking posts have sparked ideas on how they can metamorphose into convivial objects, tables or chairs… and into works of art.

Fencing serves as a physical manifestation of a need for intimacy, power or cleanliness. Whatever its form, it establishes a codified relation with the environment and the urban space. A structuring and fixed architectural element, it protects the private domain or separates the different traffic lanes. It can be mobile, like building site hoardings or what are known as "Vauban" barriers in France and "Nadar" in Belgium, which circumscribe a temporary perimeter. Today, it has a tendency to assert itself with a colour or sophisticated transparency, to invite one to see or discover through specific openings what it protects. It has several functions, integrating seats, or providing hanging for exhibitions…

The first covered benches date back to Antiquity, in the form of sentry boxes or toll gates at the entrances to cities. We find them again over the centuries in parks, before they reappear in a more urban form in the seaside resorts that emerged at the end of the 19th century in Europe, shading people from the heat of the sun. Still in the 19th century, a new furniture object saw the day, the bus shelter, linked to the development of public transport. Since its creation, it has incorporated a roof to protected travellers, this little piece of architecture also serving as a visual indication of the stop. In 1964, in France, it became a support for advertising and in this form colonised the world. Now, at the beginning of the 21st century, its physical forms are diversifying. It has tended to become a support for new technologies and for biodiversity through the integration of plants into its structure. The only urban factory model existing, it has created around itself other contemporary amusements with a convivial vocation.

riverside park south
2008
Thomas Balsley Associates
Trump/New World Holdings, Extel/Carlyle Group, City of New York Department of Parks, Recreation Country of clients
page 204 left

Peggy Rockefeller university
2009
Thomas Balsley Associates
Rockefeller University
page 204 centre and right

plugin
2008
Alexandre Mussche & Demet Mutman
Refugee camps for the victims of natural disasters are always sited far from the centres of cities, causing economic and social disconnection. To integrate them into the parts of cities that remain intact, Plugin proposes a light and mobile architecture that can be grafted onto façades.
page 205

205

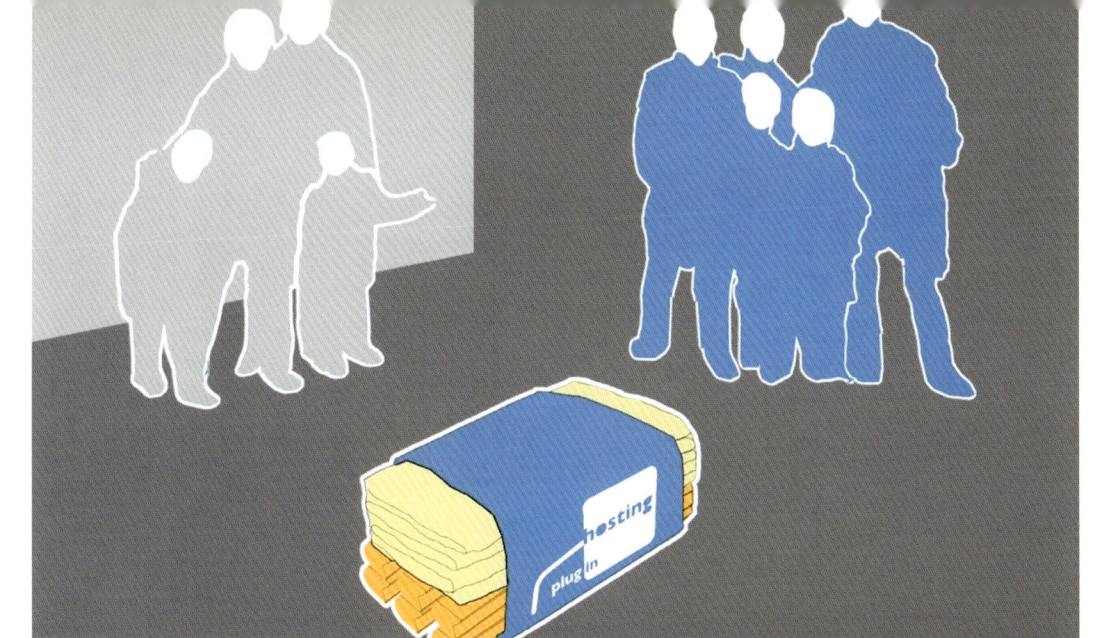

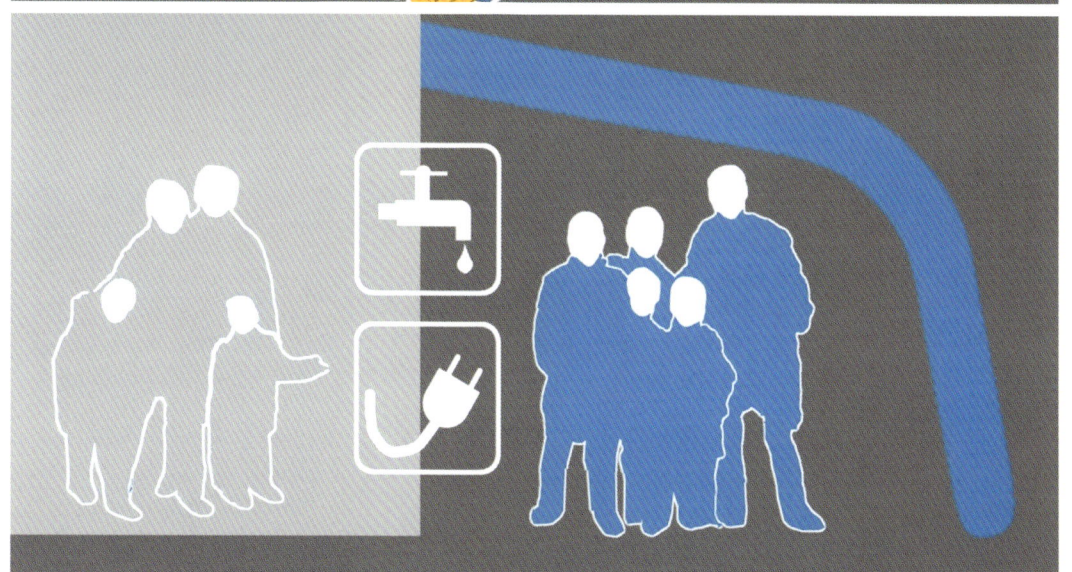

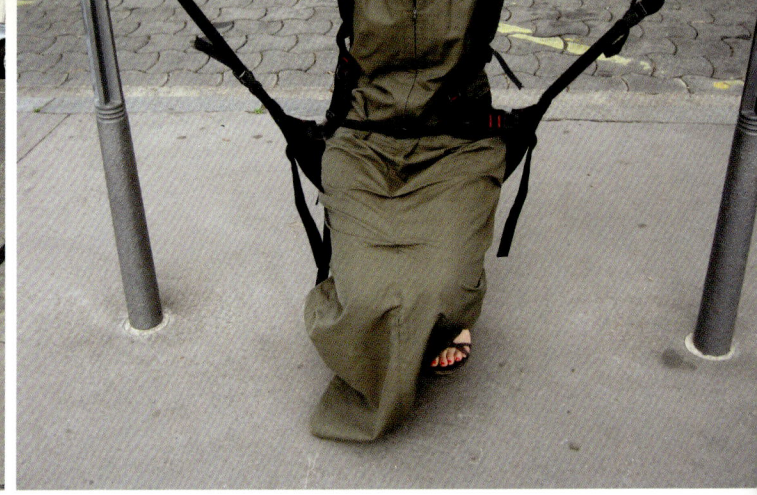

mobile-homme - 2009
Christelle Privileggio

urban jewellery - 2009
Liesbeth Bussche

potobos - 2009
Anne Maurange, Paule Kingleur, Natasha Gudermane, Catherine Videlaine...
Paule Kingleur / Paris Label
Coopérative De Rue et De Cirque (2r2c)

206 shelter / POSTS & BLOCKS

urban seat - 2009
Damien Gires, le Plan B
Designer Day 2009

207

security barriers and railings - 2006
Matthieu Theaudin, Phytolab
City of Trignac / Carene 44

cidade - 2005
Andrea Bandoni

208 shelter / FENCING

westminster presbyterian church - 2008
Coen + Partners
MS&R, Meyer, Scherer & Rockcastle

lentspace - 2009
Tobias Armborst, Daniel D'Oca, Georgeen Theodore / Interboro
Adam Kleinman, Lower Manhattan Cultural Council, New York

209

octopus - 2006
Vincent Baur, Guillaume Colboc, Gaël le Nouëne, Atelier O-S architectes & Marie Lang
Festival des Architectures Vives, Montpellier

belvedere plaza - 2000
Thomas Balsley Associates
Rose Associates

West 8
Lalou + Lebec Architectes
Lille Métropole Communauté Urbaine

Jean-Baptiste Lebas park

The City of Lille decided, aptly, to transform the historic Jean-Baptiste Lebas boulevard into a public park. This large urban conduit bore the name of an emblematic figure of the French political Left: mayor, from 1912, of the town Roubaix, where he put in place a municipal socialism and created the first council housing. He was also Employment Minister under Léon Blum in 1936, achieving notably the establishment of paid holidays in France. For the layout of this park, in a historic neighbourhood dating from the 18th century, a 4m-high railing recalls classic architecture. But, in a provocative and judicious move, it has been painted red, and integrates different elements of urban furniture such as seats, pivoting gates and information panels. Inside, three landscape spaces, with specific functions and surrounded by vegetation, welcome the local inhabitants.

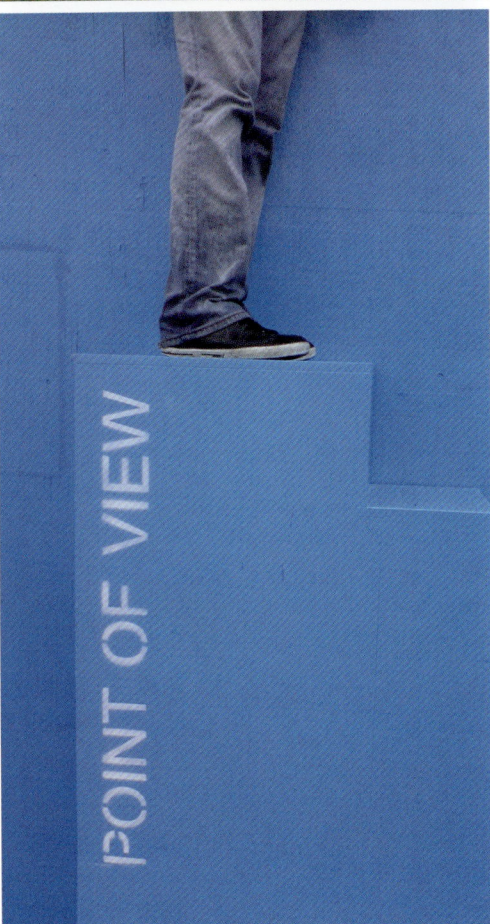

view point - 2008
Karsten Huneck & Bernd Trumepler, OSA
Blueprint magazine

212 shelter / VIEW POINTS

dymaxion sleep - 2009-2010
Jane Hutton & Adrian Blackwell
Festival International de jardins, Jardins Métis

pla-tano - 2008
Tobia Repossi
Modo

Quinhuangdao botanical gardens - 2009
Kongjian Yu & Turenscape, Beijing Turen Design Institute
The Landscape Bureau Quinhuangdao City

energy zone - 2010
Tristan Kopp
Atelier de design végétal de l'ESAD de Reims, Fondation CARI

214 shelter / UNDER COVER

**Horizons paysage
Plan 01 architectes
LAPS Design sonore
Emm.Cairo Designer**

**Compétition of
Lille Métropole Communauté Urbaine**

garden of blooms

This project, an exceptional garden full of feeling at the foot of the Lille Metropolis administration building in the Madeleine quarter of the city, integrates several types of landscape architecture, with as many welcoming canopies that are secreted as if rooted in the hollows of the undulations of harmonious grounds. First of all, the main entrance of the park offers a flower market under the foliage of a huge pergola with random forms. Further away, a big top with changeable structures adapts itself to the different entertainments that are programmed through the seasons. And the hothouse-café brings together two functions, mixing nature and conviviality. The urban furniture also seems to have grown up naturally, with undulating metallic stems like water plants that form the surrounding fence and signage supports. The benches appear like leaves fallen from a tree, but still living, as if suspended between earth and sky.

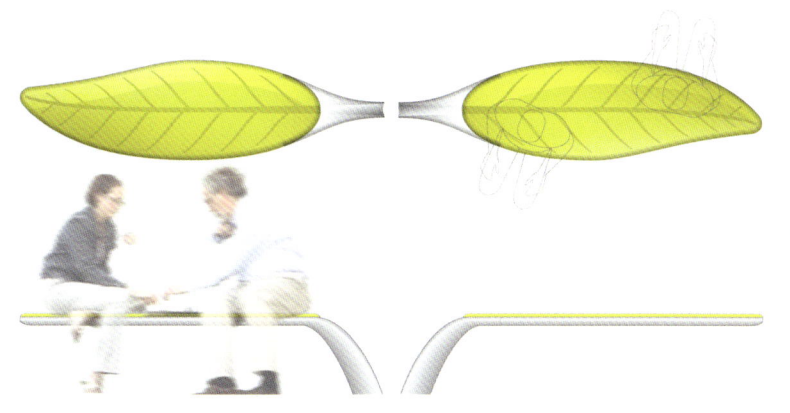

3rd collection tram-shelter - 2006
Aurel(s)studio
RATP

tram-train station in La Réunion - 2006
Aurel(s)studio
Groupe Vinci

216 shelter / BUS SHELTER

bus top

BusTop™

Patrick Jouffret & Fariba Sanaï
360

Faced with the sterilisation of the urban space that is happening today, Bus Top proposes fertilising the roofs of bus shelters over the area of one hectare in Paris. Endowing them with plants chosen for their purifying and perfumed effect, these little gardens are as many oases to be created in order to give the city back its charm. They address the sense of smell through their freshness and the scents they emit, of touch because they are within reach, and also hearing which is attracted by the sound of the wind in the plants, of flowing water... A central column offers filtered water to thirsty users, and at night Bus Top lights up, the glass panels integrating layers of LEDs, supplied by solar cells that are also on the roof.

Clothilde Huet
Partenariat ENSCI
Minatec Ideas Laboratory

eden

Eden is a new generation of bus shelter. It is also a space for the distribution of electricity, which allows the urban traveller to recharge his mobile phone. Its roof, in photovoltaic glass, provides solar energy and the ground covering, in electroactive polymer, collects that generated by passing vehicles and pedestrians. Through the design of the luminous and colourful windmill that tops the structure and attracts the eye, Eden sends out a strong visual signal, gathering people in and thus informing them about the new function that it offers. Different forms of seats and tables complete this furniture, responding to the new uses created by modern telephony, which transforms the urban space into a place for permanent personal and professional communication.

**Lorcan O'Herlihy Architects
Bruce Mau Design
Ville de Santa Monica
Big Blue Bus**

blue spots

The city of Santa Monica, California, will soon have 360 bus stops endowed with innovative structures, called Blue Spots. Made up of several modules with a simple and radical design, they offer a maximum number of ways to implant them in the urban environment, and to orient them in relation to the sun, creating welcome zones of shade. The Blue Spots entirely transform the negative image of this piece of urban furniture. They are made from recycled or recyclable materials and equipped with LEDs with a longer life than usual lighting used for bus stops, needing very little maintenance. Scattered all around the city, these blue parasols will change the ambiance, becoming an emblematic and functional symbol.

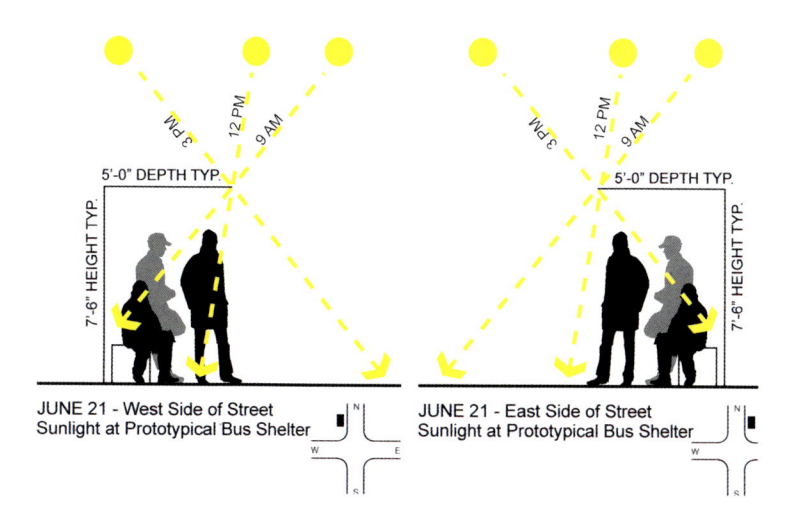

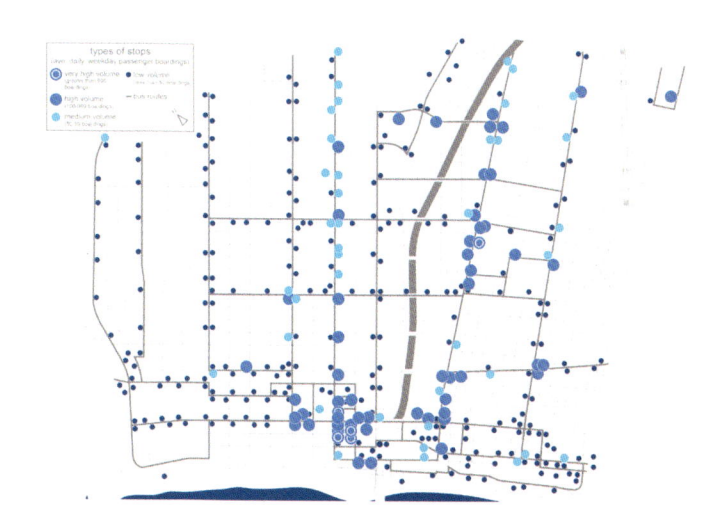

JUNE 21 - West Side of Street
Sunlight at Prototypical Bus Shelter

JUNE 21 - East Side of Street
Sunlight at Prototypical Bus Shelter

fireplace for children

2009

Completely adapted to the Norwegian climate, which is very cold in winter, easily reaching −10°C during the day, this exterior fireplace allows the schoolchildren of the city of Trondheim to play outdoors, and to warm themselves up. It also welcomes them for daily evening gatherings with fun activities and story-reading on the programme. This troll's lair, 6 m in diameter, is made from small pieces of pine and oak wood, culled from the offcuts of a neighbouring building site. Eighty superimposed circles give the teepee its form, pierced by small horizontal arrow holes which act as micro-windows and ventilation.

Haugen, ZoharArkitekter
Rani Ankori, 3D Modeling & Espen Baerheim
Rapid prototyping
City of Trondheim

220 shelter / IN THE WARM

Studio Rocco Verdult

temporary meeting places

The creation of these temporary meeting places aims to assert the personality of urban sites and to make them into appropriate spaces of conviviality for a few days. They can be created very quickly, springing up new opportunities to get together for the inhabitants. A pavement becomes an ephemeral dance floor thanks to Kliko-disco, where a series of dustbins shelters the sound system. The ramp and the entrance to a garage is transformed into a jazz club for the duration of a few concerts. And an elastic structure designed for climbing, covered with a transparent tarpaulin, is transformed into Kilmrektent, a meeting place for neighbours. Five different projects have thus reinvented the city.

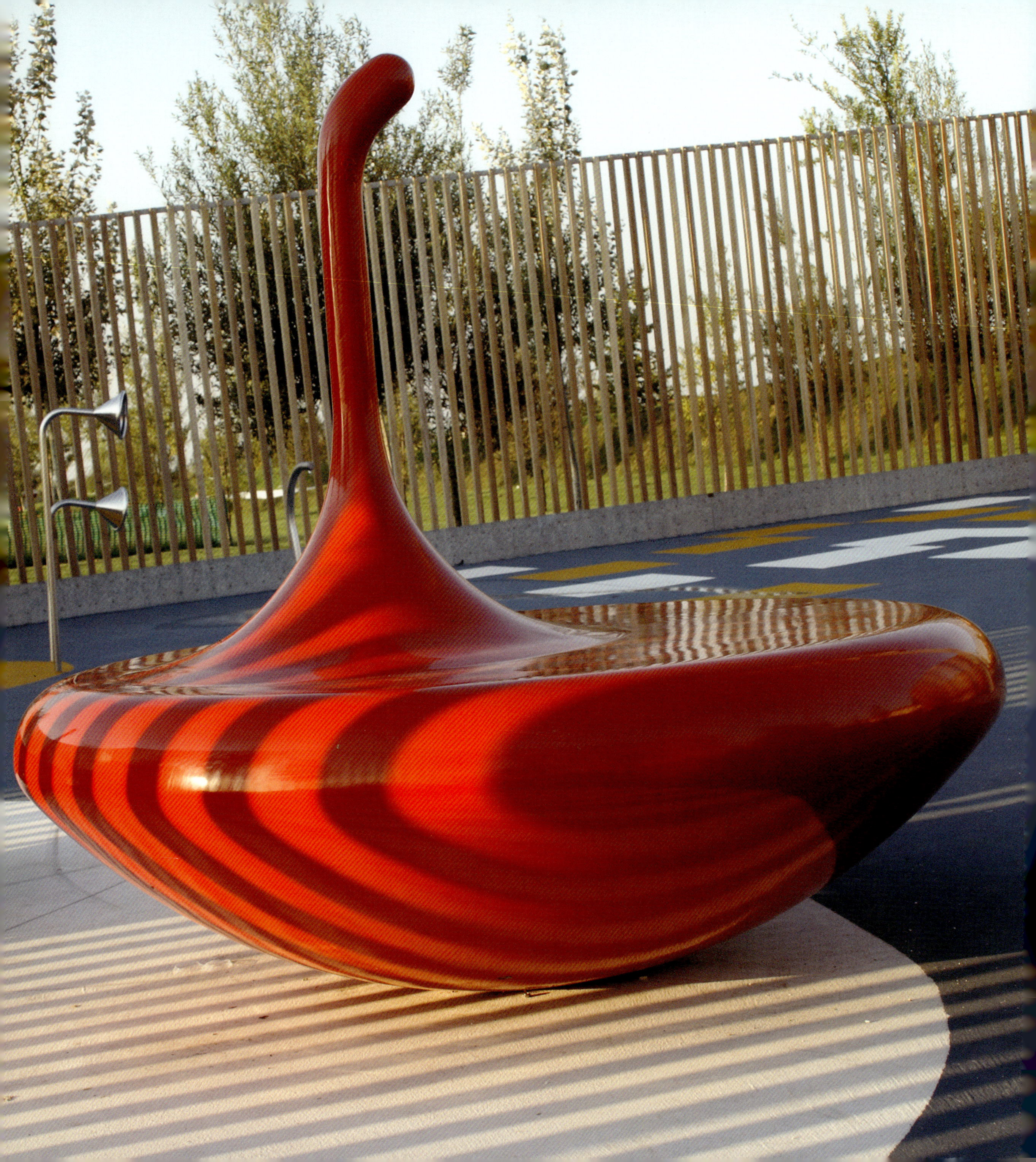

06

CITY GAMES

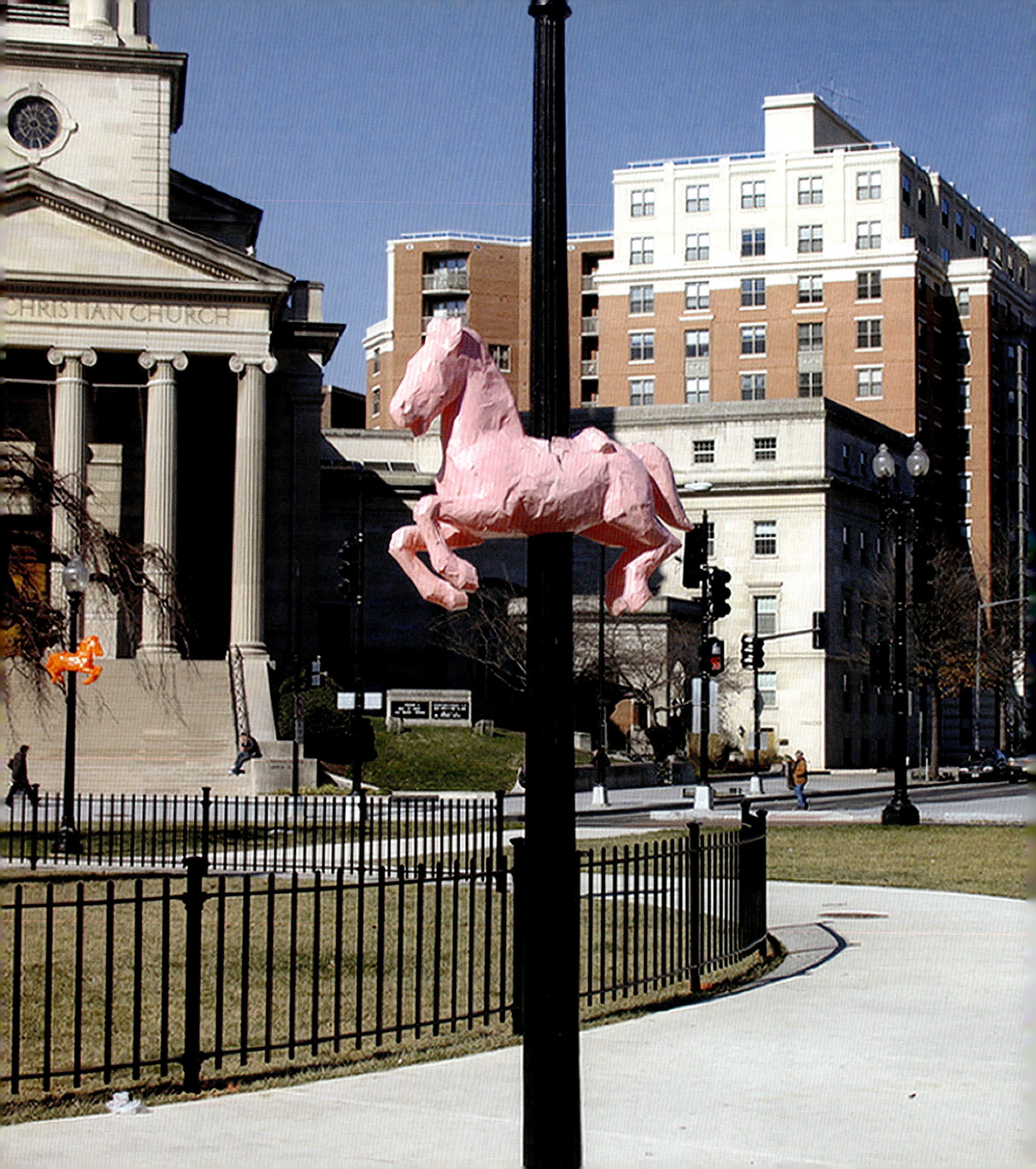
CHRISTIAN CHURCH

city games

trottola
2004
**Tobia Repossi
Modo**
page 222

traffic-go-round
2006
Marks Jenkins
page 224

untitled
2007
Marks Jenkins
page 225 left

carousel
2005
Marks Jenkins
page 225 right

In the 19th century, parks were created in the great European cities to offer city-dwellers nature, an opportunity to breathe pure air, to enjoy green spaces, even to get involved in botany. The first playground specially designed for children sprung up in Birmingham in 1854. In 1858 in Paris, the promenades flanking the Champs Élysées were for the first time punctuated by swings of different kinds. This type of apparatus grew at the end of the 19th century, particularly in the United States, with the underlying idea of controlling working class youth, often the children of immigrants, thanks to an educational tool that could be used to teach the values of democracy and prevent delinquency... But children play more naturally in the street and its was the boom in the motor car that finally provoked the creation of more systematic playgrounds that were adapted to their desires, the roads in front being cleared of anything that could limit traffic circulation!

Today, the range of apparatus offered seems to have evolved little, with the classic sandpits, slides, roundabouts, swings... But on looking closer we see that new objects have appeared and that their aesthetic has changed. Their simpler lines, with attractive colours, finally allow one to give an identity to each playground, which can also be designed individually. The environment is integrated and now we are not afraid to play with different types of ground and with the topography to give energy to the whole and create a feeling of escape.

Some very old types of playground apparatus have reappeared, revisited in a contemporary form as representations of animals, poetic and restrained, which can provoke the imagination of the youngest children. The physical interactivity already prioritised has developed thanks to new technologies appealing to other senses. For adolescents, effort and controlled risk are encouraged to promote autonomy. Skateparks, too often in raw concrete, are increasingly designed for a particular site, with specific forms, and integrated into other facilities instead of being sidelined. In another, more surprising, category, dogs also interest the designers, who are starting to create obstacle courses for them and their masters...

Alfil Set chess game
1997-2000
Diana Cabeza
Estudio Cabeza Urban Elements
page 226

distorting mirror
2002
Tobia Repossi
Modo
page 227

226 city games

227

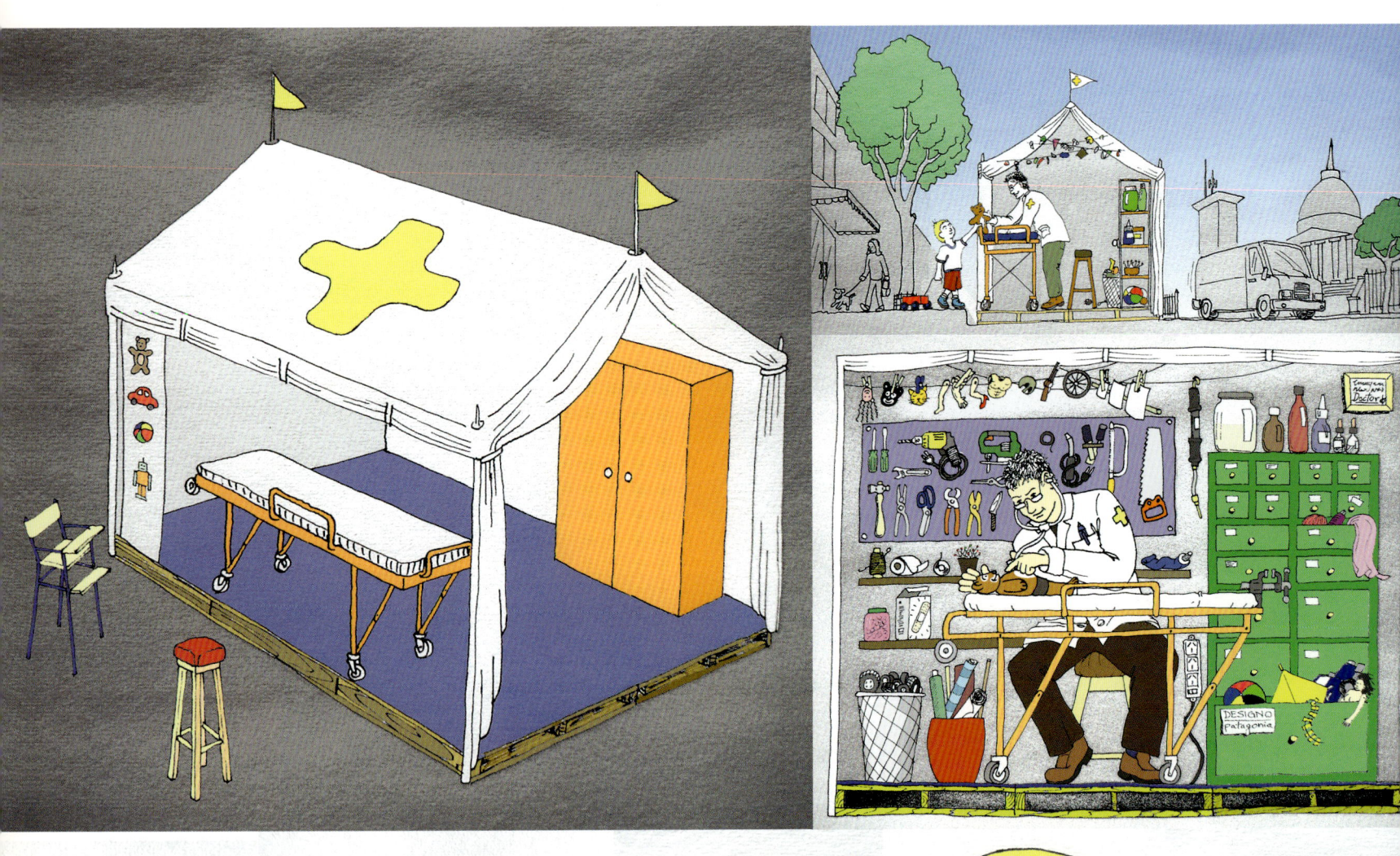

toy hospital - 2009
Manu Rapoport & Martin Sabattini, Designo Patagonia
Public Design Festival by Esterni

Manu Rapoport
Designo Patagonia
Secretaria de Medio Ambiente de la Nacion & Municipalidad de Maros Paz

Marcos Paz park

For the town of Marcos Paz, situated in the province of Buenos Aires, this project was designed with sustainable development and protection of the environment as its guiding lines. In this three-hectare park all the features of the layout have to recall a historical and economic fact, the region's exploitation of a tree with extremely hard wood, Schinopsis quebracho-colorado, which is very sought-after for making the millions of sleepers necessary for the construction of the Argentinian railways. The aim is to recall the intensive exploitation of this plant resource and the destruction of natural habitats that it has brought about. Thus, a small example of this species, which will be its hero, is to be planted, surrounded by different games constructed mainly from recycled battens and rails and other materials produced locally to limit their transport and favour the local economy. Its pertinence in terms of budget is also to be evoked, as its creation must cost three times less than that of a classic park.

bambisitter - 2005
De Oberkant, Dussen
Freeline International BV

lion cubs - 2000
David Steinfeld
Divers cité

230 city games / ONCE UPON A TIME...

Nicolas Stadler

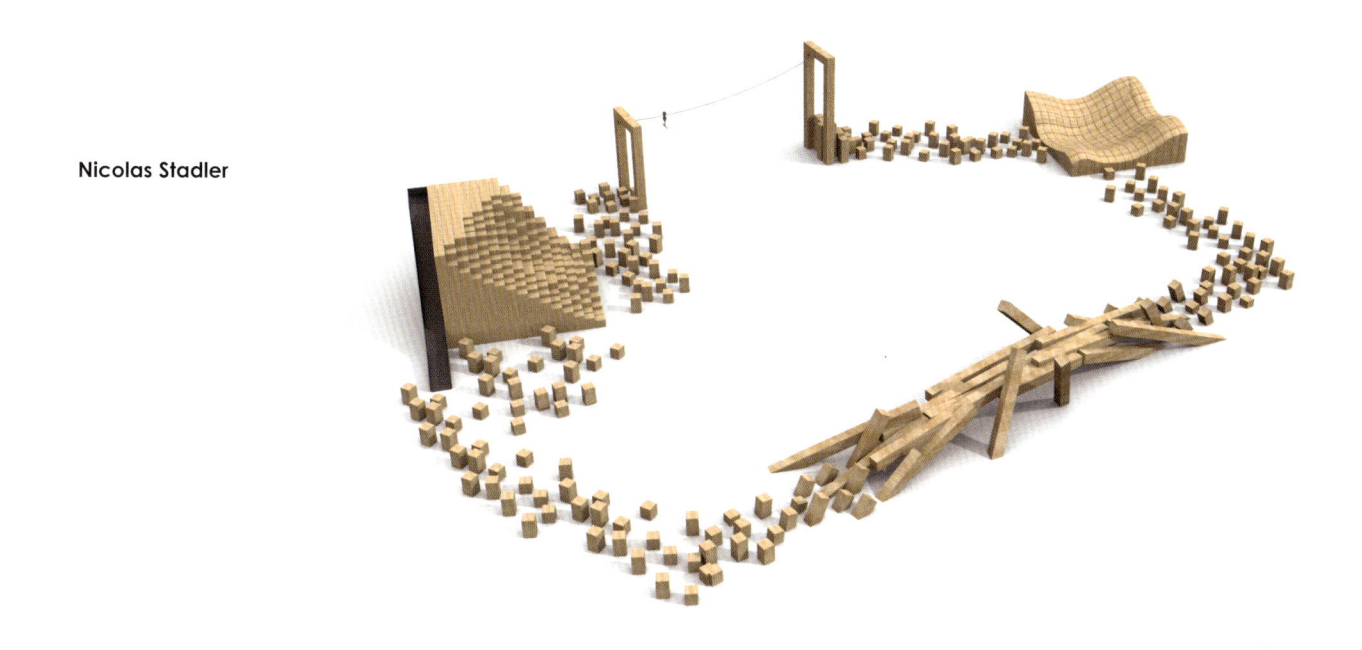

"once upon a time"

Taking the opposite direction to the current trend in playgrounds, which often represent very concrete concepts like a house, a pirate boat or a fort or castle, "Once upon a time" doesn't try to copy a world but lets children's imaginations work freely, without imposing a predefined setting. Its abstract decor allows children to invent their own adventures and to share them, just as, when he finds a large empty cardboard box, a child will transform it spontaneously into an invincible fortress or a secret hidey-hole. The principle is the same, and a trail, already an escapade in itself, offers each module a space propitious for new stories. Here a bridge under which to hide or make a den, there a climbing block like a mountain. In addition, the elements of this project give the impression, by the way they are set out, of popping up out of the ground instantaneously... This dreamlike dimension is lined with an ecological message through the exclusive use of wood.

optical illusion - 2002
Tobia Repossi
Modo

anamorphoses - 2004
Tobia Repossi
Modo

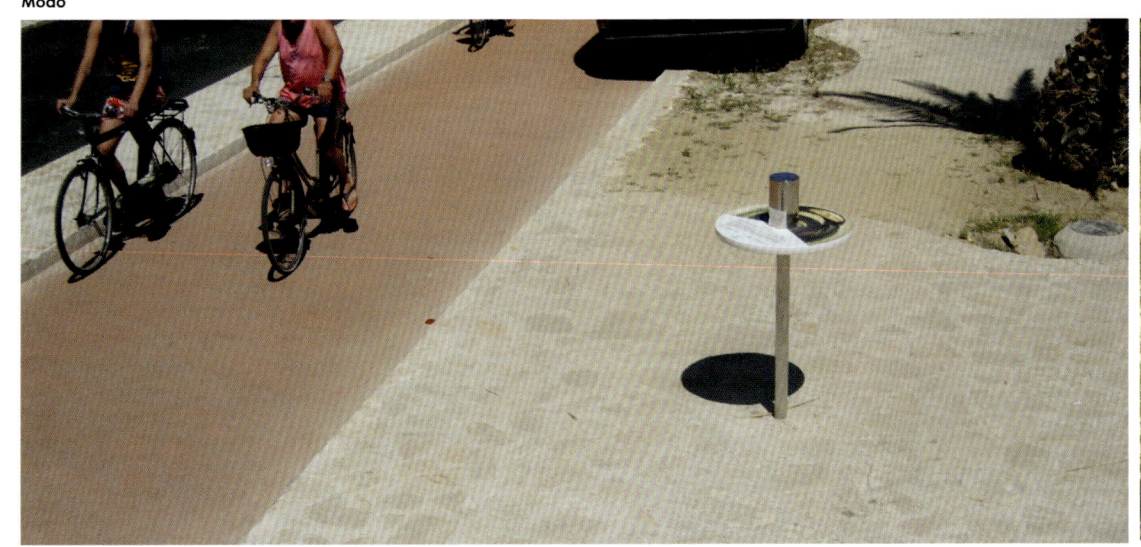

232 city games / MOBILE

Lise Capet

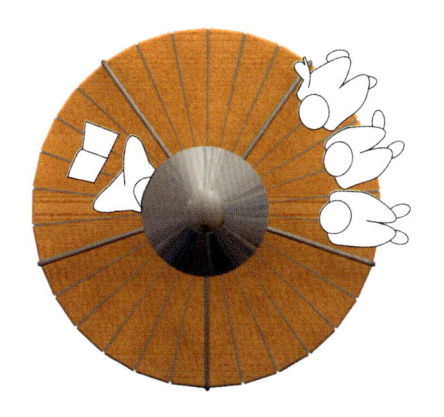

tinama

In the urban space, where one is often just passing through, how can we invite people to stop, look around them and meet people? And, at a time when we are confronted daily by questions of energy, why not use our own, through a simple gesture that could produce and offer a service to everyone? This is the challenge of this giant roundabout with its spinning-top shape, which recalls childhood memories in everyone. It allows several people of any age to get on, day and night, and has a dynamo which, over time, gathers the energy produced by the rotation. It transforms it into light, a soft, warm and convivial light created by our own movements. This interactive bench has a place in playgrounds and parks. Why not on the pavements of cities too?

Marie Denis
Galerie KernotArt

bambinos

In Montpellier as in London, in Paris at La Villette and in Fontenay-le-Comte, 1500 hoops ring the imposing trunks of trees in the sites where this ephemeral installation lands, forming as many planters with vibratory colours. Thus clad, the remarkable plants stand out differently in the landscape, which they modify through the use made of their necklaces.

Indeed, the hoops can be taken down at leisure by the public, who use them for moments of relaxation and play. Both children and adults roll them on the ground and run after them, just as they were used in Antiquity, or spin them round their waists in a rhythmic swaying, like the hula hoop of the 1950s. They also assemble them again, in different ways: piling them up or superimposing them, crossing their multicoloured lines to form sculptures or playful spaces that can be taken apart, offering an infinite field of improvisation. The dressing and undressing of the trees form part of the rules and pleasures of this new open-air game, a moment of sport that is accessible to all.

235

play engines, wall decoration and barriers - 2002-2003
Dominique Cuvelier
Recyclart

Suresh Shiva
Mark McWha
Formium Landscape Architects
City of Glen Eira

Cargenie library's "bookworms"

To complete its awakening of young children's minds, a play space has been specially laid out in the Carnegie library in Glen Eira, Australia. It's a curious zoo which houses three huge worms with shimmering colours, "bookworms" which are the characters in a story that can be lived lifesize. There is the musician worm, equipped with musical instruments, and the climbing worm, with footholds for climbing. Their rings are coloured thematically and children can climb and run over them until they reach their large head. The third, the glow worm, is in fibreglass, shining by day and lighting up the night. Interactive poles complete the system. They give their name or tell stories when you press on certain buttons, or laugh when you touch or tickle them…

Stoss LU
**International Garden Festival,
Reford Gadens (Jardins Métis)**

safe zone

Confronted, as we are today, by increasingly draconian safety standards, architects and landscape architects are permanently reined in by the "Caution principle", created initially, in 1992, for the protection of the environment. In particular, this applies to the flooring used for playgrounds, which is deliberately supple to avoid children injuring themselves. Safe Zone is designed entirely in a rubber flooring that is here used in exceptional thickness, which increases its elasticity. Small hills and valleys create a course that is fun and comfortable – maybe too comfortable. Indeed, walking on it destabilises one's steps, but allows one to jump in order to bounce back, without ever being able to master one's balance. This undulating topography adopts a dark, almost sinister colour, separated by several yellow squares which play the ambiguous role of signalling the dangers that could rise up in this garden, as in the real world, recalled by the surrounding forest.

238 city game / IN SPRINGINESS

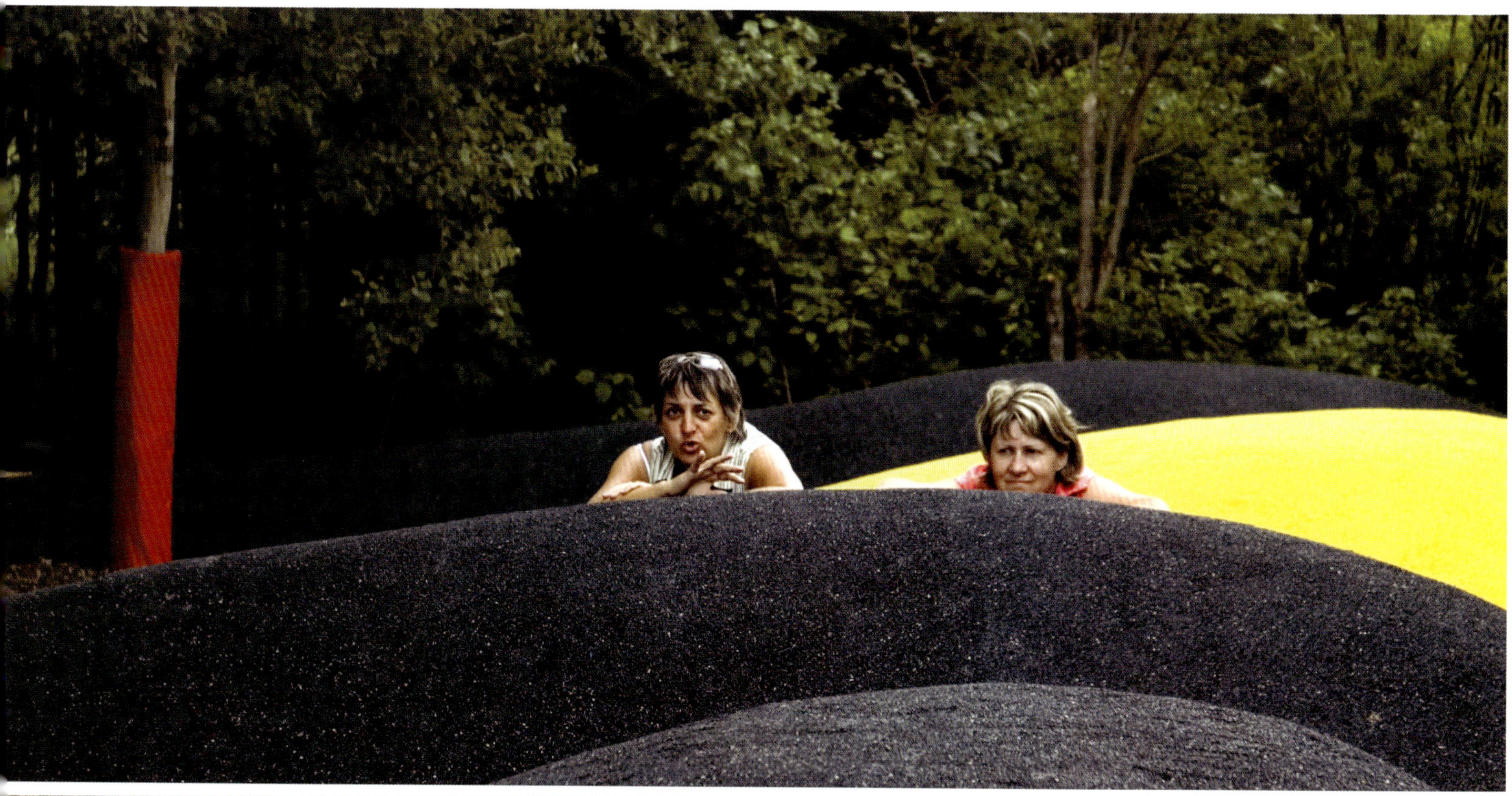

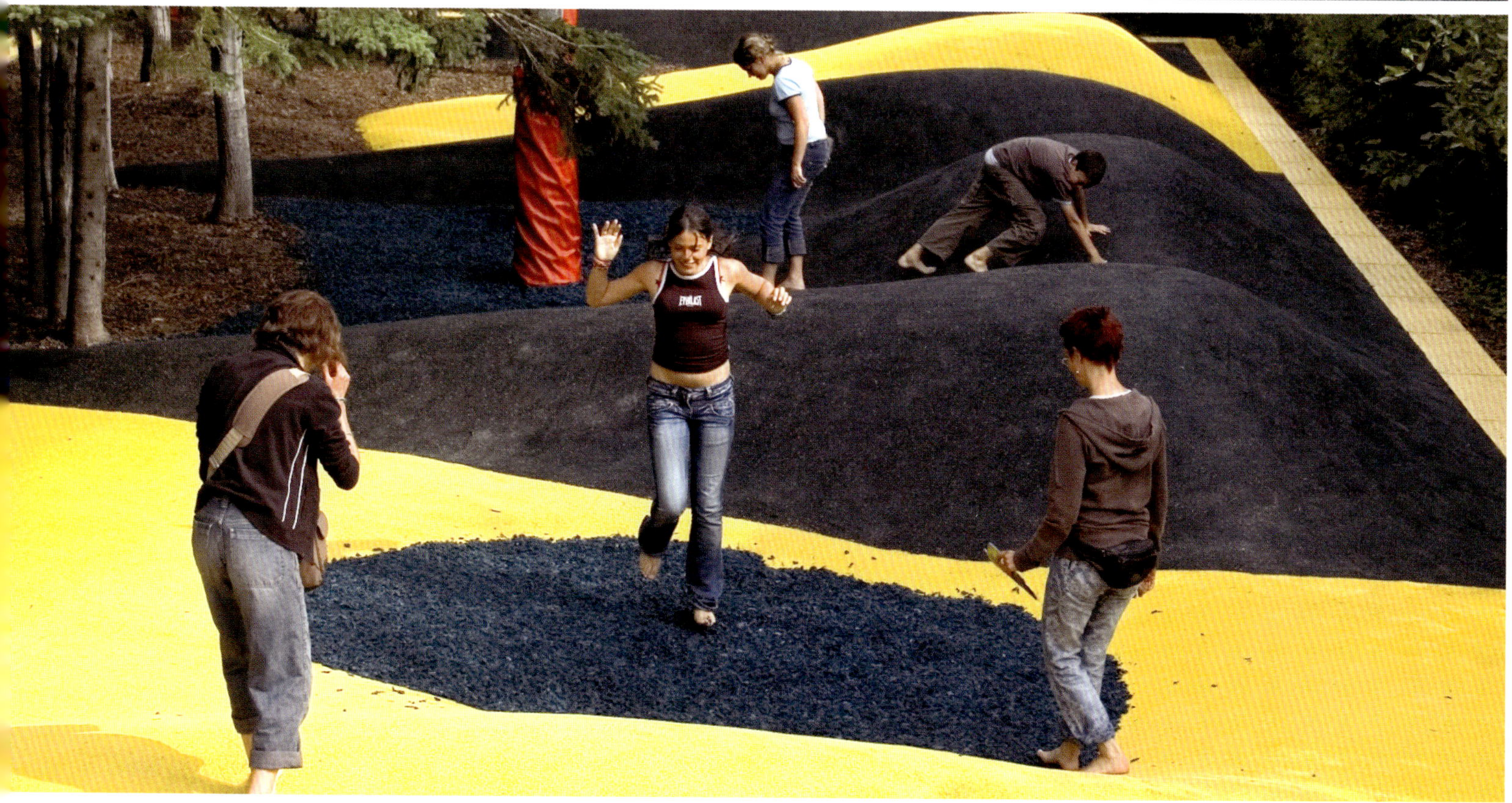

Kaptein Roodnat
Stroom Den Haag

the climclamberhangsitfootballcurtaintheatretube

This playground, open to the city, is inspired by a scene in Jacques Tati's film My Uncle. Monsieur Hulot, the hero, who works in a tube factory, falls asleep at his post. He is awoken by the visit of some dignitaries, who he tries to impress by pressing several buttons at the same time, making him lose control of the cutting machine... Here, a single tube, 5 cm in diameter, in a luminous acid green, runs amok in the space as if one had lost control. It crosses the walls, going from inside to outside, to come back again after drawing in space several playful and convivial structures. In the school, it forms coat stands, the stage of a small theatre, curtain rails and different seats. In the open air, it metamorphoses into benches, fixed bars of different heights, a slide, climbing rope and even a goal for ball games. An ingenious and simple installation, which is nevertheless very likeable.

city game / INFINITE

241

Maartje Dros
Premsela Dutch Platform for Design & Fashion Supported by SKOR ExperimentaDesign Amsterdam

city dog adventure

2006

This unusual game was created in reaction to the fact that very little space today remains available for dogs in cities, and more particularly to their physical separation from the world of children, notably in parks where signs and fences are installed leaving no ambiguity. From here came the symbolic conception of structures bearing the colour code of prohibition, red and white. Their forms are simple, recalling sports obstacle courses in green spaces, and deliberately mobile to adapt to any urban site. There is no fixed order, any combination is possible from the different elements. Pets and their masters are of course the primary users, but the small size and arrangement of this game means it can also be offered to children, skateboarders and joggers to experiment.

CITY DOG ADVENTURE

illegal furniture - 2004
Santiago Cirugeda, Recetas Urbanas

244 city games / TAKE FLIGHT

double happiness - 2009-2010
Mésarchitecture
Shenzen & Hong Kong Biennial

frogska skatable bench - 2006-2007
Cédric Carles
Atelier2CE

the ramp - 2007
Fichtre

block banks... - 2009
Block, Denis Brillet
Tetra Pak & Nantes Métropole, Estuaire Nantes-Saint Nazaire

246 city games / ON SKATES

Convic Design Pty
Tweed Shire Council

tweed skateable sculptural trail

Unlike the grey and hard concrete that is often used for skate parks, recalling the street where the first enthusiasts started to practise this sport, this one surprises with its luminous colour and its forms. Its different, sculptural structures, designed in folded metal like giant origamis, punctuate the site like landscape follies in the Romantic English park tradition. Adapted to all levels, their different faces promote numerous tricks and combinations that are sporty, even choreographic… They line an entrance path with a curved route and, in the absence of skateboarders, readily transform themselves into comfortable and unusual seats. Thus, the possible sharing of the space by several generations takes place smoothly, even sparking off interest in this activity and legitimising part of the public space being given over to those who enjoy it, here and elsewhere.

NL Architects & DS Landschapsarchitecten
Gemeente Dordrecht & CBK Dordrecht

Nicolaas Beetsplein space

2006

The Oud Krispijn de Dordrecht quarter was laid out in 1932 as a garden city for the working class, with small homes and their micro-gardens, and several green axes giving onto modest squares, the whole bordered with hedges. Little by little, the site lost its initial charm, as constructions with anachronistic architecture took their place and the population became less homogeneous and more multicultural. In the 1980s, problems of drugs and lack of safety led to a rethinking of the landscape layout to recreate the lost conviviality. Several constructions were thus destroyed to form a central, open space, the Nicolass Beetsplein.

Designed from several concentric circles, this new layout reveals itself progressively. Starting on the edge of the private zones that comprise the residential buildings, car parks resolve parking problems and make life easier through their proximity to housing. Then, once past the road, everything, bit by bit, becomes an area for relaxation or play. Benches and large trees, informally dotted around, frame the evolution of grassy lawns, which finally change into an orange ring with enveloping and amusing forms surrounding the central clearing. Ball games, being the most noisy, have also deliberately been moved away from the buildings. Every local inhabitant, young or old, can find his or her place in this trans-generational plan according to the feeling of the moment.

249

Base
Terrassol & Luc Mas
City of Paris / DEVE

new playground for Belleville Park

Belleville Park, created in 1988 in the north-east of Paris, offers a remarkable viewpoint over the capital. In 2008, one of its playgrounds opened to the public, having been completed rethought after a consultation with the local inhabitants.

With the surprising form of a wooden cliff which crushes itself into the ground in a pleat of concrete, it presents, over 12 m in height and a strong gradient of 30°, a climbing course on several surfaces with different inclines, entangled on the flank of a hill and corresponding to different levels of difficulty.

With the aid of ropes one enters into this adventure, which marries wood, concrete and bark and is inspired by mountaineering and navigation, and where there are neither horizontals nor verticals.

Multiple slides, climbs, decks, skids, secret passages, hiding places and observatories thus welcome intrepid children. Both daring and poetic, this course asserts the virtues of taking calculated risks, allowing one to channel children's need to surpass themselves against the illusion of zero risk!

251

Choblet & Associés
Agence Nez Haut
City of Paris

Paris-beaches

In 2002, Paris City Hall decided to offer a leisure space to Parisians who couldn't go away on holiday. It was a strong political act: to create a month-long space of social equality, unique in terms of its size, its function and its dramaturgy. Paris and the beach initially seem like two opposing entities. But it is the concept of the beach that allows the public to take over these spaces that are spacious, comfortable, and free in both senses of the word – not simply as a spectator, as for other offerings now and in the past, but as an actor. It is he or she that makes these specific installations exist and live, first of all on certain quays beside the Seine, then over the years developed in other waterside spaces.

Different scenographies reveal and bring about new urban uses, calling on two main ideas, imagination and experimentation, transforming the utopia into reality. Thus from dawn to the end of the day shared surprises, sensations, emotions and pleasure are on the agenda, just as if you'd gone far away... Time management no longer matters, only the present counts.

253

BOAT TOURS
TICKETS/INFO
Harbourfront centre
Harbourfront centre

07

ON YOUR BIKE

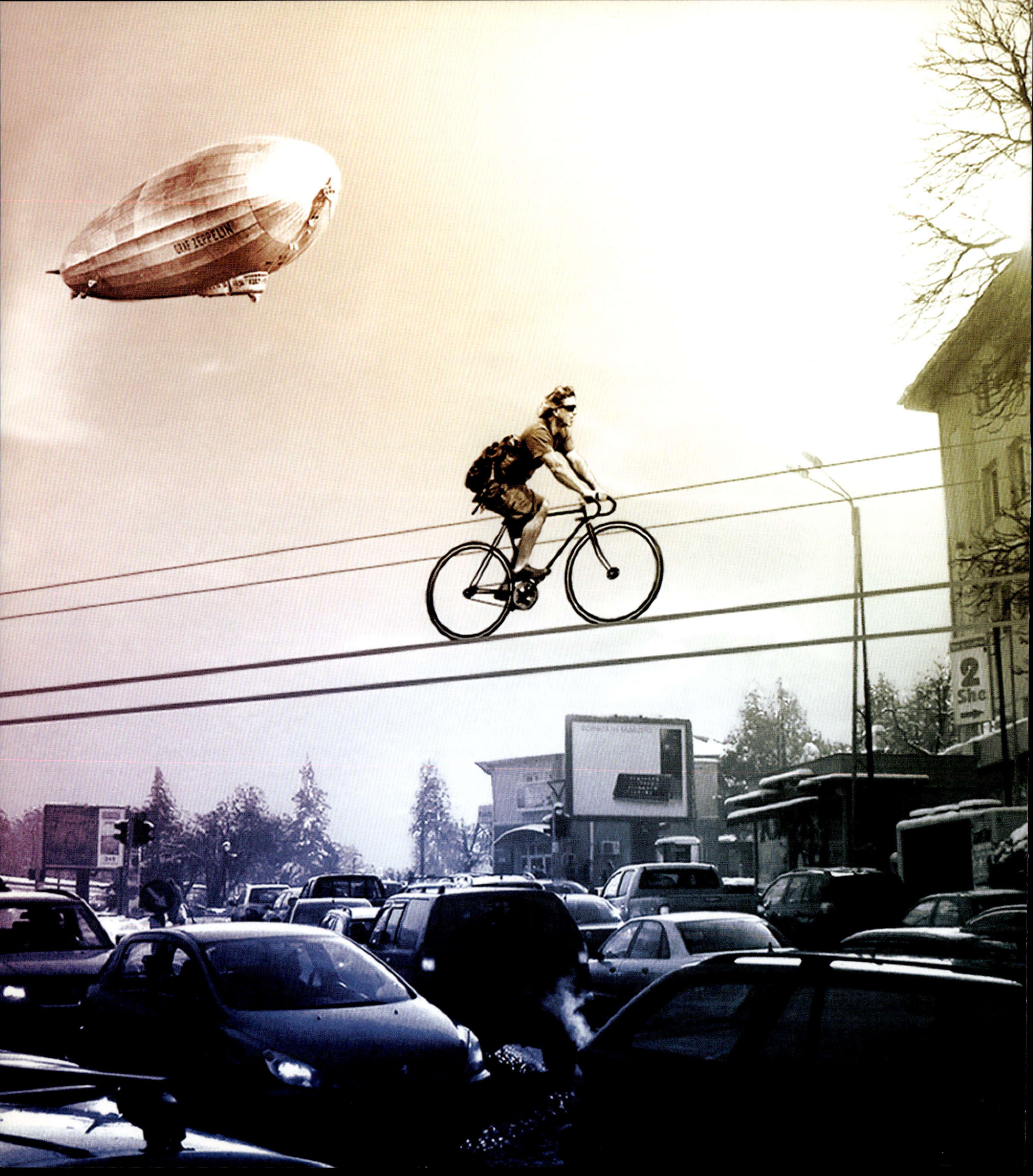
GRAF ZEPPELIN

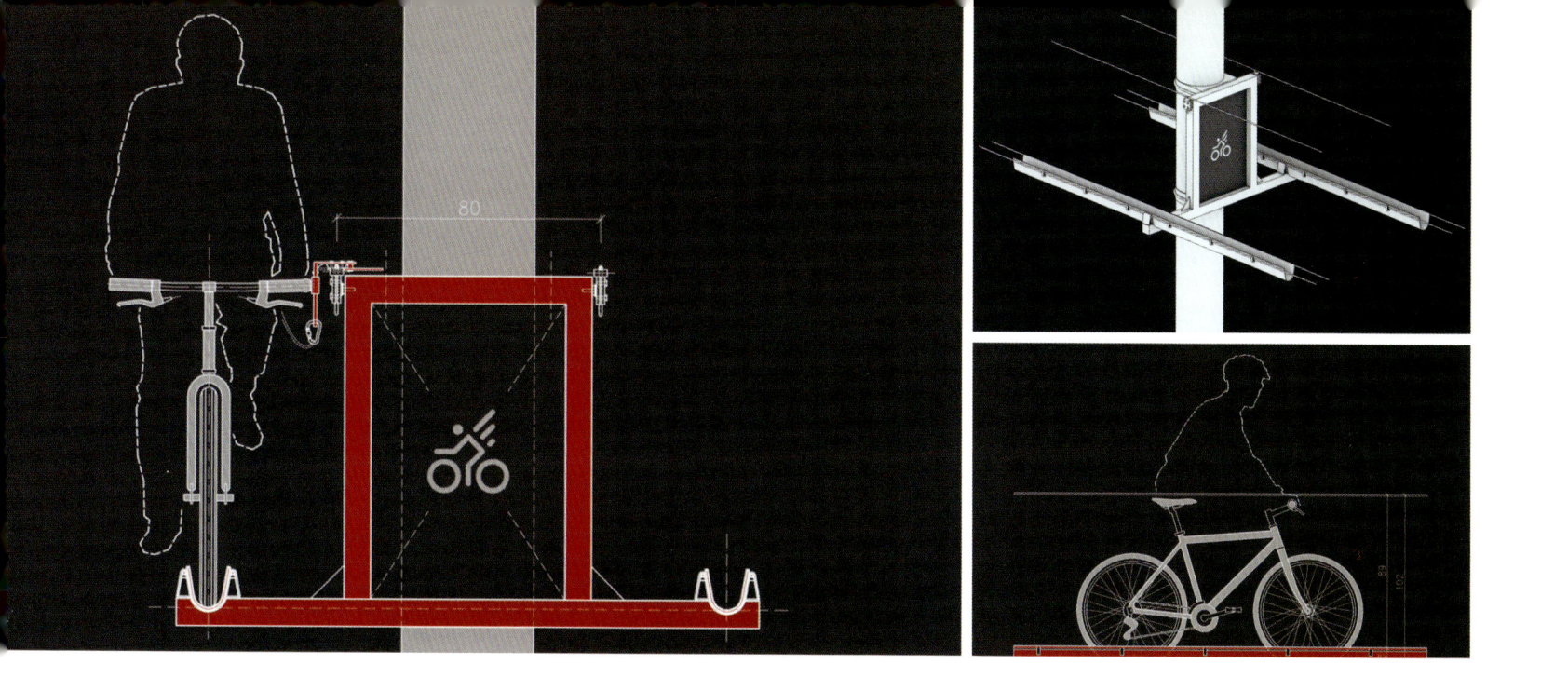

on your bike

Toronto central waterfront
2006
West 8
Du Toit Allsopp Hillier / DTAH
WaterfrontToronto
page 254

kolelinia
2009
Martin Angelov
This visionary project proposes a new type of transport channel in the form of a raised circulation rail for bikes, aimed at zones which are overcrowded at ground level, but also allowing one to prolong the existing lines or to create a tourist trail. Kolelinia offers new experiences, other points of view... while using a real and alternative economy of resources.
pages 256 & 257

Intially called a *Laufmaschine*, or "running machine", the first bicycle was created in 1817 by the German baron Karl Drais von Sauerbronn. It took the form of a large scooter that was propelled by pushing the ground with one's feet. The first pedal system to serve as a driving force emerged in 1861, designed by Pierre Michaux. The bicycle then evolved in terms of comfort and performance through modifying the size of the wheels, adding chain transmission and a braking system, then gears allowing one to go faster. By 1890 it already had its definitive form, though it remained single-speed until 1930.

In the second half of the 19th century, the number of cycling enthusiasts increased and it became an industrial product, affordable for workers and the originator of an important social evolution. In the 1890s, it accompanied a first emancipation of women, who started to leave their corsets and other constraining clothing behind in order to pedal.

257

In 1936 it also played a part in the great adventure that was the first paid holidays in France, for which the bicycle was the vehicle of predilection. Always delivering individual autonomy, the bicycle is the most common means of transport in the world today.

From the 1960s on, cycling diminished in the West, to be replaced by the car. It has grown again over the past twenty years, as a mode of transport for short distances, particularly in cities where traffic is denser and parking costs high. It is also an economical means of transport, requiring only human energy and therefore a highly environmental choice. Highly developed in northern Europe, it is currently gaining enthusiasts in the south, encouraged over the past few years by the provision of shared bike services like *Bicing* in Barcelona, *Velib'* in Paris and *Velopass* in Lausanne.

In parallel, the infrastructures necessary for its development are muliplying with the creation of cycle paths and strips along roads, which are becoming widespread, as well as the increase in the number of spaces equipped for parking and locking bikes. Several projects for bike shelters with improved security are emerging, offering other, complementary urban functions, as well as practical and visionary concepts for what could be the cyclist's world of tomorrow.

collection ensemble
2006
Roel Vandebeek
Wolters Mabeg
page 258

LightLane signposting
2008
Evan Gant, Alex Tee / Altitude

By creating a virtual cycle path at ground level, LightLane makes the circulation of bikes safer at night thanks to a simple laser projection.

page 259

259

tactil rack - 2007
Antonio de Marco
Santa & Cole

imawa rack - 2008
Urbanica
Concept Urbain

key rack - 2007
Lagranja Design
Santa & Cole

arcas rack - 2002
Tobia Repossi
Modo

dedalo rack - 2002
Tobia Repossi
Modo

260 on your bike / RACKS

Ian Mahaffy
Maarten De Greeve
New York City
Department of Transportation
DOT

NYCityRack

In 2008, an international competition was launched for the creation of the new model of bike parking in New York. It accompanies a plan for the development of free bike rack spaces and new cycle paths, to make the bicycle a truly practical way of getting around in the metropolis. Of more than 1000 projects received, 10 finalists were retained and their prototypes were installed on the pavements for users to test them in real conditions. The NYC Hoop City Rack project was finally chosen, its contemporary design appealing through its simplicity and solidity, which is indispensable for resisting urban vicissitudes. Made up of a circle with an internal horizontal bar, evoking a wheel, it offers a wide support and several possibilities for attaching. It can also lend itself as an occasional seat.

parkower rack - 2009
Kompott Studio

piano bike stand - 2008
Addi

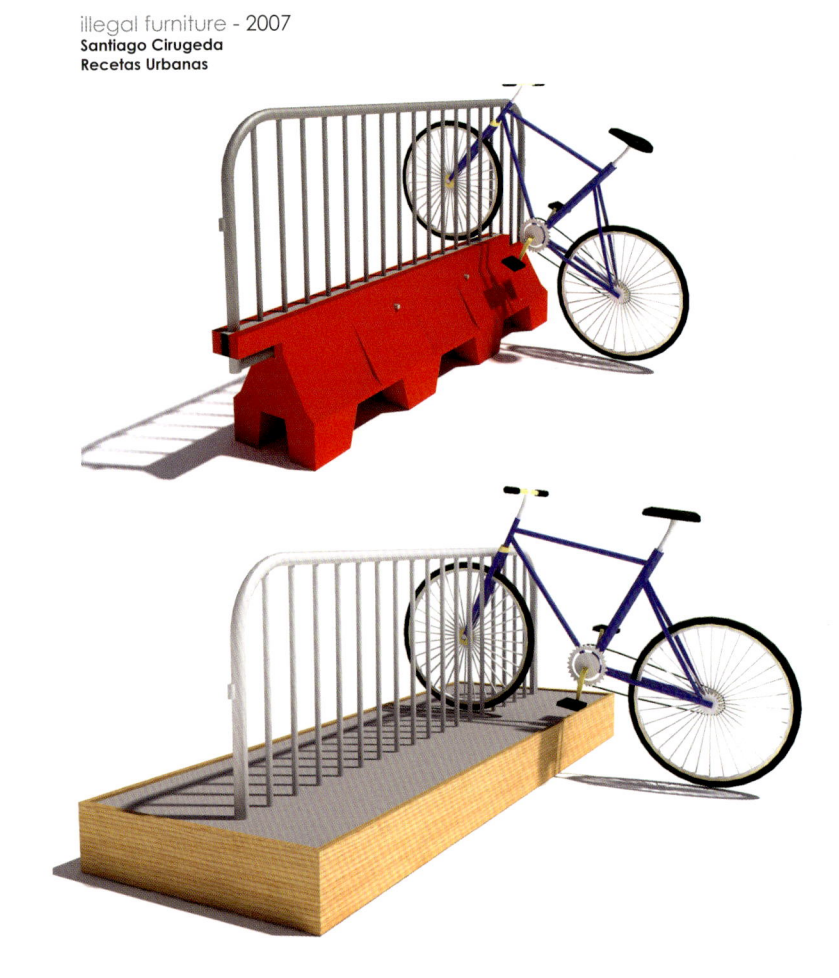

put in rack - 2006
Store Muu Design Studio

illegal furniture - 2007
Santiago Cirugeda
Recetas Urbanas

262 on your bike / MIXED RACKS

shelter-4-bikes & bike-bench / USXL

The discovery, in 1999, of a new technique for forming sheet metal has transformed the conceptual approach of numerous designers in the world. Baptised "surface (de)formation", it allows one to bend large volumes, especially self-supporting ones, without investing in a mould, offering the objects created the tight and uninterrupted line characteristic of the deformation of material. Thus the "abri-4-vélos" (shelter-4-bikes) made from a single sheet of metal envelops and protects the bicycles slotted into it, forming a sculptural ensemble. This double-function concept, economical in terms of space, has also been adopted for the bike-bench, which takes the evocative form of a strange rickshaw, in fact immobile, bringing together the comfort of a seat and the possibility of parking a two-wheeler in complete security.

Xavier Lust

bikeline - 2010
François Gustin

shelters my bikes

The City of Lille, which has for several years been considering the place of bicycles in the city, decided to equip itself with secure bike shelters. This idea originated from the number of bike thefts in France: around 400 000 each year, today the second impediment to the development of urban cycling, behind lack of road safety. Even equipped with a good cycle lock, the French cyclist has few places to lock a bike up legally, because parking on the pavement is theoretically banned as it might inconvenience pedestrians. As for bike racks, most of the time they are insufficient in numbers and often occupied by motorised two-wheelers or by wrecked bikes... In addition, the Nord region of France is quite rainy, making the seats wet, and increasing the wear and tear to bikes as well as their maintenance.

Association Kraft
City of Lille
Sustainable Development Office
Mission PDU
Plan vélo (Bike plan)

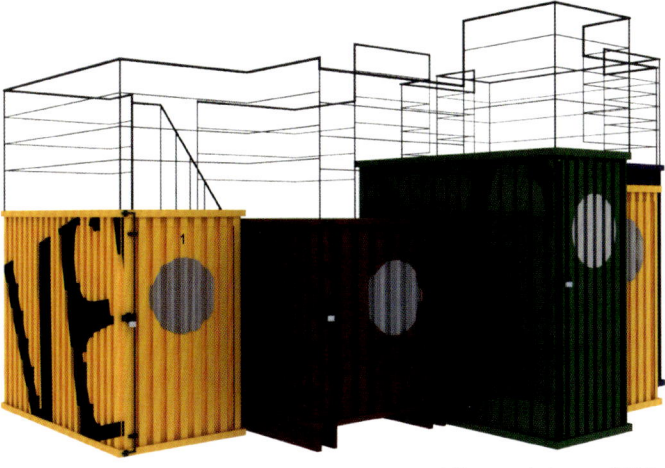

bike container - 2010
Manon Poirier

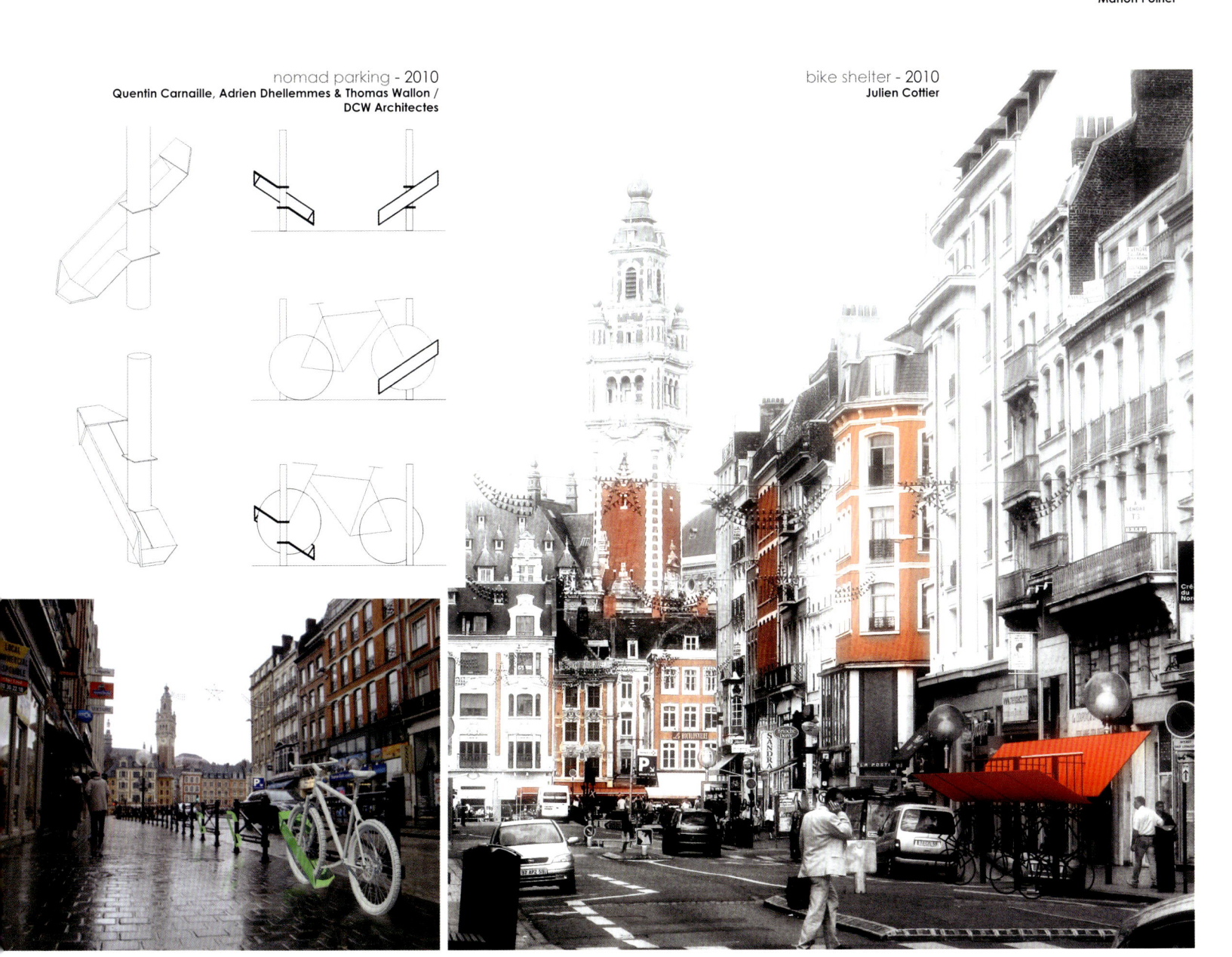

nomad parking - 2010
**Quentin Carnaille, Adrien Dhellemmes & Thomas Wallon /
DCW Architectes**

bike shelter - 2010
Julien Cottier

265

cover bike - 2010
Zurab Shavadze

bikoo - 2010
Sylvain Ory

hent, bike tree - 2010
Gaultier Bigot

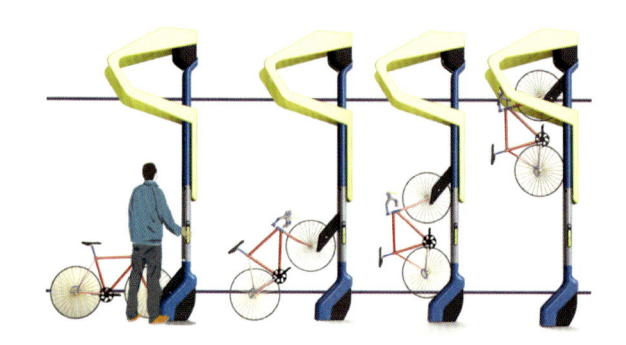

a bike shelter - 2010
Bruno Codron / Atelier Juno

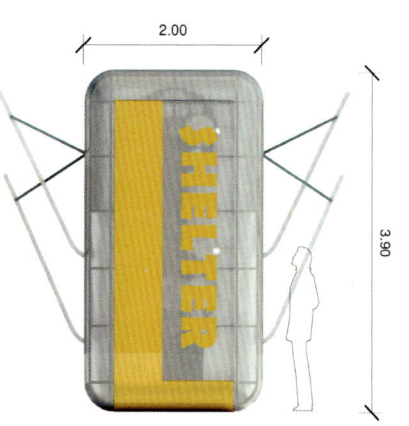

mobile hamsters - 2010
Jacques Sanselme / Design & Découverte

266 on your bike / SHELTER

On the initiative of the Kraft Association, the City of Lille, which wanted to equip itself with urban furniture that was useful against theft, vandalism and bad weather, launched a competition whose participants had to integrate these needs, as well as a creative and innovative approach in terms of eco-design and the presence of elements of communication aimed at users. Among the 115 projects received, several typologies emerged, relevant because they responded to the specific functions and contexts, targeting diverse users and offering different services.

There are two main families. The closed shelters which offer an extra guarantee (against vandalism) and sometimes storage spaces, of which some are transparent to respond to the visibility standards of French government public security measures. And the open shelters which facilitate access to bikes with child seats and limit their visual impact on the public space. They can be autonomous or grafted on to the existing urban furniture, or alternatively be mobile. Some offer new uses: places for meeting people, green spaces or viewpoints over the city, children's play facilities. All the projects are equipped with modern technology ensuring their energy autonomy, often based on photovoltaic panels. They are also designed in recyclable or recycled materials, which reduces their cost. One could imagine that all these shelters could eventually be electricity generators and even become profitable.

lill'ô-bike - 2010
Franck Dardé
Jury prize winner

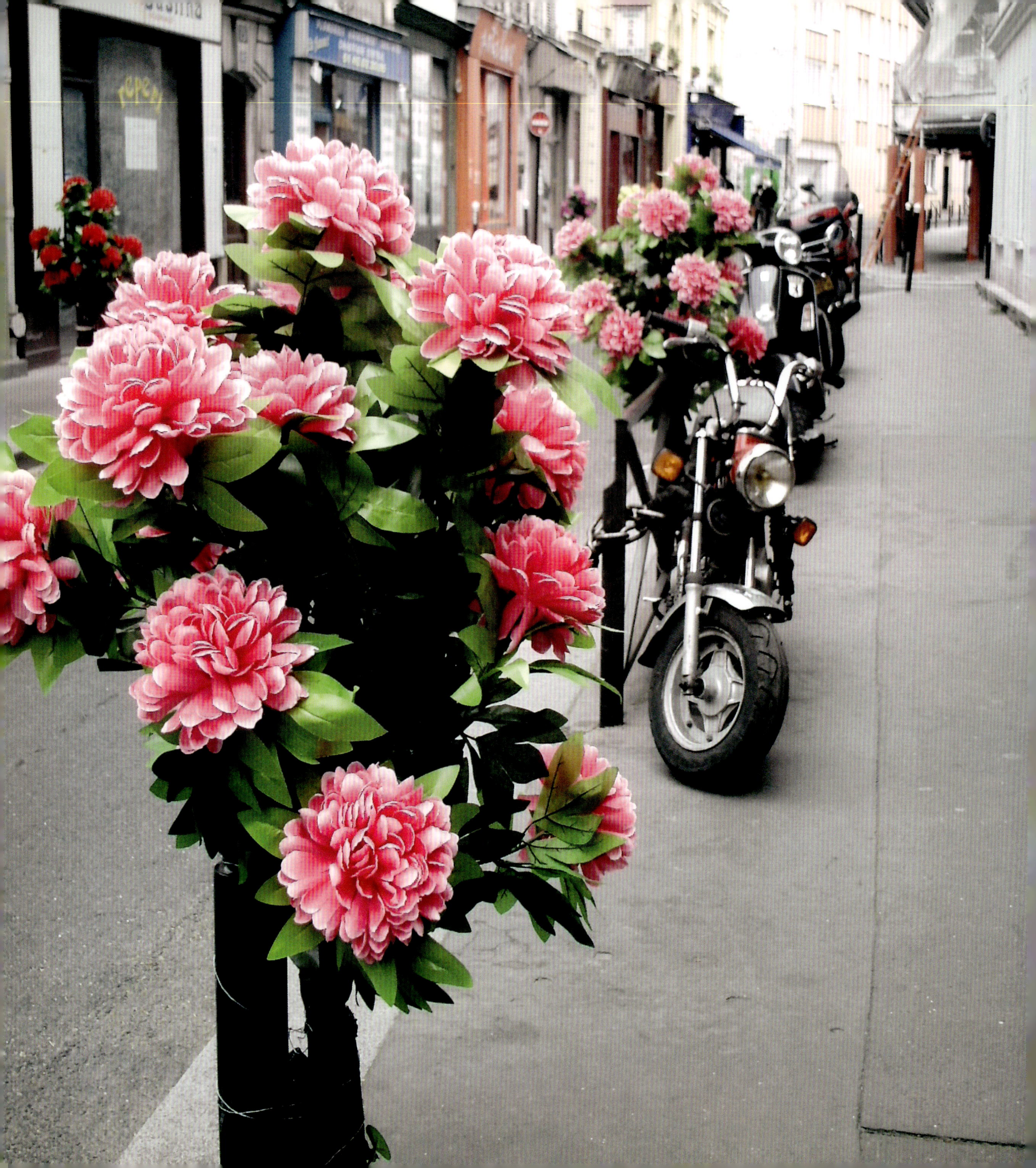

08

GREEN CITY

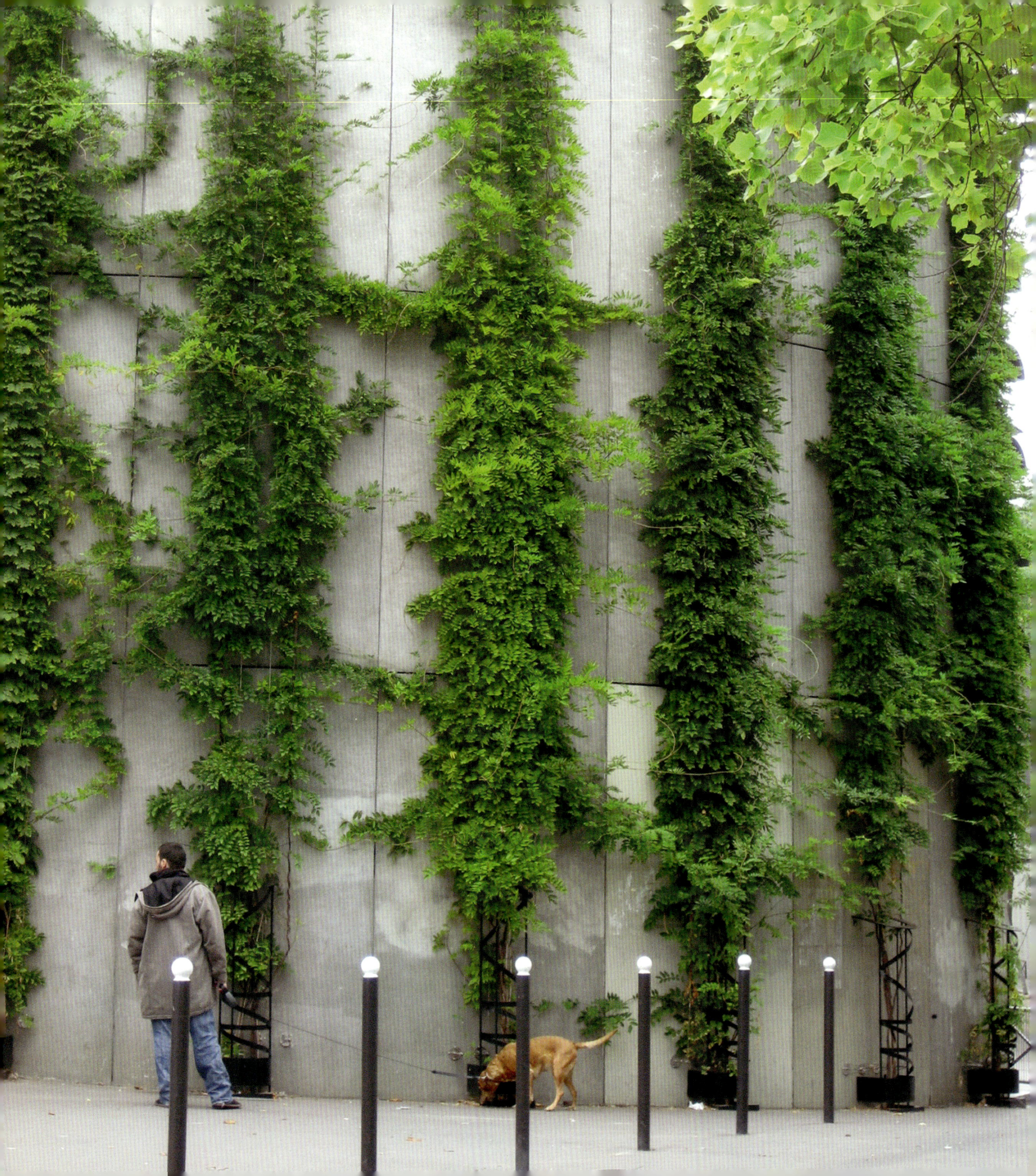

green city

rue de la Villette, Paris 19th arr.
2007
**Association des commerçants
de rue de la Villette**
page 268

corsus
2006
**Étienne Vanderpooten
Paris City Council / DEVE**

This structure was created to diversify the vegetation in Parisian public places and more particularly to adorn façades and walls with climbing species. Its forms are inspired by feminine corsets, from which its takes its Latin name. It exists in two versions, one very tall and its little sister, which is lower in order more discreetly to equip sensitive historic districts and places adjoining listed buildings.

pages 270 & 271

Beginning in the 1950s, the phrase "green spaces" was used to mean any leisure site, planted with flowers, trees or grass, situated in the urban environment and allowing one to limit the density of the cities to improve the lives of the inhabitants. Inheritors of the great history of public gardens, they reflected horticultural and landscape knowledge, linked with the new technologies offered by agricultural motorisation and the phytosanitary products created by the chemical industry. But in the 1980s people became ecologically aware and noticed the noxiousness of these products. Another relationship with the environment, one that is indispensable, began then.

The ground has gradually become a living organism again, and plant and animal biodiversity is growing thanks to differentiated management, water saving, the removal of pesticides and chemical fertilisers, resorting to renewable energies, a reduction in the noise and pollution caused by machines, the recycling of waste, the skill of gardeners and an informed public.

But the evolution doesn't stop there, and with the demand from city-dwellers intensifying, other types of natural space are developing. "Green" is invading every interstice of the city, growing, sown or planted, naturally and without fanfare…

Thus, municipal services are covering walls, even lights, with climbing plants. They respect what used to be called "weeds" and offer increasingly numerous spaces up to a public crazy for gardening, allowing them to plant on the pavements, at the foot of trees, or providing them with window boxes. Shopkeepers decorate their storefronts, and the urban space in front of them becomes a flower-filled terrace. Trees are adopted like beings with which to establish a warm and respectful rapport. Private balconies are gradually colonised by horticultural species and edible plants, while allotments are increasing in all Western cities. Artists, designers, landscape architects and architects invent new green spaces by hijacking urban objects and turning them into something new, while participating in a thought process on the future urban farms, which, through a change in scale, will mark a new stage in the ecological evolution of cities.

disurbanised furniture
1997-2010
Patrick Demazeau dit : MADE

As if they had always been there, benches let a tree grow through their heart. Designed as communication spaces, these poetic installations offer the chance of a dialogue yet to be invented between Man and nature, to talk of time, of the seasons, of ecological preoccupations…

page 272

dream projects
2008
Marie Denis
Galerie KernotArt

page 273

273

saturnia basins and seats - 2009
Philippe Negro
Piba Marmi

urban lounge - 2004
Marine Peyre
City of Lyon

Trinity college quadrangle - 2007
Gh3
University of Toronto

274 green city / SCENOGRAPHIC LAWNS

Robin Winogrond & Staupfer Hasler
Hochbauamt Kanton St. Gallen

cantonal high school Wil

This new school is situated on the outskirts of Wil, in the canton of Saint-Gall, in the north-east of Switzerland. Surrounded by industrial buildings and residential buildings from the 1980s, its exterior space is designed to welcome the 700 pupils as well as the local inhabitants. Reversing the classic concept of campus layouts, often composed of large lawns and paths, it takes the form of a landscape lounge, punctuated by enormous raised sofas, planted with lawn, whose unusual forms define and structure the wide gravel circulation paths. This abstract and convivial composition is open to the town, bordered only by a low hedge and punctuated with red American oaks, deliberately spaced out, to create a light and uniquely visual screen between the other spaces of the site, like the car park and the school with its wooden architecture, and the neighbouring constructions.

9 m² of hill - 2010
Antoine Monnet
ESAD Vegetal Design Workshop of Reims
Fondation CARI / Ecovégétal / Imaginez maintenant in Metz

park - 2009
Sean Martindale

water crater - 2007
Shigeko Hirakawa
Parcours contemporain de Fontenay-le-Comte

Piter Perbellini
Mini Design Award 2007

w² wireless square

Using the technology that allows one to find a wireless internet connection though a simple terminal installed in the public space, this symbolically unfenced square offers to bring together users who like to make the most of the open air to work or simply communicate with friends... Its form, made up of concentric circles, all of which are seats, evokes the waves that provide this autonomy and mobility. A central coloured totem pole has a fluorescent lamp that calls like a semaphore and informs people of the device. A new urban object and possibly a new icon of the landscape, this convivial system, favouring virtual communication, testifies to the importance that the internet has taken on in the life of people around the world, by offering outside spaces devoted to it.

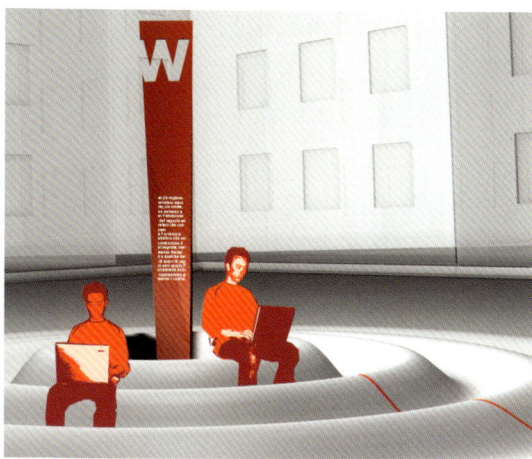

mobile green - 2009
Anja Ohliger, Stephan Goerner & Ulrich Beckefeld
OSA

278 green city / MOBILE

Comceci Architectes
Sedib
Town Council of the 2nd arr. Paris

mobîlot

In Paris' second arrondissement green or pedestrian spaces are very rare. To remedy the situation, this project aims to create breathing spaces where the city is suffocating. Playful, nomadic and economical, Mobîlot is a flower-filled mobile terrace which adopts the width and length of a vehicle and can thus be installed in a parking space. It allows one to create new urban spaces for people to meet up without obstructing the pavements, most of which are very narrow in this neighbourhood. Ecologically designed, these different structures, which can be taken apart and folded, are in metal and thermo-treated bamboo, compressed to a very high density. A first experiment in situ took place in June 2010. Watch this space…

chitchat bench - 2009
Teun Fleskens
Teunprojetcts

Romeo & Juliet bench - 2004
**Koen Baeyen, Stijn Goethals & Basile Graux,
Architenatelier Vivey & Partners
Extremis**

cisca urban seat - 2008
**Juan pablo Sammartino
Mark Iglesias Design**

theatre garden - 2001
Vincent Dupont-Rougier

280 green city / MIXED PLANTERS

Alexander Bébelin
Strate Collège

light up

Three of the main elements of the urban space are brought together in Light Up: a bench, a tree and a lamppost, reducing the influence of each and creating a multifunctional convivial space. Taking the form of a spiral of light which unfolds in space, this intelligent street light wraps itself around the tree like a second skin and floats above its summit, giving the tree back its importance and making it the centre of the device.

It also creates a convivial place, by night as well as by day, with its seat offering the chance to enjoy the shade of the branches. Ecologically equipped with LEDs, it is a leader in sustainable development, thanks to light-sensitive cells that activate illumination only when a pedestrian, cyclist or car passes by, creating a luminous zone that follows the city-dweller when he is alone or creates a continuous flux when there are several.

As lighting plays an important role in the safety of the inhabitants, as well as for the town's communication with them, the plinth of this object is anchored in the ground, strengthening its graphic identity while also spreading light in the form of specific written messages, or adopting different colours.

Landfrabrik

tempo-territorial-puzzle

2006

The urban environment is paced, trampled, crossed. With a final destination in mind, the user no longer interacts with his environment; he hardly sees it, so well does he know it. Only tourists discovering it for the first time explore it visually, look up to take in the architecture that surrounds them… The point of this installation is to change the reference points for the passive passer-by so that he becomes an actor in his city once again. Inspired by "taquin", a puzzle in which all the elements can be moved around in the same plane and must be put in a certain order, Puzzle-tempo-territorial makes the different objects of which it is made up into moveable modules. They are typical of what one finds on pavements: a bench, a street lamp, a stretch of asphalt and a grassy zone. Each is made up of several autonomous elements that form the thirty-two modules, which can be moved around anticipating their future place and the necessary movements of the other parties.

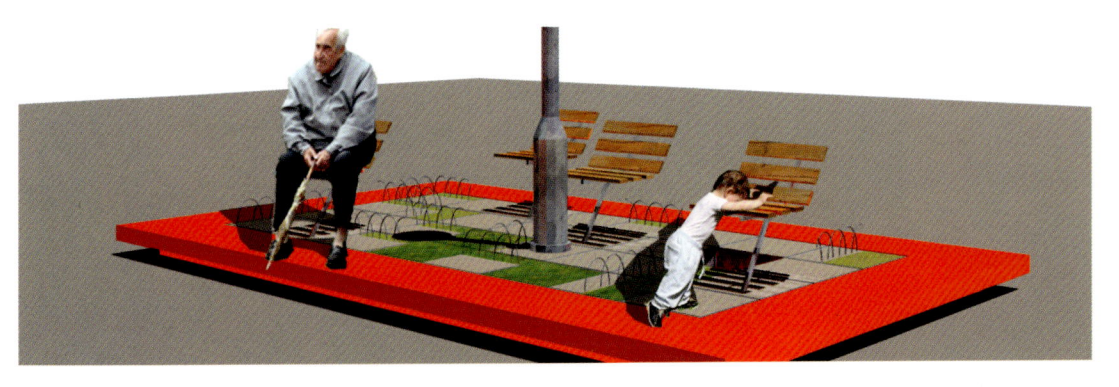

project for a terrace - 2000
Vincent Dupont-Rougier
French Cultural Centre in Parlerme

283

the Lille bouquet - 2004
Vincent Dupont-Rougier
Lille2004

the large chairs - 2004
Marie Hélène Richard & Stéphan Bohu

station square, Douais's street car line 1 - 2008
Ingérop / Reichen et Robert - Architectes / DVA Paysagistes
Andé Fournelle & Claude Chaussard
Le Syndicat Mixte des Transports du Douaisis

284 green city / AERIAL PLANTERS

Patrick Nadeau
Bernard Cavalié / Atelier de l'île
City of Rennes

Republic square

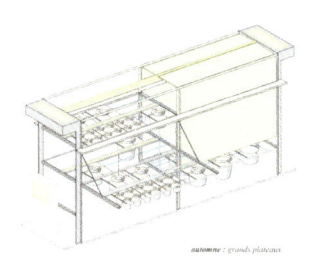

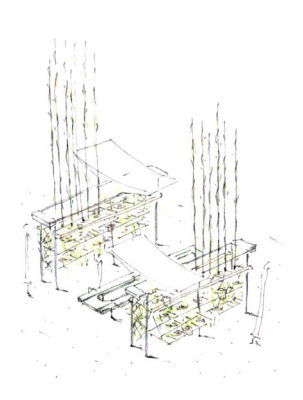

In the heart of Rennes, capital of Brittany, place de la République is a major crossroads and meeting place for pedestrians near the coach station and a new Metro station. As its concrete slab construction can't sustain excess loads, its garden has been created without beds. It has been made possible by using Ductal® for the construction of its various elements: a very light concrete that can espouse any form.

A hundred and twenty tubs contain holm oaks that define the landscape space; the latter is punctuated with double benches and suspended benches, balanced on central feet and overhanging the plants.

But the planted shelves are the most innovative part of the project, releasing plants from their purely decorative role to transform them into a truly architectural element, contributing to the definition of the place, its form and its sensory qualities. They bring together the flexibility of a garden in pots, modular and allowing for seasonal renewal, which is normally reserved for private spaces, and the rigour and constraints of a public place. In the evening, the planted shelves transform themselves into lights and diffuse a gentle illumination over the square through their foliage.

West 8
Rotterdam City of Architecture 2007

flaming city - Blooming city

At the end of 1939, at the beginning of the Second World War in Europe, Germany invaded Poland, then part of Finland. In the following spring, before France, it was the turn of Denmark, Norway, Belgium and the Netherlands to be occupied. Thus, on 14 May 1940, the Luftwaffe, the German airforce, bombed the centre of Rotterdam, which was largely destroyed, obliging the Dutch government to surrender. It is this tragic event in history that is here commemorated: fires, destruction… But it deliberately doesn't resemble a classic monument. This installation plays on the strong evocation created by these strange mountains covered with thousands of geraniums, with flamboyant colours. Installed on the main square of Schouwburgplain, this obligatory place of memory is also deliberately a place for walking, a way of deconsecrating the past while recalling it, with a strong and unusual image.

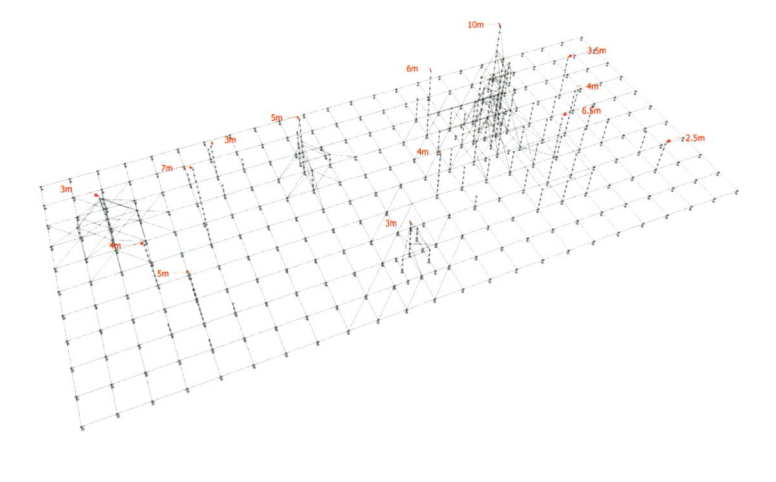

287

greenspotlight - 2009
Tjerk van de Wetering & Richèl Lubbers / Bytr
Eindhoven municipal council

green green screen - 2003
Klein Dytham architecture
Mori Building Co.

288 green city / AERIAL PLANTERS

Coen + Partners
Tulane University, New Orleans

the Lavin Bernick center for university life

In the framework of an extension to the University of Tulane in New Orleans, the Lavin Bernick Center, a central building given over to the students, has been renovated and extended, and its landscape spaces developed. The exterior, harmoniously linked to the existing buildings and shaded by majestic oaks bordering a large lawn, has thus become a new centre for campus activity, by night as well as by day. Different facilities have been created here, notably an open-air reading room, bordered by planted screens composed of cables overrun with jasmine, with the scent that is so emblematic for the region. These aerial planted structures are also found in other parts of the park, in the form of pergolas or fences that allow light and glance to pass through.

poster pocket plants

2009

Reacting to the proliferation of commercial posters on walls, bus shelters and other surfaces in large urban centres, curious plantings have started to emerge in Canada. By cutting and folding the paper of these advertisements with their catching images and slogans, small plant pot holders have been made, where different plants and their compost take root. These unexpected piracies create extra green spaces in the city, and are an act of positive subversion that offers an alternative to the invasion of cities by marketing. An internet site created to this effect gives models, instructions and suggestions free online so that this action can be multiplied and even become commonplace. Watch this space...

Sean Martindale & Eric Cheung

290 green city / MOBILE PLANTERS

guerilla gardening - 2009
Posterchild

moving forest - 2008
NL architects
Droog Design, Urban Play Event 2

291

ondine - 2007
Michaël Bihain & **Cédric Callewaert**
ParckDesign 2007 / Bruxelles Environnement & Pro Materia

Marie Denis
Gaëlle Gabillet
3D Fabrice Escalier

Galerie KernotArt
Domaine Départementale
de Chamarande
Conseil Général de l'Essonne

chamaland

In this play area designed for the Chamarande department forest, the trees are the stationary actors that structure the space and that one protects at the same time. Thus, deliberately oversized, benches surround their trunks, while preserving the typology of classic seats of public squares, known since the beginning of the 20th century. These benches form both a protective plinth and a setting that shows off the trees. With their wooden planks, displaying a range of lemon and lime tinted greens, in osmosis with the surrounding nature and offering a nod to the foliage of the park, they seem to have dawned with the spring, and evoke tea-time, Neopolitan ices or millefeuilles… These pâtisserie metaphors, both playful and poetic, welcome both children and grown-ups with the same pleasure, of rediscovering the taste of childhood. As the designer says: "You feel yourself in the process of growing up when you sit down here!"

guenus - 2004
Corentin Nicolas & Alix d'Harambure

294 green city / PROTECTED TREES

hula hoop - 2010
Thomas Joly
ERBA Rennes

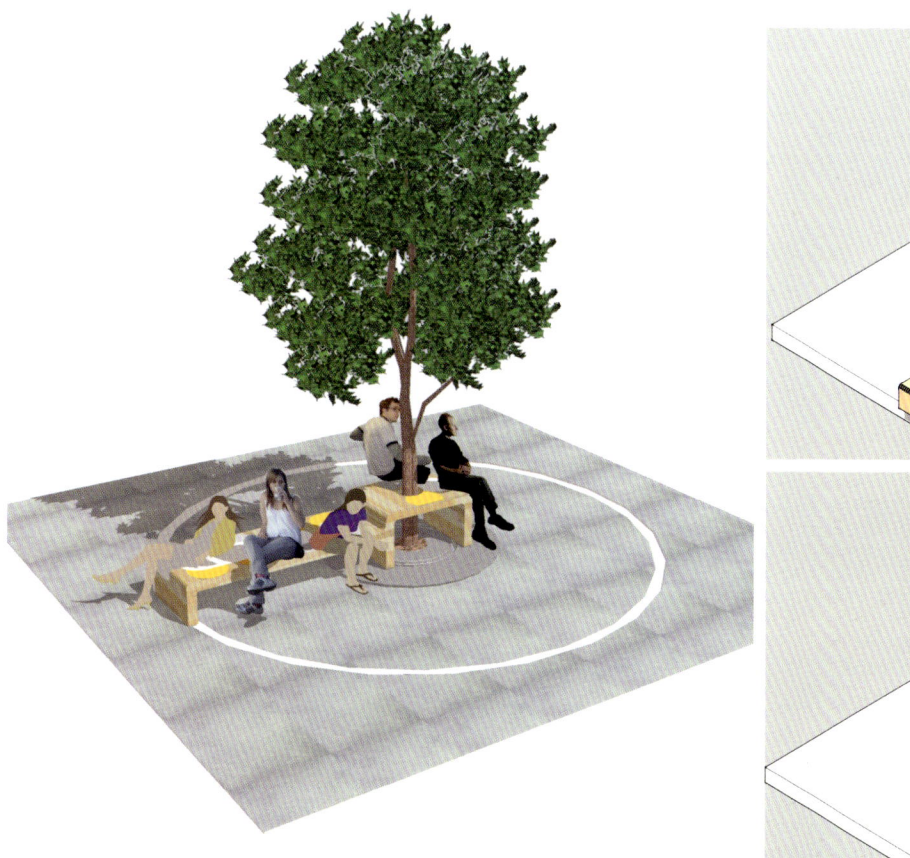

3.6 solar relaxation - 2009
Stéphane Dréville
ERBA Rennes

the shiverer, tree-sculpture

2008

As in the sacred woods of Antiquity, a tree blazes beside Lake Leman in Geneva, in the English garden. Dressed in gold and silver, it shines by day, sparkles at night, while all the time tinkling. This Judas tree was chosen for its harmonious silhouette with its trunk of young growth, formed of several branches at its base, its smooth and solid medium-sized branches, with few branchlets. Its adornment is make up of thousands of twinkling sleigh-bells, with a great diversity of shapes and sizes, in brass or copper. They are gathered together like a coat of mail on the lower part and distributed here and there, individually on in a cluster, in its crown, like Christmas baubles. Garlands of light decorate its branches and uplighting from the ground intensifies its sparkle. Everything combines to attract the attention of passers-by, who, approaching, hear the song of the tree rise progressively, provoked by a simple breath of wind. Its peculiarity and its musicality give a second kind of life to this tree, a possible place for walkers to meet and a real hyphen linking the sky and the earth…

Mourka
Trees and Lights Festival, Genève

296 green city / ADORNED TREES

Marie Denis
Galerie KernotArt
Environnementales de Tecomah

bonzaï II

In the 120-hectare wooded park of Tecomah, School of the Environment and Surroundings for Living, in Jouy-en-Josas, a single tree stands astonishingly in a plant pot. Or more exactly a giant basket, woven using the traditional basket-weave called "crocane", intersecting vertical and horizontal strands. Here they are very unusual because they are not in a plant material, but in orange irrigation tubes, 3 km of which were needed for this monumental creation. This original display vessel measures 4.5 m high and its diameter is 5.5 m. Through a simple but pertinent effect of scale, this oversizing visually transforms the large pine that it harbours into a bonsai! Through its flamboyant colour, it attracts the visitor who, the closer he comes, the more he penetrates an unusual world, like Gulliver in Brobdingnag, the land of the giants. Plunging into a childhood world, he can also think like Alice in Wonderland, in another world, with changing forms and colours, thanks to the complicity of the woods and the different lighting effects of the site.

Matali Crasset
Rhone-Alpes Region
Marianne Homiridis / Design Office

the pouffe tree

The pouf tree is one of three objects specially designed for the outside spaces of Germaine Tillion high school, recently built at Saint Bel in the north-west of Lyon, in the Rhône-Alpes region. It is a tree bearing strange, ripe fruit, in the form of poufs with a kind of handle that allows them to be put away hung in the branches, and which also forms the back of these amusing seats. Another strange creation peoples this campus, the bird dome, placed in a clearing further away. Resembling an umbrella with multiple spikes, it is the permanent home of stationary birds and symbolically protects a circular bench sunk into the ground, on which you can sit down a level from the norm.

A sound meadow completes these surreal and convivial furnishings. It is in part bordered by a circular fence to which are attached chimes. The wind controls the intensity and the rhythm of their jingles and the pupils can also play on them, transforming the space into a music room. These three installations invite relaxation and chatting, in small or large groups, transforming the usual high school ambiance by offering the possibility of sitting on the ground or almost, but comfortably and peacefully.

299

LAST ONE
by House Work

vital vegetal "last one" series

2009

This eco-design research project revolves around and is based upon an approach to an environmental challenge. Its effects aim to question the city user on reforesting, biodiversity, etc., through a specific object with a strong evocative power. Beyond the desire to reawaken the curiosity of the passer-by, this new type of furniture reweaves a privileged link between the city-dweller and nature, but also upholds a daily act of recollection. Thus Végétal Vital is an eco-design exterior tree, designed only from recycled and recyclable aluminium. This living object, symbolising life in perpetual evolution as well as its permanent cycles, is here artificially recreated and thus immortalised in order to provoke questions on the future of nature and Man. The tree thus becomes the possible metaphor for the individual finding his place in a network, a labyrinth of others, who seem the same as him.

Didier Muller
A.D.C.

the foreigner - 2009
Gaële Braun

301

Gionata Gatto

urbanbuds

Looking like trunks on wheels, these funny kitchen gardens make their way around the town. Compact and portable, they allow you to cultivate fruit and vegetables anywhere you like. Each module is made up of fine metallic structures that maintain a thick geotextile on all sides. This material, familiar to anyone used to above-ground cultivation, serves as a planting medium, on the four sides and above, thus multiplying the area available for cultivation.

In cities and metropolises, allotments and individual gardens can thus see the day, without needing spaces of earth, which are today increasingly rare. But this operation also has a social vocation, that of creating the possibility of meeting people from different backgrounds through common practices like gardening and food production, the housing estates being more and more multicultural.

The aim is to generate more communication, first of all through different culinary habits, foreign or not, and ways of sewing, watering, etc., and from there to move on to the exchange and sharing of other fields of life.

303

locavore fantasia

When New York Magazine asked several architects to offer a project for a space in Canal Street in New York, only one practice offered an urban farm. What made it unique was that it was not to be integrated into a building, but made up of a succession of retaining walls, stepped one on top of another, in order to increase the planted surface and the space for moving around. Some of them also harbour a small golf course. This autonomous structure, held up by giant stilts whose decoration would be entrusted to different artists, shelters a market under its canopy, itself planted with edible species, allowing for what is produced to be sold just beneath. Km 0.

WORK Architecture Company
NY Magazine

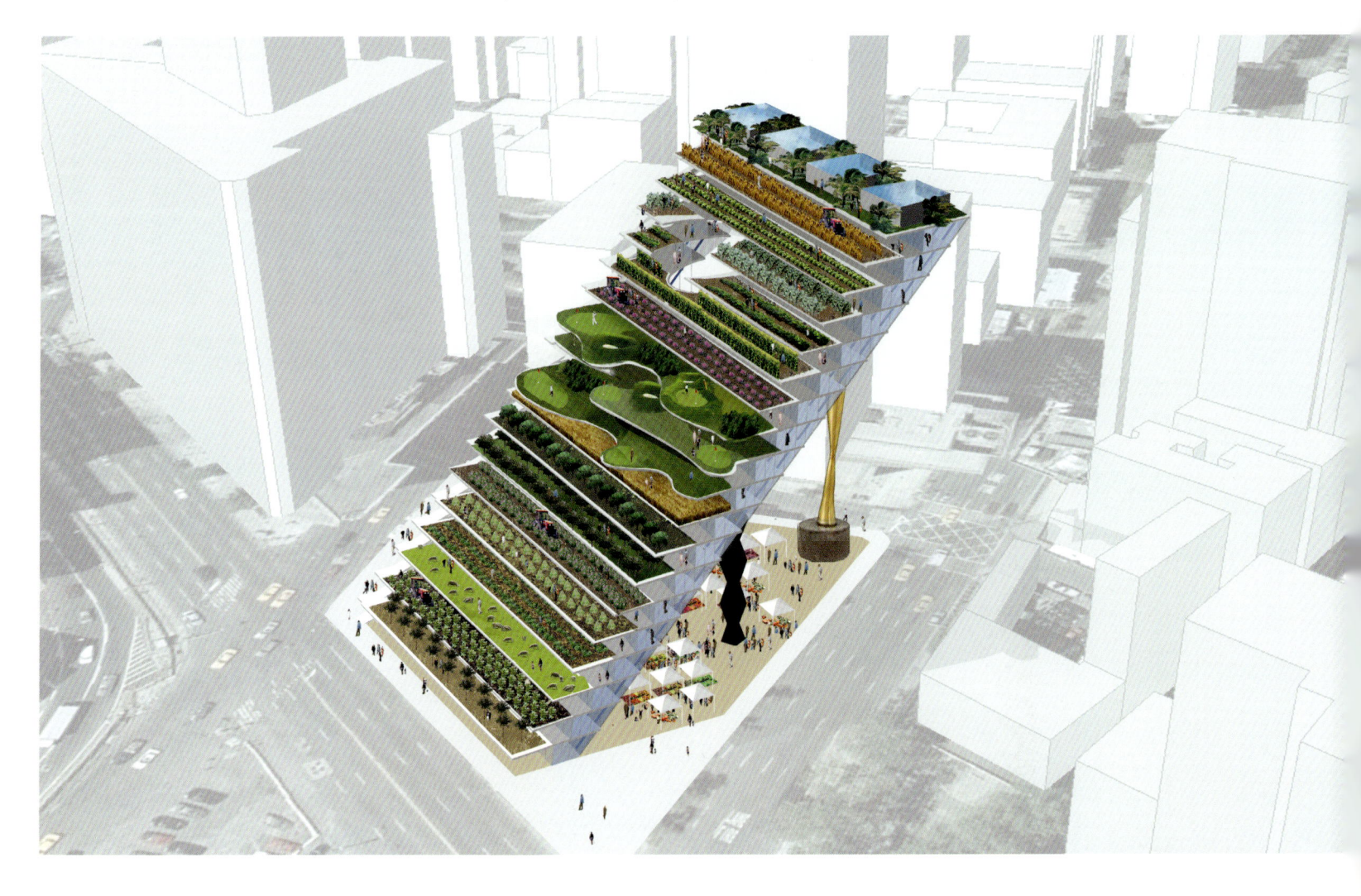

**Höweler + Yoon Architecture
Squared Design Lad
The Boston Globe**

eco-pods

In Boston, faced with the halting of several building projects because of the current world economic crisis, two agencies have got together to create an ecological and economic alternative. They propose to intervene on unfinished structures, attaching their Eco-Pods. These modules are capsule-gardens planted with specific plants, such as certain algae. Thanks to a bioreactor, they can produce biofuels while reducing the CO_2 emissions present in the air. It is also possible for them to be small units of scientific research for other solutions for replacing fossil fuels. A robot is part of the project, with an arm allowing it to place and fix the modules, directing them towards the sun. Their mobility also allows for them to be moved around in the urban space, according to when construction work begins again on the sites that have been taken over. This idea, visionary while being achievable today, opens up new fields of experimentation in the urban space, the city becoming modular and eco-responsible.

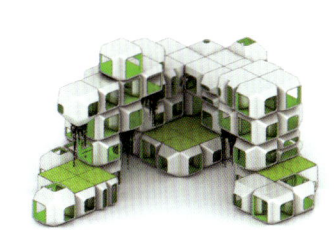

306 green city / CITY GARDENS

307

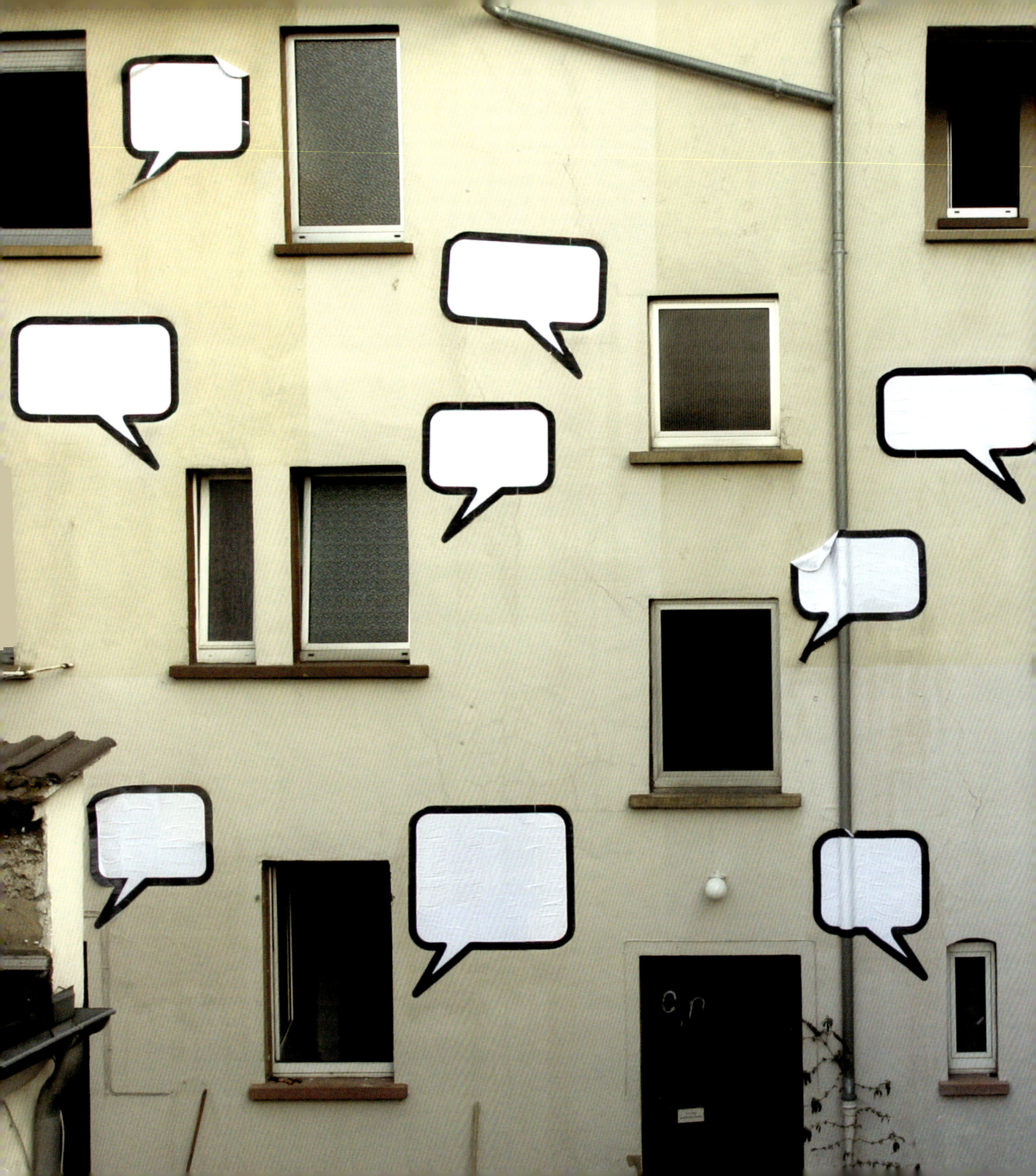

ANNEX

List of projects, contacts and iconographic credits

• Ecological projects, defined by the materials used and/or their function or purpose

dresses for Wallace fountains p.2
Contact : c_f_t@hotmail.fr
http://c-f-t.net
Photo © : Solène Couturier

the fish fountain p.4
Contact : bibi@bibi.fr
www.bibi.fr
Photo © : BIBI

Preface

reprojected pp.6-7
Contact : atelier@webblick.de
www.webblick.de
www.osram-light-consulting.com
Photo © : MSW, 2007

flight p.8
Contact : s.barbaux@orange.fr
www.sophie-barbaux.odexpo.com
roberto@mediamorphose.org
http://cabot.mediamorphose.org
Illustration © : Roberto Cabot

phonemes p.9
Contact : becheau.bourgeois@orange.fr
http://becheau.bourgeois.free.fr
Photo © : Vincent Bécheau & Marie-Laure Bourgeois

moodwall p.10
Contact : info@cube-architecten.nl
www.cube-architecten.nl
info@studioklink.com
www.studiolink.com
Photo © : Roel van Lanen

boxing p.11
Contact : linda.henry@hesge.ch
http://hesge.ch/head
Illustration © : Sarah Bittel

urban botanics pp.12-17
Contact : contact@legoville.net
www.legoville.net
www.dasein.biz
Photo © : Legoville
Illustration © : Colette Grand
Texte © : Legoville / Editions Dasein (p.14-17)

Captions of the photos in annex

speechless - 2006
Lars Herzig, Leo Volland, André Nossek, Via Grafik
page 308

hikarinoki - 2009
Philippe Morvan
Fêtes des lumières, Lyon
pages 312 & 316

1. Seats of conviviality

the banker p.18
Contact : taddeol@bdbarcelona.com
www.bdbarcelona.com
Photo © : BD Barcelona Design

flying carpet pp. 20-21
Contact : heiko.hehe@free.fr
helen.hehe@free.fr
http://hehe.org.free.fr
Photo © : HeHe

il posto seats p.22
Contact : www.thesevenhints.com
office@miramondo.com
www.miramondo.com
Photo © : Miramondo public design

the uprooting p.23
Contact : charles.e.laget@gmail.com
www.comcharles.com
Illustration © : Charles Laget

deca chaise longue p.24
Contact : info@modoarredo.com
www.modoarredo.com
Photo © : Modo s.r.l.

finferlo standing-seat p.24
Contact : info@modoarredo.com
www.modoarredo.com
Photo © : Modo s.r.l.

nigra seat p.24
Contact : informacion@escofet.com
www.escofet.com
Photo © : Escofet 1886 S.A

the poet & the loner p.25
Contact : taddeol@bdbarcelona.com
www.bdbarcelona.com
Photo © : BD Barcelona Design

wi-fi seat p.25
Contact : info@adrianodesign.it
www.adrianodesign.it
Photo © : Studio Adriano Architetti Associati

new Zgody square - Bohaterów Getta square pp. 26-27
Contact: biuro@lewicki-latak.com.pl
www.lewicki-latak.com.pl
Photo © : Biuro Projektów Lewicki Łatak

urban hammock-chair p.28 •
Contact : juliebernard@lalca.net
klobuk@ymail.com
http://localalouer.blogg.org
Photo © : Compagnie d'architectures [Local a louer]

the pallet project p.28 •
Contact : tolstrup@studiomama.com
www.studiomama.com
Photo © : Studiorama

avio chairs p. 28 •
Contact : dimmelo@vibrazioniartdesign.com
www.vibrazioniartdesign.com
Photo © : Vibrazioni Art-Design

ccc bench p. 29 •
Contact : contact@moronnoz.com
www.moronnoz.com
Illustration © : Alexandre Moronnoz

Luxembourg garden chairs p.30
Contact : info@fermob.com
www.fermob.com
Photo © : Sophie Barbaux

spinning seats p.31
Contact : info@noelblakeman.com
www.noelblakeman.com
Photo © : Noel Blakeman

urban cursor p.32
Contact : info@campion.nu
www.campion.nu
www.urbancursor.com
Photo © : Sebastian Campion

mobile chairs p.33
Contact : www.starck.com
www.villette.com
Photo © : Sophie Barbaux

signchair p.34
Contact : ken@offobject.com
www.offobject.com
Photo © : Ken Mori & Jenny Liang

playtime stool p.34
Contact : fd@fredericdedelley.ch
www.fredericdedelley.ch
www.burriag.ch
Photos © : Burri Public Elements

evolution stool p.34
Contact : fd@fredericdedelley.ch
www.fredericdedelley.ch, www.burriag.ch
Photos : Burri Public Elements

the high line p.35 •
Contact : info@thehighline.org
www.thehighline.org
Photo © : Iwan Baan, 2009 (top) ; Sara Lubtchansky (bottom)

you & me bench p.36
Contact : thomasdelussac@wanadoo.fr
www.thomasdeLussac.fr
Photos & illustration © : Thomas de Lussac

Romeo & Juliette bench p.36
Contact : thomasdelussac@wanadoo.fr
www.thomasdeLussac.fr
Photos & illustration © : Thomas de Lussac

chaise longue for two p.36
Contact : charles.e.laget@gmail.com
www.comcharles.com
Illustration © : Charles Laget

swiss benches p.37
Contact : taddeol@bdbarcelona.com
www.bdbarcelona.com
Illustration & Photo © : BD Barcelona Design

banda doblada bench p.38
Contact : informacion@escofet.com
www.escofet.com
Photo © : Escofet 1886 S.A

prat table and stool p.38
Contact : informacion@escofet.com
www.escofet.com
Photo © : Escofet 1886 S.A

set-square bench p.38
Contact : thomas.grenier3@hotmail.fr
www.latelierdethomas.com
Photo © : Thomas Grenier

310 annex

PicNik table p.39
Contact : info@extremis.be
www.extremis.be
Photo © : Extremis

company bench p.40
Contact : contact@editioncompagnie.fr
www.editioncompagnie.fr
Photo © : Christian MacManus

coral bench p.40
Contact : rob@arktura.com
www.arktura.com
Photo © : Arktura

hive bench p.40
Contact : rob@arktura.com
www.arktura.com
Photo © : Arktura

interferences bench p.40
Contact : contact@moronnoz.com
www.moronnoz.com
Photo © : Alexandre Moronooz

green oasis p.41 •
Contact : contact@MarijevanderPark.nl
www.marijevanderpark.nl
post@jomeesters.nl
www.jomeesters.nl
Photo © : Jo Meesters, 2006

illycopresto p.42
Contact : contact@o-s.fr
www.o-s.fr
Photo & Illustration © : Les Ateliers O-S architectes

glass wave p.43
Contact : contact@o-s.fr
www.o-s.fr
Photo & Illustration © : Les Ateliers O-S architectes

trek bench p.42
Contact : charles.e.laget@gmail.com
www.comcharles.com/
Photo & Illustration © : Charles Laget

burnt branches bench p.42
Contact : landfabrik@free.fr
http://landfabrik.free.fr
Illustration © : Landfabrik

115 bench p.43
Contact : charles.e.laget@gmail.com
www.comcharles.com/
Illustration © : Charles Laget

y bench p.43 •
Contact : contact@moronnoz.com
www.moronnoz.com
Photo © : VIA/Filioux & Filioux

urban adapter bench p.43
Contact : info@rocker-lange.com
www.rocker-lange.com
Photo © : Rocker-Lange Architects

memory chair p.44
Contact : info@earthscape.co.jp
http://www.earthscape.co.jp
Photo © : Shigeki Asanuma

xurret bench p.45
Contact : informacion@escofet.com
www.escofet.com
Photo © : Escofet 1886 S.A

slope bench p.46
Contact : informacion@escofet.com
www.escofet.com
Photo © : Escofet 1886 S.A

lunga mare bench p.47
Contact : informacion@escofet.com
www.escofet.com
Photo © : Escofet 1886 S.A

foundries garden pp.48-49 •
Contact : adh@doazan-hirschberger.com
www.doazan-hirschberger.com
Illustration & Photo © : ADH / Doazan + Hirschberger

puls bench p.50
Contact : martin@m-hartmann.dk
www.m-hartmann.dk
Photo © : Martin Hartmann

from one place to another 5 & 7 pp.51-53
Contact : jcnourisson@gmail.com
www.jeanchristophenourisson.com
www.valdoise.fr, www.lille.archi.fr
Photo © : Armelle Maugin (p.51),
Jean-Christophe Nourisson (pp.52-53)

the sixth hour p.54
Contact : dissardnina@gmail.com
willmina3@hotmail.com
pallatierloriane@gmail.com
www.ecole-boulle.org
www.104.fr
Illustration © : Nina Dissard, Marion Vauthier
& Loriane Pallatier

crucial collection s benches p.55
Contact : info@wolters-mabeg.eu
www.wolters.be
Photo © : Wolters Mabeg

collection benches ensemble p.55
Contact : info@wolters-mabeg.eu
www.wolters.be
Photo © : Wolters Mabeg

person parking p.56
Contact : info@springtime.nl
www.springtime.nl
Photo © : Masiar Pasquali, 2009
www.masiarpasquali.it
Illustration © : Springtime Design Team

shrinkage p.57 •
Contact : cyrielle_duprez@yahoo.fr
http://cyrielleduprez.ultra-book.com
www.retiwood.com
Photo & Illustration © : Cyrielle Duprez

university of social sciences II campus, p.58
Contact : info@kirk-specht.de
www.kirk-specht.de
Photo © : Kirk+Specht Landschaftsarchitekten

riverside park south, p.59
Contact : info@tbany.com
www.tbany.com
Photo © : Thomas Balsley Associates

capitol plaza, p.60
Contact : info@tbany.com
www.tbany.com
Photo © : Thomas Balsley Associates

325th fifth avenue, p.60
Contact : info@tbany.com
www.tbany.com
Photo © : Thomas Balsley Associates

the table of the 4 locks p.61 •
Contact : contact@atelier710.fr
www.atelier710.fr
Photo © : Atelier 710 / Xavier Coquelet,
Mathieu Gontier François Vadepied

aromatic tables p.62 •
Contact : colas.baillieul@gmail.com
s.barbaux@orange.fr
www.sophie-barbaux.odexpo.com
www.atelierdeparis.org
Photo © : Sophie Barbaux

the mobole p.63
Contact : http://lecabanonvertical.com
www.bruitdufrigo.com
Photo © : Sébastien Normand

kitchain pp.64-65
Contact : moov.email@gmail.com
www.moov.tk, www.belluard.ch
Photo © : MOOV
Illustration © : MOOV

concrete things p.66
Contact : komplot@komplot.dk, www.komplot.dk
agneta.stake@nola.se, www.nola.se
Photo & Illustration © : Komplot Design

urban furniture Roppongi Hills p.66
Contact : anbranzi@tin.it
andreabranzi@andreabranzi.it
www.andreabranzi.it
Photo © : Andrea Branzi

b love bench p.66
Contact : taddeol@bdbarcelona.com
www.bdbarcelona.com
Photo © : BD Barcelona Design

outdoor living rooms p.67
Contact : cdehove@club-internet.fr
www.workonstage.org
Photo © : Dehove & Lauro

lenivets [lab]scape pp.68-69 •
Contact : mathieugontier@yahoo.fr, vadepiedf@yahoo.fr
www.wagon-landscaping.fr, www.precarre.net
www.studiobasta.be, www.coloco.org
Photo © : Wagon Landscaping

connection p.70
Contact : elise_dek@hotmail.fr
laura.kiritzetopor@gmail.com
tijou.jonathan@gmail.com
www.ecole-boulle.org, www.104.fr
Illustration © : Jonathan Tijou, Laura Kiritze-topor, Elise Dekens

sonoptere, audio-solar armchair p.70 •
Contact : redolfi@audionaute.com
www.audionaute.com
Photo © : Michel Redolfi

boombench p.71
Contact : hello@michaelschoner.de
www.michaelschoner.de
www.droog.com
Photo © : Droog Design (top) ; Michael Schoner (bottom)

write the sequel p.72 •
Contact : benedettobufalino@yahoo.fr
www.benedetto.new.fr
http://favmontpellier.nerim.net
Photo © : Benedetto Bufalino

ljubljana chair p.72
Contact : info@asobi.si, www.asobi.si
info@movisi.com, www.movisi.com
Illustrantion © : ASOBI

aaa p.72 •
Contact : sophie@ecole-bleue.fr
www.ecole-bleue.com
Photo © : Sara Lubtchansky (left) ; Ecole Bleue (right)
Illustration © : A. Guillot, C. Mangin, C. Buccio, M. Levacher,
C-C Jaskulski, M. Coudert, S. Mallebranche / Ecole Bleue

the performance quarter p. 73
Contact : www.gpadesign.ca
www.ville.montreal.qc.ca
Photo © : Godbout Plante Associés

bushwaffle p.74
Contact : matt@rebargroup.org
www.rebargroup.org
www.droog.com
Photo © : Rebar

urban lounge pp.75-77 •
Contact : www.carlosmartinez.ch
www.pipilottirist.net
Photo © : Marc Wetli / Hannes Thalmann

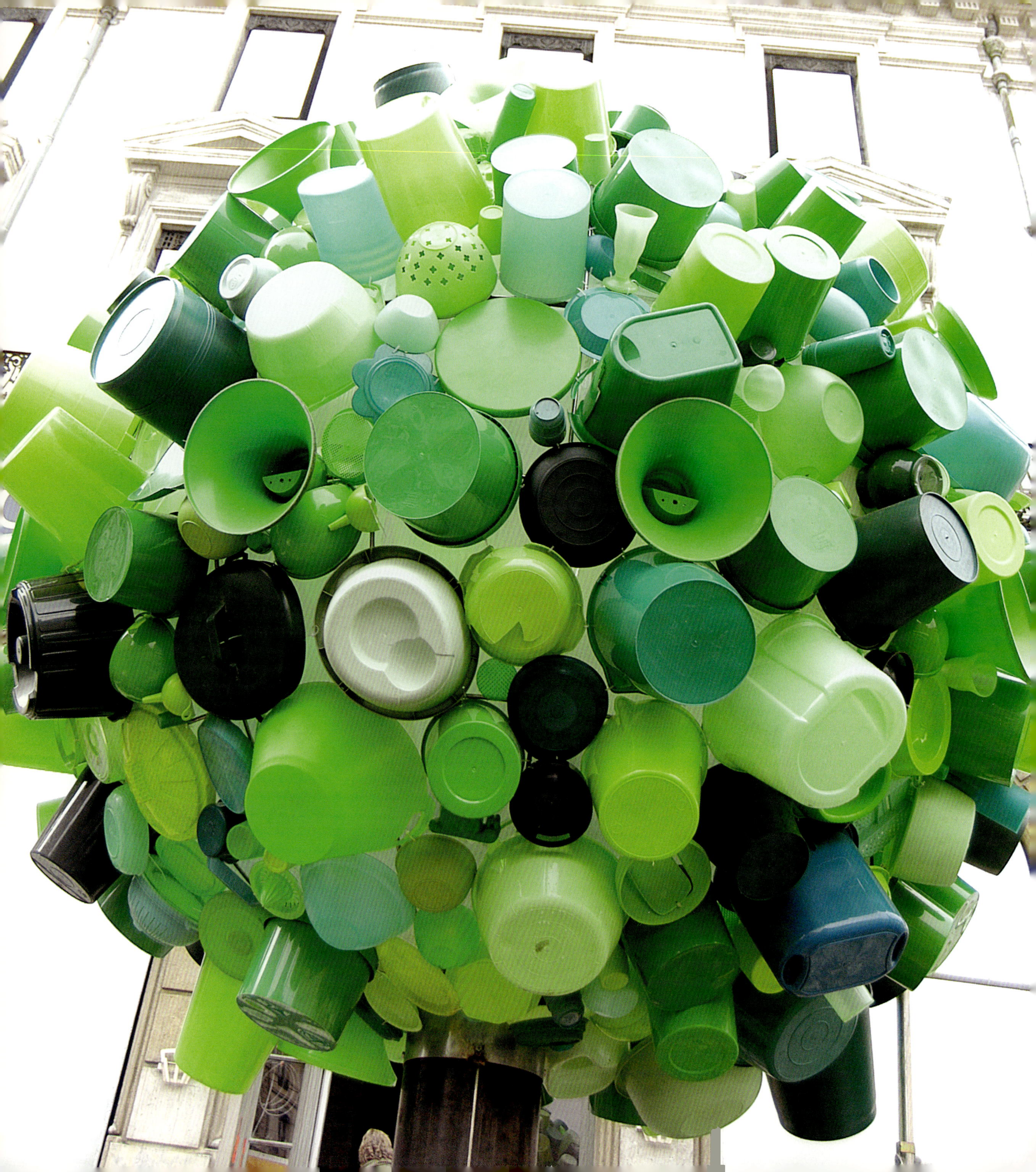

ge seat p.78
Contact : info@modoarredo.com
www.modoarredo.com
Photo © : Modo s.r.l.

rolling through time and space p.78
Contact : tdelaney@tdelaney.com
www.tdelaney.com
Photo © : Topher Delaney - Seam Studios

furniture foundation p.79 •
Contact : info@cinqcinqdesigners.com
www.cinqcinqdesigners.com
www.cg28.fr
Photo © : 5.5 designers

"mirror" bench & extract from nature pp.80-81
Contact : cecile.planchais@wanadoo.fr
www.cecileplanchais.com
www.cyria.net
Photo © : Cécile Planchais

loco bench p.82
Contact : info@allplus.eu
www.allplus.eu
Photo © : ALL+

banco catalano p.82
taddeol@bdbarcelona.com
www.bdbarcelona.com
Photo © : BD Barcelona Design

Samuel De Champlain promenade pp.83-85 •
Contact : www.daoustlestage.com
www.waa-ap.com, www.optionamenagement.com
Photo & Illustration © : Consortium Daoust, Lestage
Williams Asselin & Ackaoui Option aménagement

flow bench p.86
Contact : www.latzundpartner.de
carole.marcou@divers-cite.com
www.divers-cite.fr
Photo © : Divers Cité

timber seat p.86
Contact : west8@west8.com
www.west8.com
Photo © : West 8

gantry plaza state park pp.87-89
Contact : info@tbany.com
www.tbany.com
Photo © : Betsy Pinover Schiff

k-bench & k-baby p.90
Contact : www.charleskaisin.com
sales@abv.be
www.vange.be
Photo © : Vange

modular bench p.90
Contact : ludo.peper@gmail.com
www.ludopeper.com
Photo © : Ludovic Peperstraete

the red ribbon - Tanghe river park p.91-93 •
Contact : info@turenscape.com
www.turenscape.com
Photo & Illustration © : Turenscape (Beijing Turen Design Institute)

2. Clean city!

recycle your ideas! p.94 •
Contact : made.com@wanadoo.fr
http://nature.art.free.fr
Photo © : Patrick Demazeau dit : Made

skip waste pp.96-97 •
Contact : hello@oliverbishopyoung.co.uk
www.oliverbishopyoung.co.uk
Photo © : Oliver Bishop-Young

littershark p.98
Contact : www.zemp-objets.ch
bruco@bruco.ch
www.bruco.ch
www.littershark.com
Photo © : Brüco Swiss AG

trash p.99
Contact : www.anycoloryoulike.biz
www.artrelatedproduct.com
Photo © : Adrian K

kippe p.100
Contact : info@morgui.net
www.morgui.net
onadis@onadisrecicla.com
www.onadisrecicla.com
Photo © : Onadis Barcelona Disseny SL

cycas p.100
Contact : contact@divers-cite.com
www.divers-cite.fr
Photo © : Divers Cité

missing p.100
Contact : franckmagne@me.com
Photo © : Franck Magné

vesuvio p.100
Contact : info@manade.com
jadesign@free.fr
Photo © : Ja Design, Lui Jaramillo / Manade

canasto litter bin p.100
Contact : info@estudiocabeza.com
www.estudiocabeza.com
Photo © : Estudio Cabeza, Urban Element

koon ashtray-bin p.100
Contact : office@karimrashid.com
www.karimrashid.com
www.casamania.it
Photo © : Karim Rashid / Casamania

fold p.101
Contact : franckmagne@me.com
Photo © : Design Franck Magné

prestige litter bin p.102
Contact : contact@divers-cite.com
www.diverscite.fr
Photo © : Divers Cité

degas bin p.102
Contact : www.citydesign.it
contact@divers-cite.com
www.diverscite.fr
Photo © : Divers Cité

green palacio litter bin p.102
Contact : info@cyria.net
www.cyria.net
Photo © : Cyria

litter bin p.102
Contact : emminfo@emm-design.com
www.emm-design.com
Illustration © : Emmanuel Cairo

cestino litter bin p.103
Contact : www.bonnemazoucambus.com
www.paris.fr
Photo © : Christophe Fillioux

pink! p.104
Contact : www.villette.com
Photo © : Pierre-Emmanuel Rastoin

contradictions p.105
Contact : tt2www@hotmail.com
Photo © : Wu Wenwen & Wang Taoran

fiore bin p.106 •
Contact : contact@divers-cite.com
www.diverscite.fr
Photo © : Divers Cité

saturno bin p.106 •
Contact : info@ora.it
www.ora.it
Photo © : Ora Centurelli

marte bin p.106 •
Contact : info@ora.it
www.ora.it
Photo © : Ora Centurelli

poubelman p.106 •
Contact : thomasdelussac@wanadoo.fr
www.thomasdeLussac.fr
Photos © : Thomas de Lussac

pattumina p.107 •
Contact : www.metalsistem.com
Photos © : Metalsistem S.p.A.

anti-terrorism ecocity p.108 •
Contact : www.citydesign.it
contact@divers-cite.com
www.diverscite.fr
Photo © : Divers Cité

cube bin p.108 •
Contact : contact@divers-cite.com
www.diverscite.fr
Photo © : Divers Cité

quatroquarti bin p.108 •
Contact : contact@divers-cite.com
www.diverscite.fr
Photo © : Divers Cité

bottle bank arcade, the fun factory p.108 •
Contact : simon.higby@ddb.com
www.ddb.com
www.thefuntheory.com
Photo © : DDB

Jack bin p.108 •
Contact : Federica Fulici
www.diverscite.fr
Photo © : Divers Cité

drive-in p.109 •
Contact : mail@gillesbelley.fr
www.gillesbelley.fr Photo © : Gilles Belley

trashers, London p.110
Contact : glazedparadise@gmail.com
www.xmarkjenkinsx.com
Photo © : Mark jenkins

bin bag bear p.110
Contact : www.raw-edges.com
Photo © : Raw Edge Design Studio

garbage bag art work pp.111-112
Contact : yamasaka@maq.co.jp
www.gba-project.com
Photo © : Yoshihiko Yamasaka

fish bag p.113
Contact : sales@suck.uk.com
www.suck.uk.com
Photo © : Suck uk

dog poo bag p.113
Contact : www.poopoobags.com
Photo © : Andrea Gadesmann & Nina Dautzenberg

whippet bench p.114
Contact : info@radidesigners.com
www.radidesigners.com
Photo © : Patrick Gries

bau!haus p.114
Contact : gionatagatto@atuppertu.com
www.atuppertu.com
Photo © : Gionata Gatto

teckel bench p.115 •
Contact : autrenature@wanadoo.fr
Photo © : autre nature

the invisible dog pp.116-117
Contact : theinvisibledog.ny@gmail.com
http://theinvisibledog.org
Photo © : Katie Sokoler

3. Enchanting the city

artebeach, p.118
Contact : m-aurel@m-a-studio.fr
www.aurelstudio.fr
Photo : Aurel(s)studio

313

Schouwburg Square pp.120-121
Contact : west8@west8.com
www.west8.nl
Photo © : West 8

atlantida p.122
Contact : www.batlleiroig.com
info@santacole.com
www.santacole.com
Photo © : Santa & Cole

naia p.122
Contact : export@dae.es
www.dae.es
Photo © : DAE, S.A.

fontfosa p.122
Contact : export@dae.es
www.dae.es
Photo © : DAE, S.A

energy producing pavement p.123 •
Contact : alexandre.marciel@mairie-toulouse.fr
www.toulouse.fr
Ilustration © : Christian Guibbaud
Photo © : Alexandre Marciel

Graf-Adolf-Square 15, p.124
Contact : wesup@wesup.de
www.wesup.de
www.jsk.de/
Photo © : Wes & Partner Landscape Architects

Magdeleine lake p.124
Contact : epescher@enpleinelumiere.com
www.enpleinelumiere.com
www.ville-gujanmestras.fr
Photo © : Eric Pescher

princes Czartoryski square, p.124
Contact : biuro@lewicki-latak.com.pl
www.lewicki-latak.com.pl
Photo © : Biuro Projektów Lewicki Łatak

"starry night" atrium bench p.124
Contact : contact@area.fr
http://www.area.fr
www.toulouse.fr
Photo © : AREA

Curtis Hixon waterfront Park
p.125
Contact : info@tbany.com
www.tbany.com
www.tampagov.net
Photo © : Thomas Balsley Associates

central plaza, p.125
Contact : info@tbany.com
www.tbany.com
Photo © : Nihon Sekkei

llum-i p. 126
Contact : informacion@escofet.com
www.escofet.com
Photo © : Escofet 1886 S.A

light! p. 126
contact : info@cutting-edge.fr
www.cutting-edge.fr
Illustration © : Nicolas Marzouanlian

flames p.127
Contact : info@studiojspr.nl
www.studiojspr.nl
Photo © : JSPR / Jasper van Grootel

bora p.127
Contact : agence.michel-tortel@wanadoo.fr
www.michel-tortel.com
www.comatelec.fr
Photo © : Comatelec

live light p.127 •
Contact : valentin@monfortdesign.com
www.monfortdesign.com
Illustration © : Valentin Monfort

indalux range p.128
Contact : m-aurel@m-a-studio.fr
www.aurelstudio.fr
Illustration © : Aurel(s)studio

cristella light p.128
Contact : m-aurel@m-a-studio.fr
www.aurelstudio.fr
www.eclatec.com
Illustration & Photo : Aurel(s)studio

organic light p.128
Contact : m-aurel@m-a-studio.fr
www.aurelstudio.fr
www.rohl.com
Illustration © : Aurel(s)studio

perla light p.128
Contact : agence.michel-tortel@wanadoo.fr
www.michel-tortel.com
www.comatelec.fr
Photo © : Agence Michel Tortel

Smithfield public space p.129
Contact : info@mcgnie.ie
www.mcgnie.ie
www.dublincity.ie
Photo © : McGarry Ni Éanaigh Architects

saturno streetlighting p.129
Contact : eambaszp@ambasz.com
http://www.ambasz.com
Photo © : Emilio Ambasz & Associates

old shipyards development
p.130
Contact : emminfo@emm-design.com
www.emm-design.com
Illustration © : Emmanuel Cairo Designer

candelabra p.130
Contact : contact@distylight.com
www.distylight.com
Illustration © : Johan Sustrac / Distylight

royal light p.130
Contact : www.citydesign.it
Photo © : City design

wisps of light p.131 •
Contact : hugweill@aol.com
Illustration © : Hugues Weill

lax p.132
Contact : tedt@ttta.com
www.ttta.com
Photo © : Ted Tokio Tanaka Architects

chess park, brand boulevard passageway p.133
Contact : info@rchstudios.com
www.rchstudios.com, info@rchstudios.com
www.ci.glendale.ca.us
Photo © : Tom Bonner

dinosaurios, L'Hospitalet de Llobregat p.134 •
Contact : info@siarq.net
www.siarq.net
www.solaring.es
Photo & Illustration © : Siarq

totem p.134 •
Contact : info@siarq.net
www.siarq.net
Illustration © : Siarq Siarq

solar mallee trees p.135 •
Contact : sales@streetandpark.com.au
www.streetandpark.com.au
www.mpharchitects.com.au
Photo © : Street and Park Furniture PTY

sustainable city lights p.136 •
Contact : www.design.philips.com
Illustration © : Philips Design

sola tree p.136 •
Contact : www.rosslovegrove.com
www.artemide.com
Photo & Illustration © : Artemide

electree city p.136 •
Contact : contact@vivien-muller.fr
www.electree.fr
Illustration © : Vivien Muller

veil solar-shade project p.137 •
Contact : emily@buronorth.com; www.buronorth.com
www.ecoinnovationlab.com
Illustration © : Soren Luckins / Buro North

light wind p.138 •
Contact : info@demakersvan.com
www.demakersvan.com
Photo © : Ingmar Kramer

flow lamp p.139 •
Contact : alberto@igendesign.hu
www.igendesign.hu
Illustration © : Alberto Vasquez / Igendesign

Quincy court, p.140
Contact : info@rchstudios.com
www.rchstudios.com
Photo © : Scott Shigley

Nou Barris central park, p.140
Contact : arriolafiol@arriolafiol.com
http://arquitectes.coac.ne
Photo © : Arriola & Fiol Arquitects

via làctea public light p.141
Contact : www.batlleiroig.com
ElisaV@santacole.com
www.santacole.com
Photo © : Santa & Cole

dr jekyll & mr mouse p.141
Contact : contact@berger-berger.com
ww.berger-berger.com
wwww.104.fr
Photo © : Guillaume Ziccarelli

Marin central plaza
p.142
Contact : tdelaney@tdelaney.com
www.tdelaney.com
www.rawsonblumleon.com
Photo © : Topher Delaney

supernature p.142
Contact : www.vincentleroy.com
galerie@art-entreprise.com
www.galerie-verney-carron.com
Photo © : Art Entreprise

silent city p.143 •
Contact : info@kjellgrenkaminsky.se
www.kjellgrenkaminsky.se
www.chinaacsc.com
Illustration © : Kjellgren Kaminsky Architecture AB

Rousseau garden p.144
Contact : maro.avrabou@gmail.com
dimitri.xenakis@gmail.com
http://dimitri.xenakis.free.fr
www.arbresetlumieres.ch
Photo © : Dimitri Xenakis

recycling, a luminous idea p.145 •
Contact : www.designpackgallery.fr
Photo © : DesignPack Gallery

lighthouse, p.146
Contact : www.corneliaerdmann.de
Photo : Cornelia Erdmann

color design hôtel, p.146
Contact : reservation@colordesign-hotel-paris.com
www.colordesign-hotel-paris.com
Photo © : Color Design Hôtel

impression p.146
Contact : michiel@ruimtelijkvormgevers.nl
www.ruimtelijkvormgevers.nl
Photo © : cazemier & vankempen

advent calendar p.147
Contact : contact@cacmeymac.com
www.cacmeymac.com/
Photo © : Abbaye Saint-André,
Centre d'art contemporain de Meymac

N building p.148
Contact : info@teradadesign.com
www.teradadesign.com
info@qosmo.jp
http://qosmo.jp
Photo © : Yuki Omori

the cultural shop window p.149
Contact : info@momentfactory.com
www.momentfactory.com
http://info.lavitrine.com/
Photo © : Martine Doyon (top left and bottom),
Richard Hachem (top roght)

vertical housing scheme p.150 •
Contact : zzz@herault-arnod.fr
www.herault-arnod.fr
Illustration © : Hérault Arnod Architectes

twists and turns p.151
Contact : atelier@webblick.de
www.webblick.de
Photo © : Mader Stublic Wiermann

the altoviseur p.152
Contact : www.julienberthier.org
Photo © : Julien Berthier

resonance 2, p.152
Contact : b-l-o-c-k@wanadoo.fr
www.b-l-o-c-k.com
Photo © : Denis Brillet / Block

Minato-Mirai business square p.153
Contact : nozomi@earthscape.co.jp
www.earthscape.co.jp
Photo © : Shigeki Asanuma / Earthscape

decoys, Washington, DC p.154
Contact : glazedparadise@gmail.com
www.xmarkjenkinsx.com
Photo © : Mark jenkins

ecorafts p.154 •
Contact : http://www.parislabel.com
www.paris.fr
Photo © : Lhomme (left) ; Paris Label (right)

Tanner Springs park, Portland p.155 •
Contact : ueberlingen@dreiseitl.com
www.dreiseitl.com
Photo © : Atelier Dreiseitl (top), Doug Dacy (bottom)

Crown fountain pp.156-157
Contact : www.jaumeplensa.com
www.ksarch.com
llorca.jean-max@neuf.fr
www.jeanmaxllorca.com
Photo © : Crystal Fountains Toronto

river eyelash p.158
Contact : www.stacylevy.com
www.artsfestival.net
Photo © : Stacy Levy

Diana, princess of Wales Memorial fountain p.159
Contact : Embernardoni@gustafson-porter.com
www.gustafson-porter.com
www.royalparks.org.uk
Photo © : Jason Hawkes (top), Peter Guenzel (bottom)

François Mitterrand square p.160
Contact : site2010@grunig-tribel.com
www.grunig-tribel.com
llorca.jean-max@neuf.fr
www.jeanmaxllorca.com
www.lacommunaute.fr
Photo © : Jean Max Llorca & François Tribel

Vigan square p.161
Contact : llorca.jean-max@neuf.fr
www.jeanmaxllorca.com
Photo © : Stéphane Llorca

Rakvere central square p. 162
Contact : info@kosmoses.ee
www.kosmoses.ee
Photo © : Kosmos

Apeldoorn station square p.163 •
Contact : landscape@baljon.nl
www.baljon.nl
Photo © : Lodewijk Baljon landscape architects

watering as the wind blows pp.164-165 •
Contact : alain.faragou.paysages@orange.fr
www.faragou-paysages.com
Photo & Illustration © : Agence Faragou

urban bocage p.166 •
Contact : Estephan.design@gmail.com
Illustration © : Elodie Stephan

topic-eau p.167 •
Contact : isabelle_daeron@yahoo.fr
Photo & Illustration © : Isabelle Daeron

spruzzi d'acqua water spray p.168
Contact : info@modoarredo.com
www.modoarredo.com
Photo © : Modo s.r.l.

street fountain p.168
Contact : www.helmutsmits.nl
Photo © : Helmut Smits

Radi millennium fountain p.168
Contact : info@radidesigners.com
www.radidesigners.com
Photo © : Radi Designers

O'claire drinking fountain p.168
Contact : contact@cecileplanchais.com
www.cecileplanchais.com
www.eaudeparis.fr
Photo © : Cécile Planchais

aqua fountain p.169
Contact : comercial@urbes21.com
www.urbes21.com
Photo © : Urbes 21, S.A.

estadio fountain p.169
Contact : comercial@urbes21.com
www.urbes21.com
Photo © : Urbes 21, S.A.

by-pass fountain p.169
Contact : comercial@urbes21.com
www.urbes21.com
Photo © : Urbes 21, S.A.

lilla fountain p.169
Contact : info@modoarredo.com
www.modoarredo.com
Photo © : Modo s.r.l.

tana fountain p.169
Contact :export@dae.es
www.dae.es
Photo © : Dae

4. Urban expressions

prohibited! p.170
Contact : s.barbaux@orange.fr
www.sophie-barbaux.odexpo.com
Photo © : Sophie Barbaux

la Kommune garden pp.172-173 •
Contact : www.teurk.com
www.latlas.net
lakommune@gmail.com
www.lakommune.org
Photo © : Sandra Cremonesi & Caroline Ackermann
(p.172), Sophie Barbaux (p.173)

heads or tails p.174
Contact : contact@legoville.net
www.legoville.net
Photo © : Legoville

resident's park p.175
Contact : mail@osa-online.net
www.osa-online.net
Photo © : Osa

nails! p.176
Contact : fichtre@neuf.fr
www.fichtre.org
Photo © : collectif Fichtre

urban ways p.177
Contact : info@adrianodesign.it
www.adrianodesign.it
Photo © : AdrianoDesign

Johnny B. p.178
Contact : contact@legoville.net
www.legoville.net
Photo © : Legoville

extraordinary meeting p.178
Contact : contact@legoville.net
www.legoville.net
Photo © : Legoville

media campus p.179
Contact : contact@ruedi-baur.eu
www.integral.ruedi-baur.eu
www.mediacampus.org
Photo © : Irb Zurich

new Nowy square p.180 •
Contact : biuro@lewicki-latak.com.pl
www.lewicki-latak.com.pl
Illustration © : Biuro Projektów Lewicki Łatak

assimilation p.181
Contact : mail@osa-online.net
www.osa-online.net
Photo © : martin kaiser (top), Osa (bottom)

chronological steps p.182
Contact : nozomi@earthscape.co.jp
www.earthscape.co.jp
Photo © : Earthscape

the piano stair case p.183 •
Contact : simon.higby@ddb.com
www.ddb.com
www.thefuntheory.com
Photo © : DDB

the landing p.184
Contact : contact@sweatshoppe.org
www.sweatshoppe.org
Photo © : Sweatshoppe

space invader p.185
Contact : www.space-invaders.com
Illustration © : Invader (Map #18 Kathmandu 2008)
Photo © : Invader (top : NY_103 New York / 11-2007 & bottom :
NY_111 New York / 11-2007)

panos, fake roadsigns pp.186-187
Contact : www.you-are-beautiful.com
www.francois-morel.net
www.myspace.com/teurk
www.emilystrange.com
www.kanardo.com
www.andrewrae.org.uk
www.mikeperrystudio.com
www.meomi.com
www.freakfabric.com
http://struggleinc.blogspot.com
Photo © : Kanardo

Lyon parc auto pp.188-189
Contact : galerie@art-entreprise.com
www.galerie-verney-carron.com
Photo © : Guillaume Perret (p.188), Art Entreprise (p.189 top
left and bottom), André Morin (p.189 top right)
Illustration © : Yan D. Pennors

untitle p.190
Photo © : Sophie Barbaux

ampelmann p.190
Photo © : Leïla Garfield www.leilagarfield.com (left),
Karine Daiban (right)

315

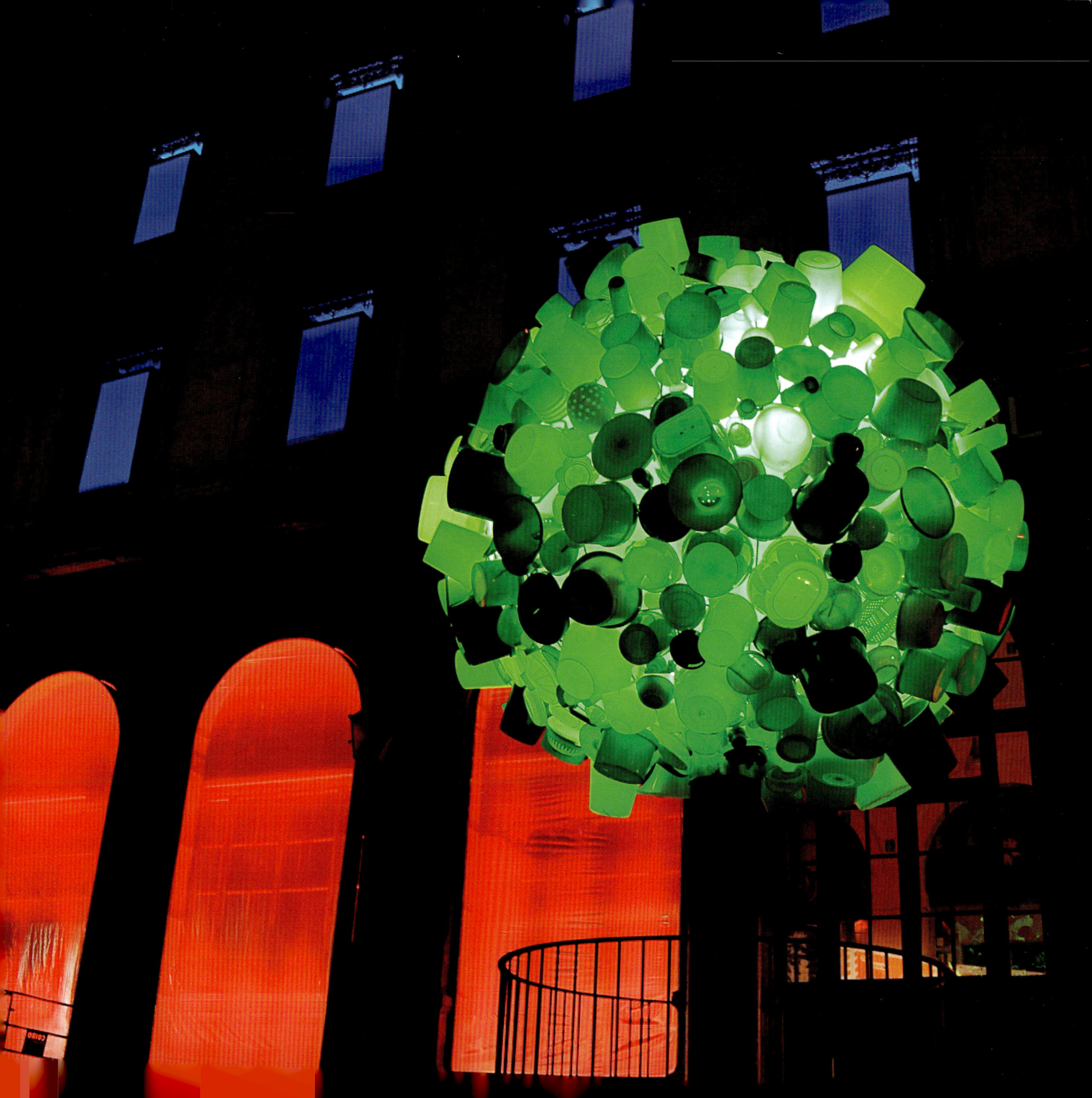

eko - traffic light concept p.191
Contact : damjan@relogik.com
stankovicdamjan@gmail.com
www.relogik.com
Photo © : Damjan Stankovic

Ambient traffic-light p.192
Contact : hbarragan@uniandes.edu.co
http://designblog.uniandes.edu.co/blogs/dise3123/
Photo © : Hernando Barragán

witness p.193
Contact : dellys.thomas@yahoo.fr
www.thomasdellys.fr
Photo & Illustration © : Thomas Dellys

118 218 p.194
Contact : benedettobufalino@yahoo.fr
www.benedetto.new.fr
Photo © : Benedetto Buffalino

nature p.194
Contact : sean.martindale@gmail.com
www.seanmartindale.com
Photo © : Sean Martindale

Paris floral park p.194
Contact : sylvie.depondt@paris.fr
www.paris.fr
Photo © : Sophie Barbaux

signage system for the park of la Villette p.195
Contact : emminfo@emm-design.com
www.emm-design.com
www.villette.com
Illustration © : Emmanuel Cairo & Thérèse Troïka

buga 05 pp.196-197
Contact : contact@ruedi-baur.eu
www.integral.ruedi-baur.eu
Photo © : Heidi Abt

lifts for the Toulouse metro p.198
Contact : contact@kld-design.fr
www.kld-design.fr
Photo © : KLD Design

taxi totem p.198
Contact : galerie@art-entreprise.com
www.galerie-verney-carron.com
Photo © : André Morin

building site hoarding p.199
Contact : marc.dolger@outsign.fr
www.outsign.fr
Photo © : Luc Boegly.

5. Shelter

business class p.200
Contact : info@radidesigners.com
www.radidesigners.com
Photo © : Patrick Gries

lace fence pp.202-203
Contact : info@lacefence.com
www.lacefence.com
Photo © : Studio Demakersvan / Idfence BV

riverside park south
New York p.204 (left)
Contact : info@tbany.com
www.tbany.com
Photo © : Thomas Balsley Assosciates

Peggy Rockefeller university
New York p.204 (centre & right)
Contact : info@tbany.com
www.tbany.com
Photo © : Thomas Balsley Assosciates

plugin p.205
Contact : alexandre.mussche@gmail.com
demet.mutman@gmail.com
Photo © : Alexandre Mussche

mobile-homme p.206
Contact : c.privileggio@gmail.com
www.christelleprivileggio.ultra-book.com
Photo © : Christelle Privileggio

urban jewellery p.206
Contact : info@liesbetbussche.com
www. liesbetbussche.com
Photo © : Liesbet Bussche

potobos p.206
Contact : parislabel@gmail.com
www.parislabel.com, www.2r2c.coop
Photo © : Brigitte Pujol (left),
A-L Chatard (3 others photos)

urban seat p.207
Contact : damien@leplanb.com
www.leplanb.com
Photo © : Justin Westover

security barriers and railings p.208
Contact : m.theaudin@phytolab.fr
www.phytolab.fr
Photo © : Phytolab

cidade p.208
Contact : andreabandoni@gmail.com
www.abandoni.net
Photo © : Andrea Bandoni

Westminster presbyterian church p.209
Contact : info@coenpartners.com
www.coenpartners.com, www.msrltd.com
Photo © : Paul Crosby www.pcrosby.com

lentspace, p.209
Contact : info@interboropartners.com
www.interboropartners.com, www.lmcc.net
Photo © : Interboro

octopus p.210
Contact : contact@o-s.fr
www.o-s.fr
Illustration & Photo © : Atelier O-S architectes

belvedere plaza p.210
Contact : info@tbany.com
www.tbany.com
Photo © : Thomas Balsley Associates

Jean-Baptiste Lebas park p.211
Contact : west8@west8.com
www.west8.nl
Photo © : West 8

view point p.212
Contact : mail@osa-online.net
www.osa-online.net
www.blueprintmagazine.co.uk
Photo © : OSA

dymaxion sleep p.213
Contact : adrian.blackwell@daniels.utoronto.ca
jane.hutton@utoronto.ca
www.jardinsdemetis.com
Photo © : Adrian Blackwell

pla-tano p.214
Contact : info@modoarredo.com
www.modoarredo.com
Photo © : Modo s.r.l.

Quinhuangdao botanical gardens p.214
Contact : info@turenscape.com
www.turenscape.com
Photo & Illustration © : Turenscape (Beijing Turen Design Institute)

energy zone p.214
Contact : tristan.kopp@gmail.com
www.esad-reims.fr
www.fondation-cari.fr
Illustration © : Tristan Kopp

garden of blooms p.215
Contact : contact@horizons-paysages.fr
www.horizons-paysages.fr
emminfo@emm-design.com
www.emm-design.com
www.plan01.com
www.laps-design.com
Illustration © : Horizons paysage (top), Emm.Cairo Designer (bottom)

3rd collection tram-shelter p.216
Contact : m-aurel@m-a-studio.fr
www.aurelstudio.fr
Photo © : Aurel(s)studio

tram-train station in La Réunion p.216
Contact : m-aurel@m-a-studio.fr
www.aurelstudio.fr
Illustration © : Aurel(s)studio

bus top p.217
Contact : p.jouffret@agence-360.com
www.agence-360.com
Illustration © : Patrick Jouffret & Fariba Sanaï / 360

eden p.218
Contact : clob3@yahoo.fr
http://clothildehuet.blogspot.com
www.ensci.com
www.ideas-laboratory.com
Illustration © : Clothilde Huet

blue spots p.219
Contact : ds@loharchitects.com
www.loharchitects.com, www.brucemaudesign.com
www.bigbluebus.com
Illustration © : Lorcan O'Herlihy Architects & Bruce Mau Design

fireplace for children p.220
Contact : marit@hza.no, dan@hza.no
www.hza.no
Illustration © : Grethe fredriksen & Jason havneraas

temporary meeting places p.221
Contact : info@roccoverdult.nl
www.roccoverdult.nl
Photo & Illustration © Studio Rocco Verdult

6. City games

trottola p.222
Contact : info@modoarredo.com
www.modoarredo.com
Photo © : Modo s.r.l.

traffic-go-round, p.224
Contact : glazedparadise@gmail.com
xmarkjenkinsx.com
Photo © : Marks Jenkins

untitled, p.225
Contact : glazedparadise@gmail.com
xmarkjenkinsx.com
Photo © : Marks Jenkins

carousel p.225
Contact : glazedparadise@gmail.com
xmarkjenkinsx.com
Photo © : Marks Jenkins

Alfil Set chess game p.226
Contact : info@estudiocabeza.com
www.estudiocabeza.com
Photo © : Estudio Cabeza Urban Elements

distorting mirror p.227
Contact : info@modoarredo.com
www.modoarredo.com
Photo © : Modo s.r.l.

toy hospital p.228
Contact : estudio@designopatagonia.com.ar
www.designopatagonia.com.ar
www.publicdesignfestival.org
Illustration © : Designo Patagonia

Marcos Paz park p.229 •
Contact : estudio@designopatagonia.com.ar
www.designopatagonia.com.ar
Illustration © : Designo Patagonia

bambisitter p.230
Contact : rianne@free-line.nl
www.enjoyfreeline.com
Photo © : Freeline International BV

lion cubs p.230 •
Contact : david.steinfeld@wanadoo.fr
www.david-steinfeld.com
carole.marcou@divers-cite.com
www.divers-cite.fr
Photo © : Divers cité

"once upon a time" p.231 •
Contact : nicolas@stadler.fr
www.stadler.fr
Illustration © : Nicolas Stadler

optical illusion p.232
Contact : info@modoarredo.com
www.modoarredo.com
Photo © : Modo s.r.l

anamorphoses p.232
Contact : info@modoarredo.com
www.modoarredo.com
Photo © : Modo s.r.l

tinama p.233 •
Contact : lisecapet@gmail.com
www.lisecapet.com
Illustration © : Lise Capet

bambinos pp.234-235
Contact : marissima@free.fr
http://marissima.labomedia.org, www.kernotart.com
Photo © : Marie Denis

play engines, wall decoration and barriers p.236 •
Contact : info@recyclart.be
www.recyclart.be
Photo © : Recyclart

Carnegie library's "bookworms" p.237
Contact : info@formium.com.au
www.formium.com.au, www.gleneira.vic.gov.au
Illustration & Photo © : FORMium Landscape Architects

safe zone pp.238-239
Contact : admin@stoss.net
www.stoss.net, www.jardinsdemetis.com
Photo & Illustration © : Stoss LU

the climclamberhangsitfootballcurtaintheatretube
pp. 240-241
Contact : info@kapteinroodnat.nl
www.kapteinroodnat.nl
Photo © : Bas Princen

city dog adventure pp.242-243
Contact : info@maartjedros.nl
www.maartjedros.nl, www.premsela.org
www.experimentadesign.nl
Photo © : Rachel Sender

illegal furniture, p.244 •
Contact : www.recetasurbanas.net
Photo © : Recetas Urbanas

double happiness p.245
Contact : bureau@mesarchitecture.com
www.mesarchitecture.org, www.szhkbiennale.org
Photo © : Mésarchitecture

frogska skatable bench p.246
Contact : atelier2ce@bluewin.ch
www.atelier2ce.org/a2ce-fr/frogska.html
Photo © : Atelier2CE

the ramp p.246
Contact : fichtre@neuf.fr
www.fichtre.orgfichtre@neuf.fr.
Photo © : Fichtre

block banks... p.246 •
Contact : b-l-o-c-k@wanadoo.fr
www.b-l-o-c-k.com, http://planete.tetrapak.fr
www.estuaire.info
Photo © : Gregg Brehin

tweed skateable sculptural trail p.247
Contact : aaron@convicdesign.com
www.convic.com
Photo © : Convic Design Pty

Nicolaas Beetsplein space pp.248-249
Contact : office@nlarchitects.nl
www.nlarchitects.nl, www.landschapsarchitecten.nl
Photo © : NL Architects

new playground for Belleville park pp.250-251
Contact : www.baseland.fr
sylvie.depondt@paris.fr, www.paris.fr
Photo © : Helbert

Paris-beaches pp.252-253
Contact : nezhaut@free.fr
www.nezhaut.com, www.paris.fr
Photo © : Choblet & Associés / Agence Nez Haut

7. On your bike

Toronto central waterfront p.254
Contact : west8@west8.com
www.west8.nl, www.dtah.com
Photo © : West 8

kolelinia pp.256-257 •
Contact : i@martinangelov.com
http:// kolelinia.com
Illustration © : Martin Angelov
Photo © : Boby Dimitrov

collection ensemble p.258 •
Contact : info@wolters-mabeg.eu
www.wolters-mabeg.eu
Photo © : Wolters Mabeg

LightLane signposting p.259 •
Contact : info@altitudeinc.com
www.altitudeinc.com
Photo © : Altitude / Evan Gant, Alex Tee

tactil rack p.260 •
Contact : info@santacole.com
www.santacole.com
Photo © : Santa & Cole

imawa rack p.260 •
Contact : s.dreux@concepturbain.fr
www.concepturbain.com
Photo © : Concept Urbain

key rack p.260 •
Contact : www.lagranjadesign.com
www.santacole.com
Photo © : Santa & Cole

arcas rack p.260 •
Contact : info@modoarredo.com
www.modoarredo.com
Photo © : Modo s.r.l.

dedalo rack p.260 •
Contact : info@modoarredo.com
www.modoarredo.com
Photo © : Modo s.r.l.

NYCityRack p.261 •
Contact : ian.mahaffy@gmail.com
www.nyc.gov/dot
Photo © : New York City Department of Transportation (top),
Ian Mahaffy (bottom)

parkower rack p.262 •
Contact : i@lovekompott.com
www.lovekompott.com
Photo © : Kompott Studio

piano bike stand p.262 •
Contact : info@addi.se
www.addi.se
Photo © : Addi

put in rack p.262 •
Contact : info@storemuu.com
www.storemuu.com
Photo © : Store Muu Design Studio

illegal furniture p.262 •
Contact : www.recetasurbanas.net
Illustration © : Recetas Urbanas

shelter-4-bikes & bike-bench / USXL p.263 •
Contact : info@xavierlust.com
www.xavierlust.com
Illustration © : Xavier Lust
Photos © : Lode Saïdane

shelters my bikes, pp.264-267 •
Contact : scrotchdesign@yahoo.fr,
julien.cottier@gmail.com, poiriermanon@orange.fr,
gaultier.bigot@gmail.com, bruno@atelierjuno.com,
zwall@hotmail.fr & quentincarnaille@hotmail.com &
addhellemmes@gmail.com (DWC), franckdarde@gmail.com
www.dpxgraphisme.com, www.z-black.com
http://sanselme.fr, b.roselle@yahoo.fr,
www.abritemonvelo.org
Ville de Lille and Association Kraft (France)
Photos & Illustration © : Franck Darde, Jacques Sanselme,
Zurab Shavadze, François Gustin, Julien Cottier, Sylvain
Ory, Manon Poirier, Gaultier Bigot, Bruno Codron, Quentin
Carnaille, Adrien Dhellemmes & Thomas Wallon &
Association Kraft

8. Green city

rue de la Villette, Paris 19th arr. p.268
Photos © : Sophie Barbaux

corsus pp.270-271 •
Contact : sylvie.depondt@paris.fr
etienne.vanderpooten@paris.fr
www.paris.fr
Photos © : Sophie Barbaux

disurbanised furniture p.272 •
Contact : made.com@wanadoo.fr
http://nature.art.free.fr
Photos © : Patrick Demazeau dit : MADE

dream projects p.273 •
Contact : marissima@free.fr
http://marissima.labomedia.org
www.kernotart.com
Photos © : Marie Denis & Fabrice Escalier

saturnia basins and seats p.274
Contact : phil@philippenigro.com
www.philippenigro.com, www.pibamarmi.it
Photos © : Philippe Negro

urban lounge p.274 •
Contact : mp@marinepeyre.com
www.marinepeyre.com, www.lyon.fr
Photos © : Marine Peyre
Ville de Lyon

Trinity college quadrangle p.274
Contact : info@gh3.ca
www.gh3.ca
Photos © : gh3

cantonal high school Wil p.275
Contact : mail@winogrond.com
www.winogrond.com
Photos © : Robin Winogrond

9m² of hill p.276 •
Contact : antoine.monnet@laposte.net
www.esad-reims.fr
www.fondation-cari.fr
www.ecovegetal.fr/
Illustration © : Antoine Monnet

park p.276
Contact : sean.martindale@gmail.com
www.seanmartindale.com
Photos © : Sean Martindale

318 annex

water crater p.276
Contact : artist@shigeko-hirakawa.com
http://shigeko-hirakawa.com
Photos © : Shigeko Hirakawa

w² wireless square p.277
Contact : piter@pprdesign.com
www.pprdesign.com
Illustration © : Piter Perbellini

mobile green p.278 •
Contact : langbein@osa-online.net
www.osa-online.net
Photos © : OSA

mobilot p.279 •
Contact : comceci@comceci.fr
www.comceci.com
Photos © : Comceci Architectes

chitchat bench p.280
Contact : info@teunfleskens.nl
www.teunfleskens.nl, www.teunprojects.nl
Photos © : Teunprojetcts

Romeo & Juliet bench p.280
Contact : architecten@telier-vyvey.be
www.architectenatelier.eu
info@extremis.be, www.extremis.be
Photos © : Extremis

cisca urban seat p.280
Contact : juampisammartino@gmail.com
www.juampisammartino.com.ar
www.markiglesiasdesign.com
Photos © : Juan pablo Sammartino

theatre garden p.280
Contact : vdr@free.fr
vincentdupontrougier.com
Illustration © : Vincent Dupont-Rougier

light up p.281 •
Contact : alexander.gebelin@gmail.com
Illustration © : Alexander Gébelin

tempo-territorial-puzzle p.282
Contact : landfabrik@free.fr
http://landfabrik.free.fr
Illustration © : Landfabrik

project for a terrace p.283
Contact : vdr@free.fr
vincentdupontrougier.com
Illustration © : Vincent Dupont-Rougier

the Lille bouquet p.284 •
Contact : vdr@free.fr
vincentdupontrougier.com
Photos © : Nicolas Héron

the large chairs p.284 •
Contact : http://www.mhr-artinsitu.com
Illustration © : Marie Hélène Richard & Stéphan Bohu

station square, Douai's street car line 1 p.284 •
Contact : d.v.a@dvapaysages.com
www.dvapaysages.com
www.reichen-robert.fr
www.ingerop.com
www.transportsdudouaisis.fr
Photos © : DVA Paysagistes

Republic square p.285 •
Contact : nadeau@patricknadeau.com
www.patricknadeau.com
paris.atile@atile.fr
www.rennes.fr
Photos & Illustration © : Patrick Nadeau

flaming city - blooming city pp.286-287
Contact : west8@west8.com
www.west8.com
Photos & Illustration © : West 8

greenspotlight p.288 •
contact : mail@bytr.nl
www.bytr.nl
Photos © : Ernie Buts

green green screen p.288 •
Contact : kda@klein-dytham.com
www.klein-dytham.com
Photos © : Klein Dytham architecture

the Lavin Bernick center for university life p.289 •
Contact : info@coenpartners.com
www.coenpartners.com
Photos © : Paul Crosby www.pcrosby.com

poster pocket plants p.290 •
Contact : posterpocketplants.blogspot.com
Photos © : Sean Martindale

guerilla gardening p.291 •
Contact : posterchilds.blade.diary@gmail.com
Photos © : Posterchild

moving forest p.291 •
Contact : office@nlarchitects.nl
www.nlarchitects.nl
www.droog.com
Photos © : NL Architects

ondine p.292
Contact : info@bihain.com
www.bihain.com
info@callewaert-architecture.be
www.callewaert-architecture.be
Illustration © : Michaël Bihain
Photos © : Pierre-François Gérard

chamaland p.293
Contact : marissima@free.fr
http://marissima.labomedia.org
www.kernotart.com
Photos © : Marie Denis

guenus p.294
Contact : codesigner@hotmail.com
info@sparkling-design.com
Photo © : Corentin Nicolas & Alix d'Harambure

hula hoop p.295
Contact : thomasjolygris@gmail.com
Illustration © : Thomas Joly

3.6 solar relaxation p.295
Contact : drevillestephane@gmail.com
Illustration © : Stéphane Dréville

the shiverer, tree-sculpture p.296
Contact : mourka@yaqua.eu
www.yaqua.eu,
www.arbresetlumieres.ch
Photo © : Mourka

bonsaï II p.297
Contact : marissima@free.fr
http://marissima.labomedia.org
www.kernotart.com
www.tecomah.fr/les-environnementales
Photo © : Marie Denis

the pouffe tree pp.298-299
Contact : matali.crasset@wanadoo.fr
www.matalicrasset.com
http://blog.matalicrasset.com
Photo © : Blaise Adilon

vital vegetal, "last one" series p.300 •
Contact : didier@hw12.com
www.hw12.com
Photo © : Claire Lacout

the foreigner p.301
Contact : gaele.braun@wanadoo.fr
www.gaelebraun.com
Photo & Illustration © : Gaële Braun

urbanbuds pp.302-303 •
Contact : gionatagatto@atuppertu.com
www.atuppertu.com
Photo © : Gionata Gatto

locavore fantasia p.304 •
Contact : office@work.ac
www.work.ac
Illustration © : WORK Architecture Company

eco-pods pp.305-307
Contact : www.hyarchitecture.com/
www.squareddesignlab.com/
Illustration © : Höweler+Yoon Architecture & Squared Design Lab

Annexes
Annex

speechless p.308
Contact : leo@vgrfk.com, www.vgrfk.com
Photo © : Via Grafik

hikarinoki p.312 & p.316 •
Contact : www.philippemorvan.com
Photo © : Roland Gouy-Paillier
roland.gouy-paillier@wanadoo.fr

©2010 by Design Media Publishing Limited
This edition published in December 2010

Design Media Publishing Limited
20/F Manulife Tower
169 Electric Rd, North Point
Hong Kong
Tel: 00852-28672587
Fax: 00852-25050411
E-mail: Kevinchoy@designmediahk.com
www.designmediahk.com

Writing: Sophie BARBAUX
Plan: Ici Consultants
Design/Layout: Linh VU
Cover Design: Karine de La Maison & Linh VU

All rights reserved. No part of this publication
may be reproduced or transmitted in any form or
by any means, electronic or mechanical, including
photocopy, recording or any information storage and
retrieval system, without prior permission in writing
from the publisher.

ISBN 978-988-19508-4-0

Printed in China